Colorado City Polygamists

An Inside Look for the Outsider

by Benjamin G. Bistline

Colorado City Polygamists: An Inside Look for the Outsider
by Benjamin G. Bistline

Copyright © 2004 by Benjamin G. Bistline

Photographs and documents used by permission.

Publisher's Cataloging-in-Publication Data

Bistline, Benjamin G.
    Colorado City Polygamists : an inside look for thr outsider / Benjamin Bistline.
– 1st ed.
        p.cm.
        LCCN: 2004109458   (pkb : alk.paper)
        ISBN: 1888106859
1. Mormon Fundamentalism–Arizona–Colorado City–History. 2. Mormon Fundamentalism–Utah–Hildale–History. 3. Polygamy–Utah–Hildale–History. 4 Polygamy–Arizona–Colorado City–History. 5. Persecution–Arizona–Hildale–History–20th Century. 7. Colorado City (Ariz)–Church history. Hildale (Utah)–Church history. Title.

BX8680.M534C64 2004   289.3'79159–dc20

Printed in the United States of America

Featured on www.agreka.com

Agreka, LLC
800 360-5284
www.agreka.com

Dedication

To Jed, Deslie and Michelle

Acknowledgements

I would like to thank my editor Linda Taylor for all her work and the support she has given me, and my daughter Diane, and my granddaughters Chelesa and Ashley for all their help with the computer and typing. I am grateful to John Llewellyn for introducing me to his publisher because without this help my book would not have been published. I appreciate and thank Bob Curran for his support.

I would like to thank the following people who provided research material: Max and Nancy Anderson, John Dougherty, Jay Beswick, Lorin Webb, Keith Pipkin, Elaine Johnson, Richard Van Wagner, Brian Hales, Don Bradley, Dorothy Zitting, and Don and his wives Earlene and Katy.

And most especially I would like to thank my wife Annie. She labored long and hard to transfer my manuscript from an old word processor into a computer program. I am most grateful for her patience, understanding, and for helping me in so many ways throughout my life and this project.

Contents

Foreword

Short Creek, Arizona, whose development from the 1920s has been a central point of polygamy in America, and from which other polygamist groups have split off, was renamed Colorado City in the 1960s.

Benjamin Bistline submitted his ten-years-in-the-writing manuscript to us in late 2003. While we were familiar with polygamy outside of Colorado City, having published three books, we soon discovered that Colorado City was in a world of its own. His writing covered seven decades of development, events, and the religious power struggles that eventually produced the scandalous abuses reported by worldwide media.

His critically important history was written to present the truth of the beginnings of the group and its original religious doctrine. Over the years, that religious doctrine had been verbally "rewritten" by religious leaders to support their claim of God's approval of their one-man dictatorship. So careful had been the rewriting that, as older people died off, the remaining polygamists believed it was indeed fact. And they had long been taught not to question their leaders; to do so put not only their eternal salvation in jeopardy, but also their homes, their jobs, and their wives and children.

Ben wrote this history to restore the truth and to tell the story of the development of the town of Colorado City, its dedicated, faithful, and trusting people, and their struggles to survive.

Not only has his book been well received by those in Colorado City who want the truth restored, but also countless others, including those who chose to leave the dictatorship, those who were evicted from their homes and cast out of the community, the girls who escaped from forced childhood marriages, the boys forced to leave the community so older men could have more wives, and those whose parents and grandparents had escaped years before.

But for "outsiders" to whom Colorado City and all its issues are new, *The Polygamists: A History of Colorado City* was overwhelming with facts, events, and deep documentation. So we offer you this book, condensed, simplified, and easy to understand.

People across America are asking how it is that girls as young as thirteen can be forced to marry, and not even to young men but old men; and how it is that women are treated as chattel and belong not to themselves or their husband, but to the Priesthood; and how it is that such wives and their children can be reassigned to a more worthy man; and how it is that tax dollars of American citizens are not only supporting many large polygamist families, but helping the community expand.

Polygamy abuses in America remain in the public eye thanks to Oprah, CNN, ABC Primetime, and other media sources, including newspapers *The Salt Lake Tribune, The Spectrum* of St. George, Utah, *The Phoenix New Times, The Arizona Republic,* and the

Deseret Morning News. With polygamists setting up an enclave in Texas, *The Eldorado Success, San Antonio Express-News, Fort Worth Star Telegram, The Dallas Morning News,* and others are working diligently to make their citizens aware.

As a publisher, we believe the public needs to know how all this developed, what methods were used and by whom, and for what purpose.

Americans are asking: How is such a society allowed to exist in this country?

Agreka Editor – Linda Taylor

Scripture References for the Reader

To assist the reader in understanding topics about the diverse positions taken by the Fundamentalists in Colorado City over the course of many decades, listed here are some of the scriptures they rely on. Most are from the Doctrine & Covenants, considered to be the Law Book for the polygamists.

The three standard works of Mormon scripture used by The Church of Jesus Christ of Latter-day Saints (LDS) are the Book of Mormon, Doctrine & Covenants, and Pearl of Great Price. And they use the Holy Bible. The polygamists claim to be the true Church, and only temporarily a sub-culture of the LDS Church. They believe that the LDS Church is out of order for discontinuing plural marriage, and that one day God will hand over the LDS Church to the polygamists and they will rule.

A critical issue within the polygamist group is "who" among them holds the "keys" or the authority to act in God's name, and how that authority is carried out.

When Brigham Young was president, he acted on his own regarding decisions for the LDS Church and its members, not necessarily consulting with his counselors or the other apostles. But after John Taylor became president, Wilford Woodruff, an apostle to Taylor, was in Arizona with a group of sheep herders and was praying about the many challenges the Church was having. He then received the 1880 Revelation regarding the leadership decision-making of the Group. It came in two parts: There was to be a senior man, by order of ordination (the prophet) who would lead the group, and they (the prophet, his two counselors, and the twelve apostles) would vote and make decisions together. President Taylor and his counselors and apostles then voted to accept this revelation as coming from God.

From that time forth this has been the policy in the LDS Church. The prophet, his two counselors, and the twelve apostles must always be in agreement regarding any action taken. The prophet does not arbitrarily act alone without the approval and support of his counselors and the twelve apostles. Nor does any person within this group do so. Within the group of twelve apostles, the senior man by date of ordination is considered the president of that group.

These are the same guidelines of leadership given to the early Fundamentalists by Lorin Woolley, who claimed to be one of five men commissioned by LDS Prophet John Taylor in 1886 to carry on the principle of plural marriage. But over the years, the polygamist leadership has evolved into a One-Man Rule that many call a dictatorship. During this evolution, various Priesthood Council Members disagreed, some strongly and others not so strongly, and eventually the early teaching of all holding common power wherein they make decisions as a group fell by the wayside. A key verse in the Doctrine & Covenants seems to explain what has happened. D&C 121:39 "We have learned by sad experience that it is the nature and disposition of almost all men, as soon as they get a little authority, as they suppose, they will immediately begin to exercise unrighteous dominion."

As the reader follows the developing and ever-changing leadership doctrines of the early polygamists, he will encounter references to "keys of the priesthood," and the question of "who" legitimately holds the keys to act in God's name: a group of men or one man assuming supreme authority over the people and their eternal salvation.

In the LDS Church, it is understood that the current prophet holds the keys delegated to him by Jesus Christ, and each prophet beginning with Joseph Smith has held the keys. Beginning with John Taylor none acted arbitrarily, but as a group with his counselors and apostles. The prophet holds the keys for the entire church and from that position he delegates a portion of the keys to various male priesthood members to carry out certain responsibilities. Also discussed is the high priesthood of the LDS Church.

The following verses address these topics.

Melchizedek Priesthood

Hebrews 5:4
And no man taketh this honour unto himself, but he that is called of God, as was Aaron.

Hebrews 5:6-10
6. As he saith also in another place, Thou art a priest for ever after the order of Melchisedec.
7. Who in the days of his flesh, when he had offered up prayers and supplications with strong crying and tears unto him that was able to save him from death, and was heard in that he feared;
8. Though he were a Son, yet learned he obedience by the things which he suffered;
9. And being made perfect, he became the author of eternal salvation unto all them that obey him;
10. Called of God an high priest after the order of Melchisedec.

D&C 107:22-27, 30

22. Of the Melchizedek Priesthood, three Presiding High Priests, chosen by the body, appointed and ordained to that office, and upheld by the confidence, faith, and prayer of the church, for a quorum of the Presidency of the Church.

23. The twelve traveling councilors are called to be the Twelve Apostles, or special witnesses of the name of Christ in all the world–thus differing from other offices in the church in the duties of their calling.

24. And they form a quorum, equal in authority and power to the three presidents previously mentioned.

25. The Seventy are also called to preach the gospel, and to be especial witnesses unto the Gentiles and in all the world–thus differing from other offices in the church in the duties of their calling.

26. And they form a quorum, equal in authority to that of the Twelve special witnesses or Apostles just named.

27. And every decision made by either of these quorums must be by the unanimous voice of the same; that is, every member in each quorum must be agreed to its decisions, in order to make their decisions of the same power or validity one with the other –

. . . .

30. The decisions of these quorums, or either of them, are to be made in all righteousness, in holiness, and lowliness of heart, meekness and long suffering, and in faith and virtue, and knowledge, temperance, patience, godliness, brotherly kindness and charity.

The Keys of the Priesthood

D&C 65:2

2. The keys of the kingdom of God are committed unto man on the earth, and from thence shall the gospel roll forth unto the ends of the earth. . . .

D&C 64:4-5

4. I will be merciful unto you, for I have given unto you the kingdom.

5. And the keys of the mysteries of the kingdom shall not be taken from my servant Joseph Smith, Jun., through the means I have appointed, while he liveth, inasmuch as he obeyeth mine ordinances.

D&C 107:64-66

64. Then comes the High Priesthood, which is the greatest of all.

65. Wherefore, it must needs be that one be appointed of the High Priesthood to preside over the priesthood, and he shall be called President of the High Priesthood of the church,

66. Or, in other words, the Presiding High Priest over the High Priesthood of the church.

D&C 81:2
Unto whom I have given the keys of the kingdom, which belong always unto the Presidency of the High Priesthood. (speaking of Joseph Smith, Jun)

D&C 110:16
Therefore, the keys of this dispensation are committed into your hands; . . . .

One Man Rule Justification (quoted by the polygamist leadership)

D&C 132:7
And verily I say unto you, that the conditions of this law are these: All covenants, contracts, bonds, obligations, oaths, vows, performances, connections, associations, or expectations, that are not made and entered into and sealed by the Holy Spirit of promise, of him who is anointed, both as well for time and for all eternity, and that too most holy, by revelation and commandment through the medium of mine appointed, whom I have appointed on the earth to hold this power (and I have appointed unto my servant Joseph to hold this power in the last days, and *there is never but one on the earth at a time on whom this power and the keys of this priesthood are conferred*), are of no efficacy, virtue, or force in and after the resurrection from the dead; for all contracts that are not made unto this end have an end when men are dead. (italics added)

The polygamist group now called First Ward in Colorado City quotes the above verse as their justification of the one-man rule.

The Reassignment of Wives

D&C 132:44
And if she hath not committed adultery, but is innocent and hath not broken her vow, and she knoweth it, and I reveal it unto you, my servant Joseph, then shall you have power, by the power of my Holy Priesthood, to take her and give her unto him that hath not committed adultery but hath been faithful; for he shall be made ruler over many.

The polygamists consider a wife to belong not to the man, but to the priesthood, and if the husband is out of favor, the wife/wives (and children) are reassigned to another man.

Holding the Women's Eternal Salvation in Their Hands

D&C 132:64
And again, verily, verily, I say unto you, if any man have a wife, who holds the keys of this power, and he teaches unto her the law of my priesthood, as pertaining to these things, then shall she believe and administer unto him, or she shall be destroyed, saith the Lord your

God; for I will destroy her; for I will magnify my name upon all those who receive and abide in my law.

A powerful verse that controls the women who fear for their heavenly salvation.

The Acceptance and Dispensing of Donations to the Polygamist Priesthood

D&C 51:2-9

2. For it must needs be that they be organized according to my laws; if otherwise, they will be cut off.

3. Wherefore, let my servant Edward Partridge, and those whom he has chosen, in whom I am well pleased, appoint unto this people their portions, every man equal according to his family, according to his circumstances, and his wants and needs.

4. And let my servant Edward Partridge, when he shall appoint a man his portion, give unto him a writing that shall secure unto him his portion, that he shall hold it, even this right and this inheritance in the church, until he transgresses and is not accounted worthy by the voice of the church, according to the laws and covenants of the church, to belong to the church.

5. And if he shall transgress and is not accounted worthy to belong to the church, he shall not have power to claim that portion which he has consecrated unto the bishop for the poor and needy of my church; therefore, he shall not retain the gift, but shall only have claim on that portion that is deeded to him.

6. And thus all things shall be made sure, according to the laws of the land.

7. And let that which belongs to this people be appointed unto this people.

8. And the money which is left unto this people–let there be an agent appointed unto this people, to take the money to provide food and raiment, according to the wants of this people.

9. And let every man deal honestly and be alike among this people, and receive alike, that ye may be one, even as I have commanded you.

A major issue within the polygamist group over the past several decades is that the leadership has evicted men from the homes they built with their own money, because the man was out of favor. Men coming into the group since the 1930s were expected to donate all they possessed, including money and lands, plus ongoing donations of money and community work to build the town. All assets were donated to and held in a Business Trust owned by the Group. Thus the land homes are built on belong to the Trust. Lawsuits were filed and fought in the courts for a number of years.

The Adam God Doctrine

D&C 107:54-55

54. And the Lord appeared unto them, and they rose up and blessed Adam, and called him Michael, the prince, the archangel.

55. And the Lord administered comfort unto Adam, and said unto him: I have set thee to be at the head; a multitude of nations shall come of thee, and thou art a prince over them forever.

There are many other doctrines among the polygamists, but these listed will aid the reader in following the course of events throughout this book.

Introduction

The Church of Jesus Christ of Latter-day Saints (Mormons) founder Joseph Smith secretly introduced the principle of polygamy (plural marriage) as practiced in the Old Testament to a handful of his closest followers in 1843. A select few would begin the practice and in time, it would be required for all members. Other doctrines openly taught by Smith and his followers had already created great antagonism and resentment among people living near Nauvoo, Illinois, a city that Smith had created for his followers. He reportedly married more than thirty wives, some young teenagers, so it is not surprising that the secret did not remain so.

When a newspaper exposed his secret polygamist relationships with several women, Joseph Smith ordered their printing press destroyed. This led to his arrest and incarceration in jail in Carthage, Illinois, about thirteen miles from Nauvoo. His brother Hyrum, John Taylor, and Willard Richards were put in jail with him. A mob stormed the jail killing Joseph Smith and his brother Hyrum. John Taylor was severely wounded and Willard Richards escaped with barely a scratch.

After the assassination of Joseph Smith, Brigham Young, president of the twelve apostles of the Church, assumed the leadership position. In the winter of 1845-46 the Mormons were finally driven from Nauvoo. Crossing the Mississippi River, they began their trek westward. Finally reaching the Missouri river and following it upstream, they stopped in the area of Council Bluffs, Iowa, and established a camp along the Missouri river bottom lands, remaining there for the summer. Many of the Saints contracted malaria and cholera, resulting in many deaths among the refugees, who were scattered in the deplorable camps among the mosquito-infested willows and marshes. Brigham Young himself became a victim of malaria, coming very close to death.

In the spring of 1847 Brigham Young led a vanguard of a little over one hundred people across the great plains, toward the great Basin of the Rocky Mountains, settling around the great Salt Lake. Thousands more would follow.

Brigham Young was sustained as the second president of the Church in 1848 and by 1852 he introduced polygamy to the people as a requirement to reach the highest place in heaven. (Before he died, some say he had more than fifty wives.) In 1862 Congress passed the Morrill law prohibiting polygamy, which the Mormons resisted on the grounds that it was unlawful interference with religious belief and practices, thus unconstitutional. This law remained practically a dead letter until 1872, when Brigham Young decided to test the validity of the Morrill law. His secretary George Reynolds offered himself as a test case to go before the Supreme Court to test the constitutionality.

The Reynolds case ascended the territorial tribunals and by 1879 was argued before the United States Supreme Court, which ruled the Morrill Act to be constitutional. Church leaders and members were greatly disappointed and George Reynolds went to prison. However, because of the failure of the Morrill Act to stop the practice of polygamy, the U.S. Congress then passed the Edmunds Act in 1882 that provided imprisonment and fines for the practice of plural marriage. It also prevented polygamists from voting and serving on juries.

Meanwhile Brigham Young had died on August 29,1877, and three years later John Taylor was sustained as president of the Church.

In 1887 Congress considered The Edmunds-Tucker Bill, which threatened to confiscate all church property (except chapels) in excess of $50,000, and to dissolve the church as a corporate entity. This law was approved in 1890 by the Supreme Court. Following that, Wilford Woodruff, fourth president of the Church, issued the Manifesto prohibiting polygamist marriages.

Many of the Mormon people did not accept this manifesto and in defiance to these laws of the land and this rule of the Church continued in the living of polygamy. In 1926 a few of these people gravitated to a spot on the Utah/Arizona border called Short Creek (the name was changed to Colorado City in 1961) and established a society based on their beliefs in polygamy. The society eventually became a United Order, where all possessions and acquisitions were owned not by the person, but by the group and were for the use of everyone participating, so there would be no rich or poor, but all would be equal. Each person would be responsible for and to all others in the group.

1

Birth of the Fundamentalists

When John Taylor succeeded Brigham Young and became the third president of the Mormon Church in 1880, there was a spirit of revolt among its members against polygamy. The Church had accepted polygamy in 1852 as a law pertaining to salvation in heaven, but the price of salvation became very high for the majority of the members. The desire for statehood was uppermost in the hearts of many members of the church, polygamist and non-polygamist alike. All were chafing under the yoke of territorial "carpet-bag" government, local self-government being denied them. Congress had enacted measures against polygamy and the Supreme Court of the nation had declared these laws constitutional.

Authorities aggressively pursued any suspected polygamist and captured men were imprisoned, leaving their multiple wives and many children to fend for themselves. Rumors began reaching people in Utah Territory that the United States would grant political emancipation if they would conform to the civil law. Also, there were new threats of a confiscation of all Church property and the disfranchisement of all church members who refused to compromise. It is understandable that concerned members would seek some kind of an agreement with the Government. The pressures had become so severe that President John Taylor was forced into hiding lest the civil authorities put him in prison.

John Taylor went into hiding in 1884 and remained so until his death three years later. While in hiding he remained in Salt Lake and Davis Counties, moving between the homes of people he could trust, often staying just one step ahead of the authorities. He was wanted because he was a polygamist but vigorously because he was the President of the Church. He had trusted bodyguards with him at all times.

The following is an account of events that a man by the name of Lorin Woolley claimed to have taken place at his father's home in 1886, when the pressure to discontinue polygamy became so intense. It alleges that a self-appointed committee drafted a manifesto to discontinue polygamy for President Taylor's consideration. One of the men Lorin claims was present for these events, who he says witnessed all that occurred, denied that he had been witness to any of this. The account by Woolley was written in 1929, forty-three years later.

This following account is referred to as The Eight Hour Meeting among polygamists.

"On September 26, 1886, George Q. Cannon, Hyrum B. Clawson, Franklin S.

Richards, and others, met with President John Taylor at my father's residence at Centerville, Davis County, Utah, and presented a document for President Taylor's consideration.

"I had just got back from a three days' trip, during most of which time I had been in the saddle, and being greatly fatigued, I had retired to rest.

"Between one and two o'clock P.M., Brother Bateman came and woke me up and asked me to be at my father's home where a manifesto was to be discussed. I went there and found there were congregated Samuel Bateman, Charles H. Wilkins, L. John Nuttall, Charles Birrell, George Q. Cannon, Franklin S. Richards and Hyrum B. Clawson.

"We discussed the proposed Manifesto at length, but we were unable to become united in the discussion. Finally George Q. Cannon suggested that President Taylor take the matter up with the Lord and decide the same the next day. Brothers Clawson and Richards were taken back to Salt Lake. That evening I was called to act as guard during the first part of the night, notwithstanding the fact that I was greatly fatigued on account of the three days' trip I had just completed.

"The brethren retired to bed soon after nine o'clock. The sleeping rooms were inspected by the guard as was the custom.

"President Taylor's room had no outside door. The windows were heavily screened.

"Some time after the brethren retired and while I was reading the Doctrine and Covenants, I was suddenly attracted to a light appearing under the door leading to President Taylor's room, and was at once startled to hear the voices of men talking there. I was bewildered because it was my duty to keep people out of that room and evidently someone had entered without my knowing it. I made a hasty examination and found the door leading to the room bolted as usual. I then examined the outside of the house and found all the window screens intact. While examining the last window, and feeling greatly agitated, a voice spoke to me, saying, 'Can't you feel the Spirit? Why should you worry?'

"At this I returned to my post and continued to hear the voices in the room. They were so audible that although I did not see the parties I could place their positions in the room from the sound of their voices. The three voices continued until about midnight, when one of them left, and the other two continued. One of them I recognized as President John Taylor's voice.

"I called Charles Birrell and we both sat up until eight o'clock the next morning.

"When President Taylor came out of his room about eight o'clock of the morning of September 27, 1886, we could scarcely look at him on account of the brightness of his personage.

"He stated, 'Brethren, I have had a very pleasant conversation all night with Brother Joseph' (Joseph Smith). I said, 'Boss, who is the man that was there until midnight?' He asked, 'What do you know about it, Lorin?' I told him all about my experience. He said, 'Brother Lorin, that was your Lord.'

"We had no breakfast, but assembled ourselves in a meeting. I forget who opened the meeting, I was called to offer the benediction. I think my father, John W. Woolley, offered the opening prayer. There were present, at this meeting, in addition to President Taylor; George Q. Cannon, L. John Nuttall, John W. Woolley, Samuel Bateman, Charles H. Wilkins, Charles Birrell, Daniel R. Bateman, Bishop Samuel Sedden, George Earl, my mother, Julia E. Woolley, my sister, Amy Woolley, and myself. The meeting was held from about nine o'clock in the morning until five in the afternoon without intermission, being about eight hours in all.

"President Taylor called the meeting to order. He had the Manifesto (to discontinue polygamy), that had been prepared under the direction of George Q. Cannon, read over again. Then he put each person under covenant that he or she would defend the principle of Celestial or Plural Marriage, and that they would consecrate their lives, liberty and property to this end, and they personally would sustain and uphold that principle.

"By that time we were all filled with the Holy Ghost. President Taylor and those present occupied about three hours up to this time. After placing us under covenant, he placed his finger on the document (the proposed manifesto to discontinue polygamy), his person rising from the floor about a foot or eighteen inches, and with countenance animated by the Spirit of the Lord, and raising his right hand to the square, he said, 'Sign that document – never! I would suffer my right hand to be severed from my body first. Sanction it, never! I would suffer my tongue to be torn from its roots in my mouth before I would sanction it!'

"After that he talked for about an hour and then sat down and wrote the revelation which was given him by the Lord upon the question of Plural Marriage. Then he talked to us for some time, and said; 'Some of you will be handled and ostracized and be cast out from the Church by your brethren because of your faithfulness and integrity to this principle, and some of you may have to surrender your lives because of the same, but woe, woe, unto those who shall bring these troubles upon you (Three of us were handled and ostracized for supporting and sustaining this principle. There are only three left who were at the meeting mentioned: Daniel R. Bateman, George Earl and myself. So far as I know those of them who have passed away all stood firm to the covenants entered into from that day to the day of their deaths).

"After the meeting was concluded, President Taylor had L. John Nuttall write five copies of the revelation. He called five of us together: Samuel Bateman, Charles H. Wilkins, George Q. Cannon, John Woolley, and myself.

"He then set us apart and placed us under covenant that while we lived we would see to it that no year passed by without children being born in the principle of plural marriage. We were given authority to carry this work on, they in turn to be given authority to ordain others when necessary, under the direction of the worthy senior (by ordination), so that there should be no cessation in the work. He then gave each of us a copy of the Revelation.

"I am the only one of the five now living, and so far as I know all five of the brethren remained true and faithful to the covenants they entered into and to the responsibilities placed upon them at that time.

"During the eight hours we were together, and while President Taylor was talking to us, he frequently arose and stood above the floor, and his countenance and being were so enveloped by light and glory that it was difficult for us to look upon him.

"He stated that the document, referring to the Manifesto, was from the lower regions. He stated that many of the things he had told us we would forget and they would return to us in due time as needed, and from this fact we would know that the same was from the Lord. This has been literally fulfilled. Many of the things I forgot, but they are coming to me gradually, and those things that come to me are as clear as on the day on which they were given.

"President Taylor said that the time would come when many of the Saints would apostatize because of this principle. He said 'one half of this people will apostatize over the principle for which we are now in hiding, yea, and possibly one half of the other half' (rising off the floor while making this statement). He also said the day will come when a document similar to that (Manifesto) then under consideration would be adopted by the Church, following which 'apostasy and whoredom would be rampant in the Church.'

"He said that in the time of the seventh president of this Church, the Church would go into bondage both temporally and spiritually and in that day (the day of bondage) the One Mighty and Strong spoken of in the 85th Section of the Doctrine and Covenants would come. (Heber J. Grant was seventh president, from 1918 -1945.)

"Among many other things stated by President Taylor on this occasion was this: 'I would be surprised if ten percent of those who claim to hold the Melchizedek Priesthood will remain true and faithful to the Gospel of the Lord Jesus Christ, at the time of the seventh president. . .there would be thousands that think they hold the Priesthood at that time, but would not have it properly conferred upon them.'

"John Taylor set the five mentioned apart and gave them authority to perform marriage ceremonies, and also to set others apart to do the same thing as long as they remained on the earth; and while doing so, the Prophet Joseph Smith stood by directing the proceedings. Two of us had not met the Prophet Joseph Smith in his mortal lifetime, and we – Charles H. Wilkins and myself were introduced to him and shook hands with him."

WAS IT FROM MAN OR GOD?

What polygamists use as a guide to determine the truth of what is claimed to be from God for direction to His people, comes from the Doctrine & Covenants, Section 128:3. In it, Joseph Smith proclaims: ". . .in the mouths of two or three witnesses every word may be established." It is understood that verbal "revelations" must be written so that people will have a record.

When John Taylor died, a copy of the revelation was found among his papers by one of his sons. It did not mention plural marriage specifically, or ordaining men to keep plural marriage alive. It spoke to the fact that John Taylor had asked God about "keeping God's law" and was told that His laws must be kept.

Page 1

Purported to be the Revelation received by LDS President John Taylor, September 1886, as found in his papers after his death.

Page 2

Purported to be the Revelation received by LDS President John Taylor, September 1886, as found in his papers after his death.

would apostatize because of this principle. He said "one-half of this people will apostatize over the principle for which we are now in hiding, yea, and possibly one-half of the other half (rising off the floor while making this statement). He also said the day will come when a document similar to that (manifesto) then under consideration would be adopted by the Church, following which "apostacy and whoredom would be rampant in the Church."

He said that in the time of the seventh president of this Church, the Church would go into bondage both temporally and spiritually and in that day the one Mighty and Strong spoken of in the 85th section of the Doctrine and Covenants would come.

Among many other things stated by President Taylor on this occasion was this: "I would be surprised if ten per cent of those who claim to hold the Melchisedek Priesthood will remain true and faithful to the Gospel of the Lord Jesus Christ, at the time of the seventh President and that there would be thousands that think they hold the Priesthood at that time, but would not have it properly conferred upon them."

John Taylor set the five mentioned apart and gave them authority to perform marriage ceremonies, and also to set others apart to do the same thing as long as they remained on the earth; and while doing so the Prophet Joseph Smith stood by directing the proceedings. Two of us had not met the Prophet Joseph Smith in his mortal life-time, and we—Charles H. Wilkins and myself—were introduced to him and shook hands with him.

Signed—LORIN C. WOOLLEY.

Daniel R. Bateman, being present while the above experience was related by Brother Woolley, testified as follows:

I was privileged to be at the meeting of September 27, 1886 spoken of by Brother Woolley, I myself acting as one of the guards for the brethren during those exciting times.

The proceedings of the meeting as related by Brother Woolley are correct in every detail.

Signed—DANIEL R. BATEMAN

In a later interview (March 18, 1938) given by Daniel R. Bateman, the above facts are re-stated and the following information added:

I was twenty-nine years of age when the revelation of 1886 was given to John Taylor, and I was permitted to make a copy of it from the original which was written by John Taylor during the meeting held September 27, 1886. I still have the Journal with the revelation in it.

I was at a meeting at Draper, Salt Lake County, Utah, when President George Q. Cannon, shortly before his death, spoke as follows:

"The day will come when men's priesthood and authority will be called into question, and you will find out that there will be hundreds who will have no priesthood, but believe they hold it, they having ONLY AN OFFICE IN THE CHURCH." (1)

At this writing, Elder Bateman, in his 84th year, resides at Salt Lake City, and will cheerfully verify the information given.

From the facts presented the unprejudiced mind will readily concede the inviolableness of the law of plural marriage and the absolute necessity of its practice, even though civil laws are enacted against it.

It should also be noted, from the Woolley-Bateman statement that provision was made not only to have the law of plural marriage perpetuated during the lives of the brethren then set apart for that purpose, but they were given authority and direction to set others apart, in order that the organization might continue without interruption.

Unfortunately, but for reasons best known to its leaders, the Church, in an "Official Statement" of June 17, 1933, repudiated this 1886 revelation in the following words:

It is alleged that on September 26-27, 1886, President John Taylor received a revelation from the Lord. * * * (but) as to this pretended revelation it should be said that the archives of the Church contain no such revelation; the archives contain no record of any such revelation, nor any evidence justifying a belief that any such revelation was ever given. From the personal knowledge of SOME OF US, from the uniform and common recollection of the presiding quorums of the Church, from the absence in the Church archives of any evidence whatsoever justifying any belief that such a revelation was given, WE ARE JUSTIFIED IN AFFIRMING THAT NO SUCH A REVELATION EXISTS.

(1) Since about 1921 the Church has followed the policy of ordaining men to the office direct and not conferring upon them the Priesthood, as was formerly the practice.

This article is found in the publication, Truth. vol. 6. pp 136-137.

Furthermore, so far as the authorities of the Church are concerned and so far as the members of the Church are concerned, since this pretended revelation, if ever given, was never presented to and adopted by the Church, or by any council of the Church * * * the said pretended revelation could have no validity and no binding effect and force upon the Church members, and action under it would be unauthorized, illegal and void. —p. 17.

This statement, loosely worded and grossly misleading, was doubtless put forth as a subterfuge to camouflage the facts and lead the masses to believe that no such a revelation was received by John Taylor. However, "murder will out." Some eight months after the issuance of the "Official Statement" (Feb. 10, 1934) A. W. Ivins, one of its signers, in a letter addressed to a member of the Church residing in Long Beach, California, admitted the existence of the text of the revelation in question. He said:

The latter purported revelation of John Taylor (of 1886) has no standing in the Church. I have searched carefully, and all that can be found is a piece of paper found among President Taylor's effects after his death. It was written in pencil and only a few paragraphs which had no signature at all. It was unknown to the Church until members of his own family claimed to have found it among his papers. It was never presented or discussed as a revelation by the presiding authorities of the Church.—Supplement to New and Everlasting Covenant of Marriage, p. 15.

This weak admission of the document's existence, cunningly and adroitly written, was evidently intended to minimize its importance, by terming it a "piece of paper found among President Taylor's effects after his death," unsigned and "containing only a few paragraphs." The feeble effort at repudiation will not escape the detection of those seeking truth; a school-boy mind can grasp it. It was on a "piece of paper" and contained "but few paragraphs," and was "without signature," therefore it could not be genuine, but it was found among the effects of President Taylor! Will the reader refer to a number of the revela-

tions given through the Prophet Joseph Smith and recorded in the Doctrine and Covenants, the law book to the Church, such for instance as Sections 22, 26, 32, 37, 43, and 116, the latter containing only one paragraph and thirty words. One may readily and correctly surmise that each of these revelations were written on a "piece of paper" and contained "but few paragraphs," and, of course, not one of them bears the signature of the Prophet! They all, including the 1882 and 1886 revelations to John Taylor, were messages from Jesus Christ and bore the unmistakable ear marks of HIS signature.

Elder Ivins, it must be remembered, was a member of the First Presidency and one of the signers of the "Official Statement" referred to and in which the existence of the document was denied, though he now, eight months later admits its existence, but makes no correction of the error.

On a later occasion (December 31, 1934), some eighteen months after the "Official Statement" referred to, and with greater frankness, Elder Melvin J. Ballard, a member of the Quorum of Twelve, admitted the existence of the record of this revelation. In a letter to Elder Eslie D. Jenson of Millville, Utah, he stated:

The pretended revelation of President John Taylor (of 1886) never had his signature added to it but was written IN THE FORM OF A REVELATION and UNDOUBTEDLY WAS IN HIS HAND WRITING; nevertheless it was never submitted to his own associates in the Presidency and the Twelve nor to the Church and consequently does not bind the Church in any sense.—Marriage— Ballard-Jenson Correspondence, p. 27.

Here is an admission of a document in the "form of a revelation" and in the "handwriting" of President Taylor, and is the "purported" revelation which the Church in its "Official Statement" said was non-existent. Elder Ballard claims it was not submitted to "his associates in the Presidency," but one of his associates in the Presidency, George Q. Cannon, was with

This article is found in the publication, Truth. vol. 6. pp 136-137.

There is no *written* testimony of anyone other than Lorin Woolley of the ordinations of the five men taking place, and the written account was not accomplished until forty-three years later in 1929.

Daniel R. Bateman, who allegedly was present for the eight-hour meeting but was *not* in the meeting where President Taylor commissioned the five men to secretly promote plural marriage, also made a written statement in 1929: "The proceedings of the meeting, as related by Brother Woolley (Lorin), are correct in every detail. I was *not* present when the five spoken of by Brother Woolley were set apart for special work, but have on different occasions heard the details of the same related by both Lorin C. Woolley and John W. Woolley, and from all the circumstances with which I am familiar, I firmly believe the testimony of these two Brethren to be true" (*Truth*, vol. 2 p. 120).

Daniel Bateman's testimony presents a question for the polygamists. If he was not present when these ordinations took place, how can he be considered as a second legitimate witness? There is no other *written* testimony of anyone witnessing these ordinations to keep plural marriage alive.

George Earl, whom Lorin Woolley claimed was present *during the eight-hour meeting*, apparently was approached many times during his life by Fundamentalists seeking corroboration of the Lorin Woolley story. Each time, he denied that he had been witness to any of the events described by Woolley, although he affirmed his respect for the Woolley family.

Lorin Woolley's father John W. Woolley, one of the five allegedly commissioned and who became involved in encouraging polygamy and in sealing those marriages, never made a written statement.

Joseph Musser was one of the men most responsible for the later ongoing development of the Fundamentalist movement. Quoting from *Truth*, a monthly magazine he began publishing in 1935, he states: "There are a number of the brethren now living who heard not only Lorin Woolley and Daniel R. Bateman, but also John W. Woolley (Lorin's father), relate the incidents of the meeting referred to, and their story agrees in all essential details" (*Truth*, vol. 2, p 126).

POLYGAMY GOES PUBLIC

The secrecy of continuing plural marriages went public in 1927. J. Leslie Broadbent and John Y. Barlow had become associated with the Woolleys and were eager to live polygamy and also wanted to get the message to the entire LDS Church membership that there was a Priesthood outside of the Church commissioned to keep the Principle (plural marriage) alive. In September of 1927, these two men published a pamphlet entitled *Celestial Marriage*, with a big question mark on the front cover. The little pamphlet was read by many and created enough controversy that some began asking questions of their bishops (pastor of a local ward/congregation) about polygamy and whether the doctrine should have been discontinued. The compilers of the pamphlet did not put their names on the first printing, because of the fear of persecution and prosecution. Many secret polygamists were still members of the LDS Church and knew they would be excommunicated if discovered.

When a third printing was put out in May 1929, the compilers did put their names on the preface page. In part it says: "Grateful acknowledgment is here made of the assistance of John Y. Barlow in searching the record for the enclosed quotations." It is signed "J. L. Broadbent, Compiler." This was the first propaganda material put out by the Group that became known as the Polygamist Fundamentalists.

John Woolley died December 13, 1928, and this, according to Lorin Woolley, left him as the only survivor of the five men to whom LDS Prophet John Taylor had given the special commission to secretly promote polygamy. Thus he felt the necessity of commissioning six more men to carry on with the work. They were ordained in the following order: Joseph Leslie Broadbent, John Yates Barlow, Joseph White Musser, Charles Fredrick Zitting, LeGrand Woolley, and Louis Kelsch.

Before Lorin Woolley died, he called these men together and spent several months giving them instruction as to what their duty and calling was to be. He also explained that as a group, they each had the same authority and that decisions were to be made as a group, not by one man. He cited the 1880 revelation Wilford Woodruff received from the Lord stating such. There was to be a senior man, by order of ordination, who would lead the group, and they would make decisions together.

He instructed them not to hold public meetings to gain followers, but to discuss plural marriage in the private homes of those interested in following their teachings. They were not to publicly seek for followers or collect tithing money (ten percent) from any of their followers. He also taught them that they were not to implement any kind of a United Order, that the Lord would not require such to be lived until He came and set the Church in order. Based on early teachings of the LDS Church, many believed that One Mighty & Strong, as described in the Doctrine & Covenants, would return to the earth and correct all the problems and bring the unrighteous to justice. Some believed this would be Jesus Christ, others believed it would be Joseph Smith, and even others believed the two would come together.

Soon after giving these six men their instructions, Lorin Woolley had a stroke and was confined to his home in Centerville. It left him incapacitated and unable to communicate. In teaching them, he had not been as specific as they wished regarding what their duties were, other than making sure that plural marriage was continued. One thing he did tell them: "Your callings into the Council of Friends (Priesthood Council) will have to be confirmed by God himself, Christ will have to lay his hands on your head himself and confirm your calling."

While Lorin Woolley lay in his sick bed, these men began to speculate as to what their duties really were. They also wanted to receive confirmation from Christ of their callings, as Lorin Woolley had instructed, so they decided to go into the mountains and spend ten days of fasting and praying, asking that a messenger from heaven come to instruct them and give them the confirmation.

On April 15, 1934, Leslie Broadbent, John Barlow, and Joseph Musser left Salt Lake City, going east into the mountains to begin their quest. In Joseph Musser's journal, he writes under the date of April 15, 1934: "Preparing to leave for God's Temple in the morning with Jno. Y. Barlow and Prest. Broadbent…the Mountains…to make inquiry of the Lord regarding his will concerning us…."

"Saturday 23: "In our camp in Lamb's Canyon where we have been sojourning for the past week, seeking the will of the Lord concerning us and his people who are looking to the Priesthood for divine guidance, we have been fasting and praying and studying for a week, having finished our notes on the "Supplement to the New and Everlasting Covenant of Marriage" (a pamphlet they later published) which has been prepared with the collaboration of Elder J. L. Broadbent." These men all had dreams during their week of fasting and praying. These dreams were interpreted by them as being instruction from God that their duty was to tell their message to any who would listen, using those who believed in them to carry on the law of polygamy.

Throughout these events, the men received no confirmation and no messenger from heaven had appeared to any of them, although some dreams had been interpreted as revelation.

Lorin Woolley died on September 18, 1934, never having recovered. Leslie Broadbent, the next recognized leader of the Group, died six months later on March 19, 1935, leaving John Barlow to assume the leadership position.

Joseph Musser writes in his journal under the date of March 16, 1935: "Brother Joseph Leslie Broadbent has passed on! …The brethren of the Priesthood attended him faithfully and pled mightily with the Lord for his restoration, but without avail…. The spirit of leadership is resting upon Jno. Y. Barlow and he will 'carry on' under the direction of heaven."

John Barlow was now the senior member of this group, who were beginning to be referred to as the Priesthood Council. He and his next in line, Joseph Musser, were now the recognized leaders of the Fundamentalist movement.

2

Trying To Have All Things In Common

The Great Depression was creating severe economic distress in the country and large secretly polygamous families were particularly affected. Their struggle to provide food and clothing for their families weighed on the minds of many. To John Barlow, it only made sense to do something to help them. He had tried on various occasions to persuade John and Lorin Woolley to organize the people and set up a United Order, where everyone would work together, sharing equally, but he was rebuked every time. After their deaths, he approached Leslie Broadbent with these same ideas but was met with the same disapproval.

After the death of Leslie Broadbent, John Barlow felt that as the senior member of the Council, and entitled to his own inspiration from God, he should be able to make his own decisions. He knew he was expected to work with the remaining four men making decisions they all could support, so he began making his case about the importance of setting up a United Order.

It would be challenging to win them over because these men believed in and were following Lorin Woolley's counsel, which was not to organize, not to set up a United Order, and not to collect tithing money, but to simply teach the law of polygamy and keep the principle of plural marriage alive. With the economic struggles of the Depression, John Barlow continued to present a strong argument for the economic and religious benefits to polygamous families that a United Order would provide. They could pool their money and resources, their time, talents, and hard work and create a haven away from the world for people who wanted to live polygamy. But they would need a place to do that.

About this time several people who lived in Short Creek, Arizona, or owned property there, came to the Brethren and offered their land to the Priesthood Council as a gathering place for the polygamists. Many LDS Church members still held fast to the United Order doctrine presented in the Doctrine & Covenants. It was a way of living that represented righteous people coming together in godliness to care for one another.

But the men on the Priesthood Council were not yet convinced. They still felt it would be improper to officially organize and declined the offer. John Barlow, however, wanted to accept the property, intended that they have the property, and he pressed the other members until they finally agreed. He got Joseph Musser's consent, Charles Zitting agreed to help somewhat, but the other two members, LeGrand Woolley and Louis Kelsch only agreed not to stand in their way. But Joseph Musser's support was all that John Barlow felt he needed, because Musser was loved and respected among their followers.

It is a popular misconception that Short Creek was chosen as a gathering place for the polygamists because it straddled the state line. In fact, Short Creek was chosen because the people there offered their property to the Priesthood Council. Leroy Johnson was one of the property owners who made the offer, and in time a lifelong bond of trust would develop between him and John Barlow.

In 1935, John Barlow, along with Joseph Musser and a few others, including Richard and Fred Jessop, made a trip to Short Creek to look at the area and apprize the situation. It was a hard trip because there were few paved roads and the automobiles of the 1930s were not too dependable. After a grueling trip through Utah and finally through Cedar City and Hurricane, the group did arrive at Short Creek. Meetings were called and plans were talked about to turn the isolated spot into a beautiful place.

While there, Joseph Musser made prophecies of things that would come to pass. Among these prophecies was that a temple would be built on a small hill south of the community called Berry Knoll, so named in memory of two brothers, Robert and Joseph Berry and Isabella, wife of Robert, who were killed by Indians nearby during the Black Hawk uprising of the 1860s. He also prophesied that Short Creek, even though presently a poor place to farm, would become a garden spot of the west, one acre of land producing more food stuff than ten acres of the best farm land in Davis County, Utah. (As of 2004, neither of these prophecies has come to pass.)

The group then went back to Salt Lake City and discussed further the wisdom of setting up a United Order. Finally, it was agreed that John Barlow would oversee a United Order group in Short Creek and Joseph Musser would oversee one in Salt Lake City.

During this time, a man by the name of Charles Owens was buying a farm in the Union area of Salt Lake Valley, but he had been unable to make the payments and was faced with foreclosure. He went to the Brethren and offered the place for a United Order movement, but they would have to redeem it. He met with John Barlow, Joseph Musser, Louis Kelsch, and Arnold Boss.

Owens stated: "It has been demonstrated to me that I cannot succeed temporally except through the spirit of the United Order and I am ready to turn in all I have, permitting the Priesthood to handle the same as they see fit. I recognize those of the Great High Priests as being the mouthpiece of God on the earth." (Charles Owens later joined a United Order group in the Bountiful, Utah, area led by Eldon Kingston. This group claims that when J. Leslie Broadbent was the President, he declared Eldon Kingston his Second Elder, thus leaving him as the next in line when Broadbent died in 1935. But that didn't happen and Kingston eventually started his own group.)

Joseph Musser was appointed to draw up a document for the organizing of a United Order. He writes in his journal, Saturday (June 22, 1935): "Working on Trust papers and met with the same six brethren (including myself) at 6 P.M. and read papers, which were unanimously approved. Name of Company – United Trust." They decided to set up the organization as a Business Trust, so donated property would be protected from confiscation by the government should they be prosecuted for being polygamists.

The "United Trust" was established in Salt Lake City and the property and operations at Short Creek would be conducted under this same Trust name and language. The affairs there were placed under the direction of John Barlow and "The United Trust" papers were later filed in the Mohave County courthouse in Kingman, Arizona. *The document listed what each participant contributed and declared that all members would be equal owners in the trust.* Also, there would be no rich or poor, but all would be equal.

Again from Musser's journal (July 20, 1935):
   "John Y. Barlow to have full charge of operations at Short Creek, using his judgment and taking action as occasion requires: J. W. Musser, with the help of the brethren here (Salt Lake) to have like jurisdiction in Utah in the absence of Prest. Barlow."

Barlow and Musser began soliciting men who were already secretly polygamists or would like to become such. Some were asked to take their families and move to Short Creek while others were solicited to consecrate money to finance the project. They were successful in getting about six men to move their families to Short Creek, joining with the original settlers there. This small Group became the nucleus Barlow needed to establish a place where people could live Plural Marriage *and* the United Order according to their religious beliefs. And John Barlow wanted a secluded area, away from government eyes, and away from the scrutiny of the LDS Church.

FIRST DISCOVERY OF SHORT CREEK

"They have been shielded…by the geographic circumstances of Arizona's northern most territory – the region beyond the Grand Canyon that is best known as The Strip. Massive cliffs rearing north of Short Creek's little central street provide a natural rock barrier to the north. To the east and west are the sweeping expanses of dry and almost barren plateaus before the forests begin. To the south is the Grand Canyon. It is the most isolated of all Arizona communities. Short Creek is 400 miles by the shortest road from the Mohave County seat of Kingman. Short Creek is unique among Arizona communities in that some of its dwellings actually are in another state."
         A description by Arizona Governor Howard Pyle in 1953.

Stephen V. Jones, assistant topographer to the second Colorado River expedition of John Wesley Powell, in describing his impression of the area, entered in his diary on Saturday, April 6, 1872: "(We) made Short Creek at 1 p.m. A dirty little stream not fit to drink."
   In 1872, Short Creek, so named because of the short distance from the canyon to the

lake bed it emptied into (a distance of about three miles), indeed seemed an unlikely place for a city to be established. There was very little water, the one most important necessity for the establishment and growth of a pioneer city. The only asset was the good grasslands in the area, making it suitable for the grazing of livestock.

During the period from 1867-1900, Short Creek Valley was "herd ground" for cattle owned by the Mormon Church. The springs in the Upper Canyon and also those at nearby Cane Beds to the southeast and Canaan to the northwest were headquarters for prosperous ranches that utilized the luxuriant forage on the Arizona Strip. The Mormon Church owned the ranch at Canaan. The Maxwell brothers owned the ranch in the mouth of Short Creek Canyon. Most of the other cattle on the Arizona strip were owned by the United Order (Mormon Church) based at Orderville, Utah.

The first permanent settlers moved to Short Creek about 1914 when Jacob Lauritzen and his family came to the valley. Eventually, with the help of his brother and sons, he installed an irrigation ditch from Water Canyon that was adequate for watering about 200 acres. James Black and his family moved to Short Creek from Ferron, Utah, in April 1918, and helped the Lauritzens complete the ditch.

Water Canyon, a left hand fork from Short Creek Canyon, about one mile from the canyon mouth, produced the most water for Short Creek. The ditch, bringing the water from the canyon, was about three miles long. It was constructed by hand with the aid of horses and scrapers and was completed in one summer. The first half-mile of the ditch was run in 8 inch concrete pipe, the pipe sections being three feet in length. These pipe sections were hand carried for this half-mile distance before being set in place. The ditch was then hand dug for the remaining two and a half miles to the potential farmland. The water emptied into a reservoir where it was stored overnight and was used to water the fields in the daytime.

One "water right" was one eight hour natural stream flow. These water rights were granted to people (besides the Lauritzens) who worked on the ditch. Some of these included James Black and his family, Isaac Carling, and Elmer Johnson. The Blacks traded their water rights in the ditch to the Lauritzens for land and water rights to springs in the mouth of the main Short Creek Canyon, just above the junction of Water Canyon. They established a small farm there and called the spot The Garden of Eden.

The first permanent settlers on the south side of Short Creek were Frank Colvin and his wife Elizabeth, who moved from Pipe Spring in the summer of 1914, where they had been living in the old Mormon fort, about 15 miles east of Short Creek. Pipe Spring Fort had been built in the 1870s under the direction of Brigham Young and the ranch supervisor Anson Perry Windsor.

The building consisted of two sandstone structures facing each other across a courtyard enclosed by wooden gates, which became known as Windsor Castle. Windsor and his family used the fort as headquarters for the cattle herds that he managed for the LDS Church. Even before the fort was completed a relay station for the Deseret Telegraph system was installed, connecting this remote outpost on the Arizona Strip to other Mormon settlements and Salt Lake City, Utah. This was the first telegraph line to enter the Arizona Territory. However, the location of the territorial boundary was not known to the builders, making them unaware of this fact.

In the 1880s and 1890s the remote fort at Pipe Spring became a refuge for wives hiding from federal marshals enforcing anti-polygamy laws. A number of women and children hid at Pipe Spring to save their husbands and fathers from prosecution. Faced with the confiscation of Church property, the Mormon Church sold Pipe Spring Ranch. Between 1895 and 1923 it remained in private hands. It was an oasis in the desert where travelers would stop to refresh themselves and several families lived there from time to time. On May 31, 1923, President Warren G. Harding signed the proclamation setting aside Pipe Spring National Monument, which it remains to the present time.

The Blacks later moved out of the canyon and settled on the south side of the Creek. Two of Elizabeth Colvin's brothers also settled at Short Creek – Leroy Johnson in 1926, and Elmer Johnson in 1932. Another brother, Price Johnson and a brother-in-law, Carling Spencer, moved there about the same time. These two were probably the first polygamists to move into the area since the Mormon Church outlawed polygamy.

EXCOMMUNICATIONS

The LDS Church was well aware that some of its members were moving to Short Creek to practice plural marriage. It also knew that some of the earlier residents of Short Creek, although members of a local branch of the LDS Church, were secretly living polygamy. Finally it began excommunicating them, calling them apostates. And the Church wanted to put an end to rampant rumors about secret polygamy within the ranks of its own church. On September 7 the Stake Presidency and High Council of Zion Park Stake met with the members of the Short Creek Branch of The Church of Jesus Christ of Latter Day Saints in the same school house where a trial of the polygamists had been held the previous day. The members of the Branch were asked to sign a loyalty oath to the Church and its leaders and to promise to refrain from living polygamy. Those who would not comply to their request were threatened with ex-communication.

The following is the loyalty oath that the Zion Park Stake Presidency asked the church members at Short Creek to sign (*Truth*, vol. 1, p. 121)

Short Creek, Arizona, September 7, 1935

To the Stake Presidency and High Council of Zion Park Stake and to whom it may concern:

I, the undersigned member of Short Creek Branch of the Rockville Ward of The Church of Jesus Christ of Latter Day Saints, declare and affirm that I without any mental reservation whatsoever, support the Presidency of the Church, *and that I repudiate any intimation that any of the Presidency or Apostles of the Church are living a double life, and that I repudiate those who are falsely accusing them*, and that I denounce the practice and advocacy of Plural marriage as being out of harmony with the declared principles of the Church at the present time. (italics added)

ARRESTS BEGIN

Also in 1935 when news of the polygamists settling at Short Creek was received by the County Officials in Kingman, Arizona, they felt it was necessary to stop this influx of lawbreakers moving into Mohave County. Arizona had no law on its books against polygamy, but its Constitution did say that "polygamy shall forever be banned." The County Sheriff was sent to Short Creek in the late summer to arrest several polygamists on the charge of open and notorious cohabitation. The trial took place on September 6, 1935, at the Short Creek School house with the local Justice of the Peace, Jacob Lauritzen, presiding. After being convened for about a half hour, the cases were all dismissed because of improper pleadings prepared by the County Attorney and the prisoners were set free. New complaints were then prepared and served on two of the men who were long-time residents of Short Creek, Price Johnson (brother of Leroy) and Carling Spencer. Their cases were moved to Kingman for final disposition.

After turning themselves in to the sheriff, Price Johnson and Carling Spencer were taken to Kingman in the fall of 1935. In a preliminary hearing they were bound over to the District Court and the trial date was set, at which time they were released on bail and returned to Short Creek to prepare for the trial.

The trial began on December 9, 1935, and lasted four days with Judge J. W. Faulkner presiding, E. Elmo Bollinger as the prosecuting attorney, and Victor J. Hayek acting for the defense. Evidence was shown that the defendants were living polygamously and raising children in that relationship. In each case the defendants were adjudged guilty and were sentenced to serve eighteen months to two years in the Arizona State Penitentiary at Florence, Arizona. On January 7, 1936, they were taken to Florence to begin their prison sentence. The defense appealed their cases but to no avail. These men had never been accused of any crime and were only living polygamy as a tenet of their religion.

Both of these men had big families at Short Creek. They had become members of the United Order and had donated all they possessed to the Priesthood Group. When they left for prison, trusting the care of their families to the United Order, they felt confident their families would be taken care of. But they weren't.

John Barlow failed to provide even the basic essentials for them; in fact, when some of their relatives in Glendale sent a few meager relief supplies to Price and Carling's families, Barlow confiscated them, using them himself, much to the disgust of the contributors. Some of the small children of these men were afflicted with lifetime maladies resulting from the malnutrition they suffered at this time.

These developments did not slow Barlow from continuing to develop his United Order. It is impossible to estimate how much donated money was spent to set it up. This was a time when the Nation was coming out of the Great Depression and any money given to the project was with great sacrifice to the donors.

The United Trust established in Salt Lake had a measure of success in providing help to struggling families. The situation at Short Creek was a different story. There were about ten male members of the Group and they soon began complaining about John Barlow's management of affairs and the complaints reached Joseph Musser in Salt Lake City. Joseph Musser then wrote Barlow a letter offering some advice. "I.W. Barlow (John's brother) came up on 4th. and informed me in detail of conditions at Short Creek, and certain threats Bro. Barlow made against me for imaginary wrongs. Am non-plussed. It has annoyed me beyond expression. Will have the matter settled before my council if necessary." This disagreement between John Barlow and Joseph Musser led to a confrontation over the situation and John Barlow was "invited to come up with a view to adjust matters at Short Creek." (Musser's Journal, August 24, 1935).

Musser did indeed have the matter settled before the council. They decided that Barlow should be removed from the managing position at Short Creek. From Musser's Journal: "Friday 18th.(1936). On 13th. we held Council meeting, and decided John should discontinue his active management of affairs at S.C. except in spiritual matters, and that the brethren locally there should organize and manage their own affairs, free from domination of the Priesthood."

This was a hard blow to John Barlow, but the United Order Movement at Short Creek was his dream venture and he was not about to give up his control there. After meeting with the Priesthood Council and hearing their position that he should step down, he returned to the community and related an altered story. He told the locals that the Council had decided to let the members choose who they wanted for their leader, that while Joseph Musser wanted him out of the leadership position, the rest of the Council thought he should remain in control, that if the people did what the Council wanted, they would vote for him to continue to run things. And they did. Whether they liked the way he was running things or not, they did believe he held the "keys to the priesthood." And in their minds, if everyone on the Council supported him, as he claimed, then they felt they must as well.

When Joseph Musser learned of this, he, along with Louis Kelsch and Daniel Bateman, made a trip to Short Creek to confront Barlow on his actions, and what appeared to be developing – a one man rule domination.

Musser's journal, November 8, 1936:
"Thursday Louis and I had a personal talk with Bro. John Y. Barlow. We pointed out our fears that under the present set-up the group could not prosper; that there seemed a disposition toward a one man rule; that many of the Saints were complaining; that the present arrangement was not in accordance with the spirit of the action of the Priesthood

recently taken, whereby it was advised that Bro. Barlow resign from the management of the affairs of the group and confine his labors more particularly to the spiritual field; That our work was especially along the line of keeping faith in patriarchal marriage alive, and not in the directing of colonizing.

"Bro. Barlow was asked if he claimed to hold the Keys of Priesthood, which he answered in the negative, saying, however, that he had dreamed of a personage coming to him and handing him a bunch of keys, and leaving without explanation. He did not know that that had any significance."

In later years after his death, the sons of John Barlow changed the original account of his dream to say that the man who appeared to him was Joseph Smith, and that the keys he gave him (in this dream) were indeed the Keys of The Priesthood (which gave him supreme authority over the people).

Musser's journal continues.

"On Friday 13: Priesthood met at 9 a.m. at home of Sister Colvin. Twelve of the local brethren were present, also Elders Kelsch, Bateman and Musser.

"Elder Kelsch stated the purpose of our visit, asking several questions of the brethren, and eliciting the following information: The action taken by the Priesthood in Salt Lake had been voted (by the members at Short Creek) adversely, mainly on account of supposing it to have been the submission of Bro. Musser and not the action of the Priesthood.

"That, ignoring the action and recommendations of the Priesthood, they (Short Creek members) had organized, using the form of United Trust, placing Bro. Barlow at the head, and were now operating under that agreement....

"The majority expressed the belief that Bro. John Y. Barlow held the keys to priesthood and was the mouth-piece of God on earth, and with some this was the only reason for accepting Bro. Barlow's management of affairs. Elders Covington and I.W. Barlow expressed emphatic dissent, stating they did not believe Bro. B. held the keys to Priesthood, but that he did have authority to seal and was the senior member in the Priesthood group, and as such presided at the meetings of the group, etc." (Sealed used herein describes marriage for eternity.)

J.W. Musser explained to them his views on Priesthood matters:
"That the special mission and labors of the Priesthood group was to keep plural marriage alive; that we were not called upon to colonize only as the Lord might dictate such a move; that it was the feeling of the Priesthood that the affairs of the Saints should be conducted by them in their local communities and not by the Priesthood,...that the time had not come for the establishing of the United Order...the Lord had not revealed to him who held the Keys to Priesthood, but that Bro. Barlow, by reason of his seniority in ordination presided over the group;.... There must be no autocratic rule. The agency of every individual must be respected. That no man should refuse his neighbor help when it was needed, even though the neighbor may not be a member of a TRUST GROUP."

Barlow continued experiencing problems in Short Creek. To have all things in common proved to be an impossibility. Those who controlled the money and supplies were living better than the lay members, many of whom were living on the verge of starvation. This situation caused bitter feelings and led to distrust of their leaders.

On November 8, 1936, Price Johnson and Carling Spencer were released from prison, after serving eleven months of their sentence, which was shortened through good behavior. The men felt they had spent their prison time pretty much ignored, and their families had been unjustly treated, especially by the leaders. Carling Spencer withdrew from participation in the Group. He eventually sold his property in about 1945 and moved to Mexico.

Price Johnson, in the spirit of brotherhood, went to John Barlow and, in humility, confessed his feelings of betrayal and some of his shortcomings, hoping to bond their relationship. He was a little critical of the action of the brethren, especially that of John Barlow, but supposed he had spoken with Brother Barlow in confidence. Much to his disappointment, he heard the things come back to him from other people of the community. John Barlow had told other members that Price was complaining and was weak in the faith. Of course, this undermined the confidence of the people towards Price Johnson. When Price learned what had happened, he withdrew from the society and moved to Glendale, Utah.

The main criticism of these two men was the unjust treatment of their wives and children while they were in prison. This touched them deeply, for they had supposed that by donating their property and consecrating all of their worldly possessions to the United Order, the Order would take care of their families while they were suffering as martyrs for the cause.

THE UNITED ORDER REVOLT

Soon after this, Leroy Johnson received an offer to go to a place on the Colorado River called Big Bend, where Riveria, Arizona, now stands and share crop on a farm. He moved his family and began farming, hopeful of helping to supply the pioneers of Short Creek with food stuff. John Barlow made a trip to Big Bend to visit with Leroy and offer encouragement. Before he left he put Leonard Black, one of the natives of Short Creek, in charge of the Sunday School class. It was only a short time after Barlow's leaving until other members felt that he did not have the authority to leave Leonard Black in charge of anything. A special meeting was called. Because each person joining the United Trust was designated a member *and the members could vote on who would govern the Trust*, these men voted to remove the current trustees and replace them with other members.

Warren Black, older brother of Leonard, was called to Kingman for jury duty. He went by way of Big Bend and informed John Barlow and Leroy Johnson of these developments. John Barlow's comment: "We organized the Trust and we can dissolve it." They claimed they went to Kingman and officially dissolved the United Trust, but there is no written record they did so. John Barlow returned to Short Creek and returned the deeds of the property to the owners, but the money donated had already been spent.

Because of a water rights dispute concerning the use of the Colorado River water, Leroy Johnson was forced off the farm and moved back to Short Creek where a few of the polygamists were still struggling to survive under John Barlow's leadership. The Woolsey ranch near Cedar City, Utah, was leased and Leroy Johnson, John Barlow, and their families moved there. Richard Jessop leased a farm nearby in New Harmony. These men stayed loyal to Uncle John (Barlow). (Within the polygamist community, it is customary to call people "Uncle" or "Aunt" as a matter of respect.)

With John Barlow and Leroy Johnson in Cedar City, and Richard Jessop in New Harmony, things in Short Creek returned to much the same as it was before the United Order experiment. While John Barlow had given the deeds of property back to the former owners, some, Leroy Johnson being one, had told him to keep the property, saying, "I have consecrated this to the Lord and I want you to keep it." The operations at Short Creek, by the people who remained working with Barlow, were still carried on under the name of the United Trust for several years. It is suggested that Barlow probably told the dissenters that the Trust had been dissolved so they would leave the community.

Being able to farm in New Harmony and the Woolsey Ranch, they survived the conditions of the times. Because of the property that was owned by the Trust at Short Creek, they continued their ties there, trying to farm some of the land, but not with much success because of lack of water. An effort was made to bring an irrigation ditch from the canyon to the fields on the south side of the creek, but there was very little water coming from this source and the hope was to mostly catch the flood waters when it rained. This project did not succeed and the old ditch line remained unused for several years.

Warren Black bought out the little store that had been started by John Spencer and with the help of his mother, Sara Black, ran the store and the U.S. Post Office.

The next few years were a struggle to survive. The hardships and trials they endured together forged a strong bond of kinship between the families of John Barlow, Leroy Johnson, and brothers Richard and Fred Jessop. These ties were also strengthened by intermarriage between families. John Barlow, Leroy Johnson and Richard Jessop each married another new wife, and Fred Jessop became a polygamist. The close bonds developed between these inter-marrying families and their progeny would prevail into the 21st Century, and would play a significant role in changing the original doctrine.

Along with the financial struggle to survive, another event occurred to hinder their progress. In 1939, Richard and Fred Jessop were arrested at New Harmony for unlawful cohabitation. Their trial began on September 19, 1939, at St. George, Utah. Richard Jessop chose to be tried before a jury and in just six minutes of deliberation he was declared guilty. He was sentenced to serve from one to five years in the State Penitentiary at Salt Lake City. Execution of the sentence was stayed pending an appeal to the State Supreme Court.

Fred Jessop waived his right to jury trial and was acquitted by the Court (Judge Will T. Hoyt) on lack of evidence. On March 27, 1940, the Utah Supreme Court reversed the lower Court's decision in the case of Richard Jessop. Among the points of error cited was insufficiency of evidence.

This victory created hope among the struggling group. Their faith was renewed and with optimism and hard work, they set about the job of establishing a city at Short Creek.

3

Failed United Order Now A United "Effort"

In June of 1935, Joseph Musser, the second in line after John Barlow in the Priesthood Council, had sent out the first issue of the monthly *Truth* Magazine. A front page paragraph read:

"A complete breakdown threatens the monogamistic order of marriage, the boast of modern civilization, has failed. Gnawing at its very vitals, to which the glorious principle of marriage is slowly but surely succumbing, are the death dealing agencies of infidelity, birth control and divorce. The remedy is comprehended in God's order of marriage known today as Celestial or Patriarchal Marriage (polygamy). It was revealed to Abraham by the Lord and in the present Dispensation was restored through the Mormon Prophet, Joseph Smith."

The magazine was circulated widely among the members of the LDS Church throughout the Inter-mountain region. Joseph Musser used the magazine as a forum to promote the ideas of the Priesthood Council. The Lorin Woolley story was told of how the former Church president John Taylor had set a group of men apart to keep polygamy alive in the event the Church abandoned it. Statements from the early presidents of the Mormon Church on the necessity of living polygamy were quoted extensively.

It was not long until Musser acquired a number of followers who began seeking him out for counsel and advice. Little groups of people sprang up throughout the Western region of the United States, from Idaho to Southern California.

Joseph Musser spent much of his time traveling throughout the region teaching the small groups that began asking to know more. One group was located in Eastern Idaho around the St. Anthony area. It was in December of 1938 that Musser made his first trip to Idaho to meet with the small group. A man by the name of Jonathan Marion Hammon was a member of this group and was to become a very prominent figure in this history.

Marion Hammon had always been an active member of the LDS Church. When he first heard the story of polygamy being lived in his day and time, he became interested and began to investigate the claims of the Priesthood Group.

After several trips to Idaho, Joseph Musser advised the five families there to move into northern Utah to be closer to the main Group in Salt Lake City. In June of 1940 Marion Hammon moved to Millville, Cache County, Utah, where a handful of polygamist families were living. He lived there less than a year before moving on to Salt Lake City. One day after Sunday meeting, Brother Musser asked him to come over to his house. Marion had recently entered the "principle" and due to the problems this had caused in his household, he was afraid Brother Musser was going to chastise him for not doing better with managing his family affairs. Imagine his surprise when Joseph Musser informed him he had been selected to be a member of the Priesthood Council.

In 1941 John Barlow said he "felt inspired" to call two new men into the Priesthood Council. Joseph Musser wanted Marion Hammon and John Barlow wanted Leroy Johnson, his close friend.

The other Council Members gave them a certain amount of opposition. Lorin Woolley had taught them how new members should be selected, which is documented in Charles Zitting's autobiography: "A man must be suggested by the Council on the *other side* (heaven) first and then presented to the senior or key man of the council on the earth and he takes it up with *his council* and when they pass on the man then word is sent back, by a messenger if you please, to the council on the other side, who in turn would send word back to set that man apart." When Barlow was asked by the other Council members, "Have you had a revelation?" He answered, "No, I just feel inspired that we should call them."

As president of the Priesthood Council, Barlow believed he had the authority to act on his own volition, not necessarily needing *revelation from heaven*. Since the late 1930s he had been teaching his close friends and associates that only one man held the power and authority to manage the affairs of the Polygamists and *since he was now that one man*, it was within his right to choose these men to be in HIS council.

Louis Kelsch and LeGrand Woolley never did endorse the proposition, they only agreed to not stand in John Barlow's way. LeGrand Woolley, a doctor who delivered many babies over the years, steadfastly held to the teachings of Lorin Woolley, a distant relative. He remained on the priesthood council until his death, hoping to provide resistance to the increasing one-man authority of John Barlow. Louis Kelsch felt similarly but tried to maintain his influence among council members.

As it turned out, John Barlow ordained his friend Leroy Johnson in a private meeting at Woolsey Ranch on May 21, 1941; then on June 6, two weeks later at Salt Lake City, he and Joseph Musser ordained both Leroy Johnson and Marion Hammon, in that order. Some speculate that Barlow wanted to take no chance that Hammon would be ordained first, putting him ahead of Leroy Johnson on the Council. He may have been looking to the future, knowing that his close kinship with Leroy could serve him and his sons.

WORLD WAR II & PROSPERITY

World War II came to the United States in 1941 and with it a time of prosperity for the whole country. Members of the group in the Salt Lake City area became involved in war time production, earning high wages. Many families had husbands, sons, and brothers in the service of their country. Joseph Musser's monthly magazine kept him in close touch with many of these people.

In spite of the failure of his first venture at Short Creek, John Barlow and most of the Priesthood Council members were now ready to try again to create a place where people could live and be taught how to one day live a true United Order. They began by establishing The United Effort Plan (UEP), which would provide their "place of refuge."

The Priesthood Council decided it would be safer to organize the association as a business trust to protect members' property from mortgage foreclosure or confiscation by the government because of polygamy.

The stated intentions of the Leaders for establishing the United Effort Plan was *for the security and protection of the members*, both from outside influence as well as unjust management within the Group itself.

On March 15, 1941, Joseph Musser and others left Salt Lake City for Short Creek. They made it to the Woolsey Ranch (near Cedar City) that day and spent the night with John Barlow. The organization of the new United Effort Plan was discussed among the Brethren. Leroy Johnson, Richard Jessop and Fred Jessop were a part of these planning sessions. The group of Brethren went on to Short Creek the next day. On March 26, a special meeting was called and the community members were presented with a letter dated March 20, listing the assets for the previous United Trust. Listed: Leroy S. Johnson land, 640 Acres (three homes), Richard & Fred Jessop 130 acres, Total: 770 acres (Deeded land.).

LEASES – New Harmony: 165 acres, three years to run. On 30 acres lessees get full crop for 1941 and 2/3 on balance. 70 acres from Mr. Smutz for 1941, on 2/3 crop basis. 70 acres from Mr. Taylor for 1941, on 2/3 crop. 25 A. Planted. Cedar Ranch: 470 Acres of which 150 A. Are cultivated: 3/5 basis. 33 head of cows with bull-same basis. Group Owns Outright: 9 head two year old heifers, some with calf, 10 yearling calves, 3 work horses; 3 saddle horses and pony, Threshing machine, Hand plow, Tractor, Drill, Plows, Silo cutter, Disc, 3 and a half sets harness, Harrow, Wagon rack, Potato planter, Trailer, Mowing machine, 2 canning outfits.

Indebtedness: Taxes on Short Creek property $215.00; Due on threshing machine $65.00; On Government loan (drawing 5%) $1568.26; On Government loan (drawing 3%) $4226.15; Current bill for gas and oil $106.15.

Now due on above: Taxes $215.00, Store $106.15. Due December 1st: On Government loan $824.00. On thresher $65.00 = $889.00

The letter was a plea to the people to help raise money to pay the indebtedness of the old Trust, so the new Trust could be established. Also the letter made it clear that "pending a more complete organization, or of entering into a united order under instructions of the Lord, the contributors proceed under a United Effort Plan." A Board of Control would manage the plan: John Y. Barlow, Joseph W. Musser, Charles F. Zitting, Louis A. Kelsch, Otto Holm, Carl Fischer, Leroy Johnson, Richard Jessop, Joseph Jessop, and Moroni Jessop.

One and one-half years later in October of 1942, a committee arrived in Short Creek to set up the new trust. Some of the men in this committee: John Barlow, Joseph Musser, Marion Hammon, George Dockstader, Guy Musser (son of Joseph), and Rulon Jeffs. After returning to Salt Lake City, the trust document was drawn up and an association was formed called The United Effort Plan. The trustees were: John Y. Barlow, president; Leroy Johnson, vice-president; Joseph W. Musser, secretary and treasurer; Marion Hammon and Rulon Jeffs as trustees. The document was signed by these trustees and officers on November 9, 1942, and not filed and recorded in Mohave County Courthouse, Kingman, Arizona, until August 8, 1944.

This new trust document of the United Effort Plan was different from the old Trust. The old United Trust had given the members power *to vote who the trustees and officers would be.* But John Barlow had learned his lesson and the new United Effort Plan *did not allow this protection to the members.* "Trustees" were appointed by the organizers of the trust and *new trustees would be appointed by these trustees. The members would have no say or control in matters governing the association in any way.*

After the document was drawn up and filed, one of the committee members, George L. Dockstader, who had assisted in its creation, made this statement:

"It (the trust document) is straight from Hell. A man would be absolutely crazy to ever subscribe to such a document." (It is interesting to note that George L. Dockstader did indeed join the United Effort Plan and move to Short Creek, where he taught in the public school for five or six years).

After the earlier incidents with the United Trust, the organizers believed that strict control was necessary. They claimed it was to insure the survival of the association, and was for the benefit and good of the members.

New converts throughout the Inter-mountain region sold their homes, moved to Short Creek, and donated the money to the Priesthood. Some who had small farms would "turn them in" (donate) thinking the Group would use them for production of food to help the people. To the sad disappointment of the contributors, any real estate or property outside of Short Creek consecrated to the Priesthood was almost immediately sold and converted to cash. Thousands of dollars were obtained this way, and the money was given to the trustees as salaries for their support.

4

Developing Their Religion And Town

Young, energetic, master organizer Marion Hammon was appointed by the UEP Board of Trustees to be the General Manager of affairs at Short Creek. He moved his family there in late 1942 and became active in this managing role. Under his direction the UEP flourished, and the next few years at Short Creek were a time of growth because of new members turning in (donating) property and money.

Some of these new members were already polygamists. Those who were not hoped that by giving all they possessed to the UEP, they would earn the "blessings" of obtaining additional wives so they could become polygamists. As it turned out, obtaining plural wives would not be easy. Even after a man would make donations to the UEP, he still had to prove himself in the eyes of the Priesthood. All marriages within the Group had to be sanctioned by one of the Priesthood Council members, but getting their approval became complicated.

THREE PRIESTHOOD CLIQUES

From the beginning, a member of the Group would approach one of the Council members to perform a marriage, but approval was often held hostage. In time this caused little cliques to spring up among the Group, with each council member having his own following, and competition developed between them. If a man wanted another wife, the first step was to give more money, property or service to one of the council members, thus winning favor enough to receive the "blessings of the Priesthood." And a man needed not just one more wife, but at least three to reach the highest degree of heaven.

During the 1940s the people of Short Creek were divided into three cliques. One clique followed John Barlow and Leroy Johnson, one followed Joseph Musser and Marion Hammon, and a third group believed that to worship a "man" was a false principle. This group supposed they could be honest men, living the commandments as outlined in the Doctrine & Covenants and still gain the blessings of living the Principle (polygamy). It was this third group that suffered the most. By not aligning with one of the council members and accepting all they said as scripture, "without any mental reservations," they cut themselves off from further blessings. The men who did receive the blessing of more wives were those who sided with either John Barlow's or Joseph Musser's clique.

As the General Manager of the UEP, Marion Hammon felt the responsibility of improving the standards and living conditions of the people in the community. Young in age and experience, he had high hopes and ideals. One project he felt important was to build a meeting house, where the people could be called together and taught how to obtain the high goals he envisioned.

He began construction on the meeting house in February of 1943. As the General Manager and a Council Member, he supposed that he would receive full support from the people and the other council members. He was supported by Joseph Musser, but John Barlow opposed the project and he began to undermine Hammon's efforts. As was his custom, Barlow did not go to him directly and state his disagreement, but rather talked among the members of his clique, saying, "We are not a church house building people. The county school house is sufficient for a meeting place for us." He felt that building efforts should be spent on homes and industry.

John Barlow had more influence among the people at Short Creek than did Marion Hammon, and he approved construction on a home for Fred Jessop, with a chicken coop next to it. Their idea was to raise chickens as a commercial venture. The work on the church house was abandoned, while Fred Jessop's house and chicken coop were soon completed. This was the first building of any importance to be completed by the United Effort Plan at Short Creek.

GASOLINE-POWERED WASHING MACHINES

Back in the 1930s the Civilian Conservation Corps (CCC) had established a camp at Short Creek.

The CCC brought a 2" water line from Jans Canyon to the camp. The water rights of the spring belonged to the Lauritzen family (not members of the Group) and when the CCC left the area, the pipe line became the property of the Lauritzen's. This new house of Fred Jessop's was built close to this pipe line, and he obtained permission from the Lauritzens to use the water. His house had the one luxury that few other Group members had – running water.

In the 1940s, before electricity came to Short Creek, there were only two gasoline-powered washing machines in town. Leonard Black had one on the Arizona side of town and Genevieve Stubbs had one on the Utah side of town. Interestingly, Genevieve Stubbs had taught herself to pull teeth and even had the equipment to make false teeth for people of the town.

It was up to the women to transport their laundry to one of these washers once a week. They would use whatever means of conveyance they could come up with, be it little wagon or wheelbarrow or in some cases, just carrying the many clothes in a gunny sack. They would take turns on the washers, heating the water they needed in a barrel over an open fire. When finished washing the clothes, they would haul the wet laundry back home and if they were lucky enough to have a clothesline, hang it up to dry, or just drape it over the fence. Unfortunately, Marion Hammon would chastise them in church for hanging their clothes on a fence. Several women later commented that if Hammon would provide them a clothesline, they wouldn't have to use the fence. It was always easy for a leader to proclaim what must be done, when he himself did not have to do it and did not know the price of what he was asking.

In my short experience of living in a Polygamist home for about four years as a child, my memories of the mother in the home is one of admiration. These women would labor hard from morning until night just trying to keep the household together. The biggest chore for them was finding enough food to fix meals for the family. Breakfast was cracked wheat cereal or mush with a little milk from the small herd of about twelve milk cows. This milk was distributed throughout the whole community after the cows had been milked by two or three boys. Lunch was usually potatoes and gravy, if potatoes were available, and if not, just gravy. If lucky, the gravy would have corn or string beans in it, having been canned the summer before. We usually had bottled peaches, also canned from the summer before. Supper would be a vegetable soup, canned the summer before, or pinto beans. The only meat we ever had was venison that had been poached from the ranches at Widtsoes or Hatch, Utah.

AUNT EMMA DIGS A WELL

Much has been said about the plight of women in the polygamist community. In fact, it was the women who often held the fabric of the community together. And there were many who did unusual things. Emma was a divorcee who moved into the community in 1946, and she received a small check every month from either welfare or child support. The priesthood decided she should marry a blind man named George, a widower.

They were given a house to live in that was up on a slight ridge and about a quarter of a mile from the nearest culinary water hydrant. So to have water, she had to walk a quarter mile to get to the hydrant, fill the bucket and carry it back through the field and up the hill. Finally she asked the brethren if they would dig a well for her. They told her that because the house was on a hill, it would be unlikely they could find water, plus there would be a rock ledge to go through. So they declined.

Aunt Emma did not let them stop her. She began talking around that she intended to dig a well and needed volunteer help from boys in the community. Six teenage boys became very enthusiastic about the project. Under her direction, an A-frame was erected over the spot where they intended to dig the well, a pulley was attached to the A-frame, and a rope was run through the pulley to a five-gallon bucket that could be lowered into the hole. As the boys dug, they would empty their shovels into the bucket and when it was full, they would lift it out of the hole and empty it.

Sitting in a chair and pulling the rope, blind George was able to help. And this was the only adult help the boys received. Six weeks later, they found water at forty feet. Surprised at her tenacity, and even more shocked at her success, several adults came to help. They lowered three-foot concrete pipe sections and did the finish work for the water to gather at the bottom of the well.

Next Aunt Emma purchased a windmill. With the help of the boys, she constructed a wooden tower about thirty feet high and secured the windmill on top. The next step for the boys was to construct a holding tank to catch the water when the wind blew. By using a "go devil" (a piece of boiler plate measuring about four feet by eight feet with a chain attached to a tractor), they were able to transport sandstone from a nearby hill, to construct this holding tank.

Using the stored water in the tank, Aunt Emma was also able to grow a small garden. This was a great achievement for any woman in the male-dominated society. Few men in the community had the fortitude to dig wells for themselves. This well of Aunt Emma's stood as a monument to her tenacity even after she had died.

Along with the chicken business, the UEP obtained a sheep herd. For summer range, the sheep were kept at a ranch in Johns Valley, near Bryce Canyon. This ranch had belonged to Newel Steed, who had donated it to the Priesthood. For winter range, the sheep were moved to Short Creek, where they could forage on the desert. A sawmill was also on the Steed Ranch at Johns Valley and the Polygamists operated this mill to supply lumber to build homes. The sawmill was moved to the Kaibab Forest, near Jacob's Lake, Arizona, in about 1946 and lumber was sold to help bring in money for the Group. Also some agriculture ventures were acquired, not so much at Short Creek because of the lack of irrigation water, but other places such as a farm at Bloomington, and another at Widtsoe. The Widtsoe Ranch was also in Johns Valley, near the Steed Ranch. Mostly it was used for raising cattle, but some crops such as potatoes and alfalfa were raised. Assets for the UEP continued to grow.

Fred Jessop was appointed to act as bishop for the United Effort Plan, his responsibilities being to look after the members. A storehouse was established at his home, located on the Utah side of the town, and the Group began living closer to the principles of the United Order. Fred would purchase groceries and bring them into town. On Monday, Wednesday and Friday, he would pick up grocery lists of the members in the morning and in the afternoon he would deliver to the people the items the storehouse had. This was the system for the people "having all things in common," a United Order.

All income made by families was turned in to the Order and each family would receive back through Fred's storehouse what they needed to survive. Times were hard, but the people were willing and they believed progress was being made. Just as it seemed they might be experiencing a degree of success, law enforcement stepped in again.

CHARGES FILED AGAINST KEY PRIESTHOOD LEADERS

On the morning of March 7, 1944, F.B.I. agents and U.S. Marshals raided the polygamists, both at Short Creek and in Salt Lake City. Forty-six people were arrested on charges of conspiracy and the Mann and Lindberg Acts. The defendants were placed in county jails to await their trial dates, or for bonds to be raised. March 20th was set for the day to hear their pleas. While the defendants were in jail, they were re-arrested on charges brought under state statutes, fifteen of them being charged with unlawful co-habitation and thirty-four with conspiracy to promote the practice of unlawful co-habitation.

The federal charge of conspiracy was based upon an alleged violation of Federal code "which denounces as a crime the mailing of obscene matter." It was alleged that the mailing of the *Truth* Magazine came under this statute, that the magazine was "obscene, lewd and lascivious." The Mann Act cases were based upon a husband traveling from one state to another with his alleged plural wife. The kidnaping cases against three of the defendants resulted from a man taking his intended wife to another state for marriage. The man driving the car and his wife, who was with him, were included in the indictment.

On March 18, 1944, the conspiracy indictment against the *Truth* Magazine was quashed. U.S. District Judge L. Foster Symes ruled there was nothing in the *Truth* Magazine that could be construed as "obscene, lewd or lascivious, and *Truth* Magazine only teaches what the early Mormon leaders taught, that polygamy was and is a necessary part of the Mormon religion. In conclusion it might be said that the natural reaction to reading a publication setting forth that polygamy is essential to salvation is one of repugnance and does not tend to increase sexual desire or impure thoughts."

The decision of Judge Symes was appealed by the Government to the U.S. Supreme Court, but the High Court refused to hear the appeal. On June 7, 1944, Judge T. Blake Kennedy, U.S. Federal Court, passed sentence on the six Mann Act and the three kidnaping cases, having been previously declared guilty. Prison terms of from one year and a day to four years and a day were ordered. The men at Short Creek convicted on the Mann Act charge: Lawrence Stubbs, Theral Dockstader, and Vergel Jessop. These men were sent to Federal prison at Tucson, Arizona.

While these persecutions were being carried out against the polygamists, the Brethren attempted to comfort the Saints at Short Creek with a letter of encouragement, dated August 30, 1944, and signed by John Barlow, Joseph Musser, Leroy Johnson, and Rulon Jeffs. Guy Musser (son of Joseph) and Rulon Jeffs had been called into the Priesthood Council during 1943.

The letter was an apology for the lack of financial support from the Brethren at Salt Lake City. The burden of hiring lawyers to defend the men in court cases was using all the resources the leaders could raise. This left the Saints at Short Creek to try and earn their own support. The people had a hard time surviving, and at one point they were reduced to eating rutabagas that a sympathetic farmer from the little town of Antimony, Utah, gave them. All the members of the Group were suffering because of the persecution. This only forced them to stick together, to try and help each other and, in so doing, brought them closer spiritually.

On October 10, 1944, thirty-one defendants were adjudged guilty of conspiracy to encourage the breaking of the laws of the State (Utah) with reference to unlawful co-habitation. Each was sentenced to serve a year in the county jail in Salt Lake City. Notice of appeal was given to go before the State Supreme Court and the defendants were allowed to remain free on bail. On February 7, 1945, the cases of Fred Jessop and Edson Jessop of Short Creek, charged with unlawful co-habitation, were dismissed for lack of evidence by Judge Will L. Hoyt, at St. George.

On May 12, 1945, fifteen defendants appeared before Judge Van Cott. They had been found guilty of unlawful co-habitation about one year before and had been sentenced to an indeterminate term of from one to five years in the State Penitentiary, Salt Lake City, Utah. The defendants had exhausted all appeals and on this date were committed to the custody of the sheriff to carry out the sentence. Among these fifteen men were John Y. Barlow, Joseph W. Musser, Charles F. Zitting, Louis A. Kelsch, and Alma A. Timpson. It was a sad day for the polygamists at Short Creek when their leaders were sent to prison.

The leadership at Short Creek was temporarily left to the newly appointed members of the priesthood council: Leroy Johnson, Marion Hammon, and Richard Jessop (Richard Jessop was called to the Priesthood Council in early 1945). The publishing of The *Truth* Magazine was left in the hands of Guy Musser (son of Joseph) at Salt Lake City.

PAROLE BY DECEIT

After only seven months, some of the leaders who had been sent to prison were released on parole. On December 15, 1945, the Utah Board of Pardons granted parole privileges to eleven of the prisoners after they signed a statement agreeing "To refrain hereafter from advocating, teaching or countenancing the practice of plural marriage or polygamy." John Barlow, Joseph Musser, and Alma Timpson were among the eleven who signed to get out. Four of the prisoners, including Charles Zitting and Louis Kelsch, refused to sign the Manifesto and remained in prison to serve their full time.

Charles Zitting talks about the experience in his Autobiography, p. 88:

"The brethren had been suffering the jail sentence for three months or more.... Little hints had been circulating around concerning a Manifesto in the making, which if signed would let the brethren out on parole .... When this paper was presented to one of the leading brethren (John Barlow), he and three others, (Joseph Musser, Charles Zitting, and Louis Kelsch) spent the afternoon discussing it out behind the prison barn.... Before they presented it to the others, the leading brethren explained that they wished to make it an individual matter and wanted everyone to use his own free agency in deciding whether he should sign it or not. They all agreed on that. I read it over and felt that I couldn't sign it and told them why. When I went to my cell a little later than the rest I found that five of the brethren had already signed it. I went in tears and prayed more earnestly than I had ever prayed before in all my life. I felt that I could not sign it and I thought I was alone in my opposition. Several of the brethren worked late at the cannery that night. When they came to their cells they informed me they couldn't sign it either. It was the first time in my life that I had ever stood on the opposite side to John Y. Barlow and Joseph W. Musser....

"When I saw the signatures already on it (John Y. Barlow and Joseph W. Musser), I went to one of the brethren (John Y. Barlow) and asked if we shouldn't have prayed about it first before signing as the meeting behind the barn had not been opened nor closed with prayer.

"He answered: The Prophet Brigham Young said to pray about anything where you are in doubt and if the Lord doesn't answer you then use your best Judgement and he will uphold you in it. I have prayed about this for three months without him answering me and this is my best judgement.

"I then spoke to another (Joseph W. Musser) and he argued he couldn't see any harm in signing it. He said he felt we would have to do something like this and he believed this was the best we could do. I left and went to my cell feeling very blue and alone. I was awake most of the night pleading with the Lord to keep me from making a mistake as I wished to do nothing but his will. I stayed in my cell all the next day reading chapters in Daniel and other parts of the Bible, also revelations of Joseph Smith Jr., John Taylor and Wilford Woodruff. In the late afternoon the Lord gave me a personal revelation for my family and me which convinced me not to sign." Charles states that it was just fifty-five years ago on the very same day, September 24, 1890, that Wilford Woodruff signed his manifesto.

The signing of this Manifesto by the Group leaders caused bitter feelings among some members at Short Creek. They felt the leaders had betrayed them. After all, the reason they had left the LDS Church was because of the Manifesto signed in 1890. They wanted to know how these men could justify themselves in what they had done. The best explanation given: "We (Barlow and Musser) had to get out to carry on Our Work."

The conditions in the prison were such that the health of the older Brethren was fast deteriorating. If they were required to serve out their full sentences, it was questionable whether or not they could live them out. These reasons did little to satisfy the feelings of those criticizing their actions. That was not all. After the Brethren returned to their homes, they didn't live up to the agreements of the manifesto they had signed. They went back to cohabiting with their plural wives, to performing plural marriages for others, and they continued preaching and teaching it to their followers.

This made it even harder for the ones questioning their behavior, especially those of the third clique who began questioning the worthiness of leaders that would make agreements with no intention of living up to them. They concluded that maybe they did not really hold the High Priesthood they claimed. Within a few months, this dissension spread throughout the community.

Many became unhappy with the way the leaders had squandered the money. Several began asking for some kind of security for property and work equity they had put into the Trust. They wanted something in writing to guarantee what they had donated, if the UEP were to break up. By trying to protect themselves, these dissenters only caused more discord, especially when they confronted the leaders with a scripture from the Doctrine & Covenants about the United Order, to support their requests.

But the leaders were not willing to "Give unto him a writing that shall secure unto him his portion." Their defense: "We are not living the United Order, but only a step toward it, thus we are not bound by the commandments in the written word." No written guarantees were given.

DISSIDENTS DEMAND WRITTEN LEASES

In June of 1946, John Barlow called thirty-two year old Carl Holm to be the sixth member of the Priesthood Council. Carl was born in Ammon, Idaho, on May 14, 1917. He married Marjory Morrison on July 5, 1940, at Salt Lake City, Utah. Carl had inherited a large farm from his father in Ammon, Idaho, and in the 1940s he donated it to the United Effort Plan and moved to Short Creek. By the 1950s he would become the UEP General Manager.

As a member of the Priesthood Council, Carl was automatically recognized as a Trustee of the United Effort Plan. The dissidents were very critical of Barlow calling such a young and inexperienced man to be a leader over them and demanded changes be made in the operation of the UEP. They went to Joseph Musser with their grievances, and the leaders finally relented.

In order to keep the United Effort Plan together, the leaders decided to make a compromise with those followers who were unhappy. In March of 1948, a letter was distributed among the people of Short Creek, signed by John Y. Barlow, Joseph W. Musser, J. Marion Hammon, Guy Musser, Rulon T. Jeffs, and Richard S. Jessop (Leroy Johnson was in Old Mexico, having been sent there by John Barlow to start another Community. Dare LeBaron, father of Ervil LeBaron, had started a group and they invited people from the Barlow Group to join them. It may be that John Barlow wanted to set up a place where he could have greater control, if the situation became difficult enough in Short Creek).

The leaders agreed it was time to issue "inheritances" to those requesting them as described in the Doctrine & Covenants, by granting *perpetual leases on property to the members* to come under: "The exclusive management of the members receiving the same. . .this, then, places every man on his own, to reap the benefit of his labors and the more energetic he is the more he is entitled to for the support of his own family."

The proposed draft to the Dissidents, stated in part: "Terms: In consideration of past consecrations; a lifetime lease, not subject to termination by reason of conscientious beliefs. . . .That for and in consideration of all consecrations, gifts and contributions heretofore made by lessee to lessor, and for the further consideration of $1.00 per year to be paid by lessee to the lessor yearly in advance, the lessor has let and by these presents does grant, demise, and let unto the lessee and his heirs, for the life time of lessee and his heirs, the following described tract of land. . . Subject to the following terms and conditions: It is agreed that if default shall be made in any of the covenants herein contained, then it shall be lawful, upon thirty days notice, for the lessor to re-enter said premises and to remove all persons therefrom.

"The lessee hereby covenants to pay to the lessor the rent as herein specified, and to pay the annual rent or charge assessed or imposed on said premises and for the use of water, if any water assessment (where irrigation is included), and to pay all taxes assessed against said land.

"The lessee covenants that he will not assign this lease, nor any interest therein, or let or underlet the whole or any part of said premises, without the written consent of the lessor, under penalty of forfeiture and damages.

"The lessee covenants that he will live on said premises in peace with his neighbors and members of the United Effort Plan; and so long as lessee continues to live in peace and conduct himself as a Christian, lessor covenants that the lessee, in paying the said yearly rent and performing this and other covenants aforesaid, shall and may peaceably and quietly have, hold, and enjoy the said demised premises for the term aforesaid. . . ."

The letter further explains, "Our plan is to satisfy those *only who feel it desirable to have exclusive jurisdiction leases* – these latter people are now placed on their own." There was mention in the letter to "clear off all indebtedness as quickly as possible." Further the members were told to support their own families, pay their tithing (ten percent of all income) to the bishop, and each head of household was to give Fred Jessop thirty dollars a month to take care of the widows (Fred was still acting as the Bishop).

This threatened breakup of the UEP was a hard trial for John Barlow. He had hoped the people would support him, and the UEP. He said he endorsed the actions of the other council members in allowing members to have leases, but then changed his mind. The dissidents soon learned Barlow refused to allow these leases to be honored. Anyone who insisted on getting a lease was simply told he was no longer a member of the United Effort Plan. Because there was *nothing in writing* (no certificates of membership had been issued), they knew it was impossible to get any security on the homes they had built and paid for. These discouraged members began to move out as best as they could, and the UEP leaders refused to assist them in any way. These disillusioned men left the community, most of them going to Salt Lake City, working for up to two years in some instances before they earned enough money to move their families there.

Richard Jessop, J. Marion Hammon, and Joseph S. Jessop were appointed by Joseph Musser and the Council to oversee the Short Creek operations. They also recommended that problems be taken to them and not to Brother Barlow because of his poor state of health.

By the beginning of 1949, most of the dissatisfied members were gone. Leroy Johnson was in Old Mexico with a small group of people John Y. Barlow had sent there to try another experiment. But conditions there were so hard that after a month, Marion Hammon and Newel Steed loaded their belongings and returned. Hammon told John Barlow that he would go back only if he were shown a revelation from the Lord telling him to do so. John Barlow, to his credit, did not supply the revelation. Marion Hammon then left Short Creek and moved back to Salt Lake City. Joseph Musser stayed in Salt Lake City and had very little to do with Short Creek, leaving John Y. Barlow to do as he pleased.

Before Newel Steed was sent to Mexico, he had turned in his ranch at John's Valley

(Widtsoe) to the UEP. John Barlow had mortgaged the farm to the bank and spent the money. When Newel Steed returned from Mexico, the mortgage payment was past due. John Barlow had no way of making the payment, and intended to just let the bank foreclose. When Newel Steed learned of this, he became irate, went to the bank and made arrangements to take over the payments. It took him twenty years to pay it off, but he was able to reclaim the farm. He withdrew from the association of the United Effort Plan and ran his own business, becoming quite successful.

Meanwhile, John Barlow's dropsy had left him pretty much bedridden, and he moved to Salt Lake City, putting the affairs at Short Creek in the hands of Richard Jessop, Carl Holm, and Fred Jessop.

With the dissidents gone, Marion Hammon out of the picture, and Joseph Musser no longer bothering him, John Barlow made one last effort to make sure the United Effort Plan would continue after his death. In late 1949 he made one last trip to Short Creek. Every man over the age of sixteen was called to a special Priesthood meeting one Sunday morning at the local home of John Barlow, a small house where one of his young wives (age fifteen) lived.

John Barlow quoted scriptures and gave a moving talk, telling them "it is up to you now." He gave each the opportunity of uniting with the UEP in this last struggle for its survival. All chose to support him and they were placed under solemn covenant that they would support the UEP and its leaders with everything they had. They agreed to devote their full time, their money, property, and talents to its up-building and survival. The men were mostly young and zealous. They had grown up in the association of John Barlow, Leroy Johnson, and Richard and Fred Jessop. They were willing to accept whatever they were told by any of these men, without question.

After this meeting Barlow asked Fred Jessop to make him a promise that when he died, Fred would take care of his sons, seeing to it that they would never suffer for lack of material things. Also to see to it that they would be included in the managing of affairs of the UEP. Fred made him this promise with a sacred covenant that he honored for the rest of his life. John Barlow had extracted this same promise from Leroy Johnson a few years before. John Barlow then returned to Salt Lake City, and never returned to Short Creek again.

JOHN YATES BARLOW PASSES THE TORCH

John Barlow saw that his time on earth would soon end, and towards the end of 1949, he called off the experiment in Old Mexico, and sent for Leroy Johnson. But it took over a week for the mail to reach him in Mexico. He hastily finished up affairs and started for Salt Lake City. But he didn't arrive in time. He was grief stricken that he had not been able to talk with his very close friend in the closing minutes of his life. And he had expected to receive special instruction as to the running of the UEP and the Priesthood Work.

A few days before he had died on December 29, 1949, John Barlow sent word to Alma A. Timpson that he wanted to see him. When he arrived, the other Council

Members were quietly gathered around Brother Barlow. When he told the Brethren to ordain Timpson a member of the Priesthood Council, they went into the next room and the ordination was carried out.

This brought to seven the men John Y. Barlow had called: Leroy S. Johnson, J. Marion Hammon, Guy H. Musser, Rulon T. Jeffs, Richard S. Jessop, Carl O. Holm, and Alma A. Timpson. Of the council that Lorin Woolley had called in the 1930s, four men were still alive: Joseph W. Musser, Charles F. Zitting, LeGrand Woolley, and Louis A. Kelsch.

As next in line, Joseph Musser became the recognized President of the Priesthood Council. But the other Council Members felt he was no longer the capable man they had known, because of a series of strokes he suffered, beginning when he was released from Utah State Prison in 1945.

JOSEPH MUSSER & RULON ALLRED CREATE A NEW GROUP

Soon after Barlow's death, ailing Joseph Musser attempted to call a new member to the Priesthood Council, to fill the vacancy. He presented the name of Rulon Allred to the Council, but the other members would not sustain him in this decision. Even so, he decided to call Allred anyway, following John Barlow's example of One Man Rule.

In April of 1950 in Salt Lake City, Joseph Musser stood before a general meeting of the polygamists and announced he had received a revelation to call Rulon Allred into the Priesthood Council. He told the other Council members who were present that he wanted them to help with the ordination after the meeting. When the meeting was over, Richard Jessop was the only one to come forward. With the other Council members milling among the congregation, Joseph Musser and Richard Jessop placed their hands on the head of Rulon Allred and ordained him to the office of Patriarch and Apostle (High Priest Apostle).

Later that evening, Richard Jessop was "called on the carpet" by the other Council Members for his actions. According to Jessop's beliefs and teaching he had done no wrong. The original instructions by Lorin Woolley that all decisions were to made as a group had slowly eroded. It seems that while the Council tried to operate as a group, John Barlow's day-to-day example weakened that direction. The other council members did not approve of Allred's calling and they spent all night and until noon the next day convincing Jessop of his error in following Musser's leadership. Richard Jessop finally gave in. In later years he would say that when he assisted Joseph Musser in Allred's ordination, all they gave him was a blessing. This was probably the only concession of conscience that Richard Jessop ever made on Priesthood Matters.

After the ordination of Rulon Allred, the other Council members turned against Joseph Musser, explaining to the people that due to his sickness he was now incompetent to be the leader. This caused a split among the followers, with some following the Council, and others following Musser. And unfortunately, Joseph's own son Guy was his most bitter opponent.

Joseph Musser finally realized he had been openly rejected as president. So he decided to create a new council, leaving those who would not accept his leadership to go their own way. The old Council now consisted of Charles Zitting, LeGrand Woolley, Louis Kelsch (of the original council called by Lorin Woolley), and those called by John Barlow: Leroy Johnson, Marion Hammon, Guy Musser, Rulon Jeffs, Richard Jessop, Carl Holm, and Alma Timpson.

In 1952, Joseph Musser called six men to the Apostleship, thus establishing his new Priesthood Council. These six, along with Rulon Allred, filled the Council to the required number of seven: John Butchereit, Eslie Jensen, Owen Allred, Marvin Allred, Joseph Thompson, and Lyman Jessop (Owen and Marvin Allred were brothers to Rulon, Lyman Jessop was a brother to Richard Jessop). This new council constituted a new Group, and was referred to as the Allred/Musser Group.

Of all the polygamist followers, half stayed with Joseph Musser, and the remainder stayed loyal to the old Council. The Group at Short Creek followed the old council almost one hundred percent, because the controversy had taken place in Salt Lake City and none of them were firsthand witnesses. Joseph Musser was portrayed to them as senile and incapacitated, no longer capable to lead the Lord's Work.

In July of 1952, Joseph Musser, along with Lyman Jessop and Wayne Handy, made a trip to Short Creek to justify his actions to the people. He met with Leroy Johnson, Richard Jessop, and Carl Holm, asking them to call a meeting so he could talk to the people. They were reluctant to do so. Lyman Jessop, in his journal, states:

"Brother Joseph asked Roy (Leroy Johnson) to state how he felt toward him, so Roy said that he knows that Joseph holds the keys to the Priesthood and he (Roy) will sustain him in that position in love and loyalty. (Leroy said) 'I stood by John (Barlow) until the end. I will support you as I did him'. Joseph responded, 'That's fine'."

Leroy then said to Musser: "We are under covenant to do what we are doing and we cannot change from that course and we have no arguments to make. If the Lord wants to use an incapacitated leader (referring to Joseph Musser standing before him) to lead some people astray, that is the Lord's business." These bitter feelings surprised Musser.

After a few quiet moments, Musser told Leroy that the time would come when he (Leroy) would be in the same incapacitated condition and that the Group at Short Creek would be split to smithereens.

Joseph Musser and his companions returned to Salt Lake City and it was the last attempt made to regain the loyalty of the people at Short Creek. The two polygamist groups became split and a wide gap came between them. As time passed, the Joseph Musser/Rulon Allred group grew more in numbers than the John Barlow/Leroy Johnson group. And while the Musser/Allred group tried to maintain warm and friendly feelings toward the Barlow group, it was not reciprocated.

Even with all the controversy over the Priesthood Council, the people of Short Creek continued their daily lives, still trying to live the United Order, and had been getting commodities from the UEP storehouse. The present building with the little store and post office was sold to David Broadbent (son of J. Leslie Broadbent), and a new store building was constructed on the corner of Central Street and Township Avenue, and named Short Creek Supply. The Post Office also moved to a room there. Aunt Fawn Broadbent was appointed postmistress and also served as the store clerk.

Having a store where people could "purchase" goods was a paradox because the members of the UEP were all living the United Order. Most had no money to spend, because they turned everything over to the Priesthood. But the store and gas station did serve the few outsiders who braved the rough dirt roads (it was 30 miles to Hurricane, the closest town) to get to the isolated area. These were mostly cattlemen who operated ranches in the area. Interestingly, there was a certain class of local people who always had money to purchase goods not available in Fred's storehouse; and, of course, they were the ones in Leroy's clique.

Besides the new store, a few new homes were also built. To develop UEP resources some of the Lauritzen property was purchased. And a farm at Hatch, Utah, and one near Alton, Utah, were also purchased, from E. J. Graff of Hurricane. Payments on these ranches at Hatch and Alton were made by the UEP, the money being earned from work projects sponsored by the leaders and managers, and carried out by people in the community. The payments on the Lauritzen property were made by Bill Cooke and his son Lynn, who were farming the property, raising chickens, and selling the eggs in the outside communities.

This was a time of growth at Short Creek, and most everyone was encouraged. It appeared that nothing could stop the progress of the Priesthood in the building of the Kingdom of God.

5

The Infamous Short Creek Raid

In the early morning hours of July 26, 1953, Arizona Highway Patrolmen, Mohave County Sheriff's Deputies and Arizona National Guardsmen moved in on the people of Short Creek in military might. With red lights flashing, sirens sounding, and brandishing firearms, the military caravan in a cloud of swirling dust pulled up at the school yard fence where the citizens of the community had gathered to wait for them.

Speaking over a loud speaker to those in the school yard, Mohave County Sheriff Frank Porter announced, "This is the sheriff. You are all under arrest. Stay where you are." The invading officers then moved cautiously into the yard surrounding the group and began serving arrest warrants.

The officers had hoped they could surprise the polygamists, break into their homes, and catch them in bed with their unlawful wives to gather evidence to convict them. But the polygamists at Short Creek had been warned that the raid was coming.

In 1953, Charles Zitting was the senior man on the Priesthood Council for the group in Short Creek. But it was the Allred/Musser Group in Salt Lake City that someone in law enforcement or the press warned of the impending raid. Lyman Jessop, a member of Joseph Musser's Priesthood Council, quickly drove to Short Creek to warn the polygamists. Charles Zitting, living at Salt Lake City, had no home at Short Creek, but when he learned of the coming raid, he and his wife Elvera drove to Southern Utah to meet with the Priesthood Council members. He told them to take the women and children and leave Short Creek, to go into hiding with friends at Salt Lake City or other places. He had just spent three years in the Utah Penitentiary and knew firsthand the consequences of arrest. And, there were women and children involved. He believed they could then negotiate with the Governor and reach a compromise.

Leroy Johnson refused to take this message to the people. He said, "We are not going to run. We will stand up to them and ask the Lord to fight our battles. I will take responsibility."

Charles did not contend with Leroy over the issue. "If that's your decision, Roy, and you are willing to take responsibility, then I will stay here and be with the people when the law arrives."

Because of Leroy's decision, the Polygamists of Short Creek did not run; they had been given no choice in the matter. Leroy said they were going to stay and meet the invading force on the morning of July 26th; so putting on a brave face, they obeyed. This decision would cause much suffering for the women and children over the next two years.

The Short Creek Raid was carried out after more than two years of investigation by the Arizona State Attorney General's office. The radio address on Sunday morning, July 26, 1953, by Arizona Governor Howard Pyle made the state's case to the public:

". . .The evidence accumulated included alleged instances of statutory rape, adultery, bigamy, open and notorious cohabitation, contributing to the delinquency of minors, marrying the spouse of another and an all embracing conspiracy to commit all of these crimes along with various instances of income tax evasion, failure to comply with Arizona's corporation laws, misappropriation of the school funds, improper use of school facilities and falsification of public records. . . ."

POLYGAMY OR TAXES?

But was the raid *really* just about the practice of polygamy, or was it motivated by something else.

The Polygamists were, in some degree, guilty of almost all of these charges. The one charge that was most responsible for the Raid was the *alleged misappropriation* of school funds. And that charge came about because of tax money ranchers were having to pay to help support the Short Creek School District.

In the 1950s, to support the schools in Arizona, funds came from the state, *and* from the local school district by way of a special tax levy. About the only taxable asset in the small school District of Short Creek was the cattle industry on the Arizona Strip.

The ranchers who owned the permits to graze their cattle on the public lands in the Short Creek School District mostly lived in Utah, but they were expected to pay this tax levy and meet this tax burden. Due to the high birth rate in the polygamist community, the number of students grew each year. The ranchers felt it was grossly unfair that they should be paying extra taxes to educate the increasing number of polygamist children.

In 1950, Louis Barlow, son of John Barlow, was hired by the Short Creek School Board as principal. The school property and buildings were run down when Louis took over; the only water supply was a shallow well with a windmill to pump the water. There was only a faucet in the school yard for drinking water, the water coming from a wooden storage tank on a tower by the windmill. The toilets were outhouses. There were no lawns or shrubbery of any kind.

Louis felt it necessary to improve these conditions a little. He went to the School Board and requested them to raise the Special School Fund. This in turn caused the tax levy to go up for the Cattlemen. Louis used this extra money to purchase a pressure pump for the well (with the help of the upper class boys, he was successful in digging another well, where the new pump was used). An army surplus generator was purchased, an old car motor was rigged to turn it, and the new pressure pump was used to successfully pump the water. Grass and shrubbery was then planted, greatly improving the school grounds. A 16mm movie projector was purchased and movies were brought into the community. Also, a school lunch program was established.

These were improvements that most other schools in Arizona had taken for granted, but they were a big advancement for the school children at Short Creek. The Cattlemen might not have complained about the cost increase of these improvements, except that in their opinion, Louis went too far and bought a school vehicle, an old 1946 Ford pick-up truck. Louis' younger brother Truman, an upper class student, spent time *and school money* for gasoline, driving all over town for any excuse, whether it was school business or not.

The ranchers complained to the Short Creek School Board, but it did no good. Only then did they take their complaints to the County level at Kingman.

July 24th, the anniversary of Brigham Young's 1847 entry into Salt Lake Valley, is celebrated by the Mormons as Pioneer Day. In the 1950s era, the 24th of July was probably the biggest holiday celebrated by the Polygamists at Short Creek. Group members would gather from far and wide to attend this event. The day would be spent with such activities as playing games, running foot races, and other general sports. A barrel of lemonade, cookies baked by the young ladies, and other refreshments were available throughout the day. In the afternoon a community dinner was served at the school house (the only place large enough). After everyone had eaten their fill, the school house would be cleared out, tables removed, and the hall prepared for an evening social. Old and young alike would enjoy dancing until midnight. Then they would gather on the dance floor and sing their theme song "Give Me A Home In The Heart Of The Mountains." All would then retire to their homes, feeling much lifted up because of the day's recreation and go to sleep with joy in their hearts. The Arizona State Officials knew of this day of celebration, and planned their raid knowing that all Short Creek Polygamists would be there.

Although Short Creek straddled the Utah/Arizona state line, Utah state officials did not participate in this raid. But one of the two roads leading into town came in from Utah. The Arizona task force divided into two contingents, sending one to come in from the Utah side, thus blocking any escape route.

The detachment coming from the Arizona side stopped at Fredonia, about 40 miles east of Short Creek. After cutting the telephone lines (this telephone line only went about halfway to Short Creek, stopping at Pipe Spring National Monument and the small community of Moccasin), they moved out toward Short Creek on 40 miles of dirt roads.

The group was made up of 100 law enforcement officers, including highway patrolmen, county sheriffs and deputies, superior and juvenile court judges, the state attorney general and his associates, policewomen, nurses, doctors, the Arizona National Guard, together with all the equipment to house, feed, and clothe the task force, as well as the citizens of Short Creek. There were also 25 carloads of news media and twelve Alcohol, Tobacco and Firearms (ATF) officers.

In the early morning hours of Sunday, July 26, 1953 (during the darkness of a lunar eclipse), the officers and their entourage stopped about two miles outside of Short Creek, both from the Utah and Arizona sides of town. They were waiting to coordinate their move on the community. What they didn't know is that the citizens were gathered at the school yard waiting for them. The Polygamists had dispatched sentries to the outskirts of town to wait for the invaders' arrival.

A warning signal had been arranged for these sentries to set off dynamite blasts when they had determined that the officers were ready to move into town. When these blasts were set off, it not only warned the citizens at the school yard, but also frightened the officers of the invading force. Not knowing what to expect, thinking perhaps they were being met with armed resistance, Mohave County Sheriff Frank Porter said, "Well, it looks like they want to fight, so let's go."

Turning on their sirens and flashing red lights, the caravan began moving in on the Polygamists at 4:00 a.m. Prepared for the worst, with weapons drawn, they were stunned to find the citizens gathered around the flag pole, singing patriotic songs. The officers, still with firearms drawn, began moving through the crowd making arrests. All adults were taken into custody. Any that were not named on warrants were arrested as John or Jane Doe.

At daylight a court was set up in the schoolhouse. Each man was questioned and then booked under arrest. Judge J. Smith Gibbons from Apache County was there to read the charges against them. All the men were charged with the same crimes regardless of whether they were polygamists. They were turned over to Sheriff Frank Porter of Mohave County and locked in one of the school rooms to await transportation to the County Jail at Kingman.

The mothers and their children were presented to Judge Lorna Lockwood (Maricopa County) acting as Juvenile Judge. The children were declared wards of the state, then released into the custody of their mothers, who were told to take them home and wait for instructions. The mothers themselves were never arrested or taken into custody. Nine older women were arrested, who had no minor children, and one of these was Elvera Zitting, the wife of Charles Zitting. She was arrested on a Jane Doe warrant.

The National Guard set up camp in a vacant field about one block from the school house. A mess tent was assembled to feed the officers, and the people of the community. The one small store in town was not allowed to open and everyone was forced to go to this compound for meals. This proved so cumbersome and impractical that mothers were allowed to get food from the field kitchen and take it home to their children.

That evening the men were escorted to supper at the National Guard Camp. Buses had been ordered to take them to Kingman, but they never arrived. The men were loaded, three each, in the back seat of a patrol car, with two officers in the front. The seven hour trip to Kingman began at 7:00 p.m. Traveling all night, they reached their destination at 4:00 a.m., twenty-four hours since the raid began. Thirty-one men and the nine older women were transported.

The State had planned to hold the children's hearings at Short Creek, bringing in the fathers from Kingman to confirm the identity of their children. On Wednesday, July 29, the first two men were flown to the Kanab, Utah, airport, and then taken by automobile to Short Creek. They were returned to Kingman that same night. The next day three more men were flown up to their hearings. On Friday, five men came.

Leroy Johnson sent word with these men to have those who were still at Short Creek (the teenage boys who had not been arrested) to bring vehicles to Kingman, because bail had been raised for their release.

They expected to be out of jail the next day.

UTAH WOMEN & CHILDREN FLEE

Three men at Short Creek had not been arrested (Dan Jessop, Joe Barlow, and Jack Cooke). Warrants had been issued for their arrest, but these were Arizona warrants and by staying in Utah, they were able to avoid being picked up. Because of rumors that Washington County officials in St. George were planning to arrest those on the Utah side, Council Members at Salt Lake City directed these men to evacuate the women and children from the Utah side of the community. Word was sent to the families, telling them to take only a small pack of clothing, a few blankets, and a little food and milk for their babies. They did not tell them where they were going, only that they would be walking quite a distance.

About 100 people gathered around midnight Thursday, July 30th, and began walking west, staying on the Utah side of the state line. After hiking along the foothills, through sagebrush and trees, climbing through gullies, washes, and crossing through several fences, they crossed into Arizona about three miles west of Short Creek. Arrangements had been made for a truck to meet them, but it was not there. Rhea Kunz, a member of the Polygamist Group who lived in Hurricane, Utah, was there, however. She only had a small car, but used it to transport these tired souls a little further west, back into Utah and into the seclusion of trees and rocks.

It had rained all night while they were hiking and the people were soaked through. When the sun came up in the morning, they spread their wet clothing and blankets on the rocks to dry. The babies were out of milk and the food was gone. About 10:00 a.m. one of the three men, who had escaped arrest brought water and milk, and also food for the older children and adults.

Feeling safe on the Utah side, they waited for the truck scheduled to arrive sometime in the afternoon. But something went wrong and the men and older boys fled the area, leaving the women and children behind to wait for the truck. They soon learned that the driver of the rescue truck had been apprehended. Officials told these women and children they had to return to their homes in Short Creek. They promised that if they went back to their Utah homes, they would not be arrested. They convinced them that it was safe to return to their homes, so these women allowed the officers and matrons to transport them back, reaching home about sundown.

REMOVING THE CHILDREN

Due to the escape attempt of Utah women and children, Arizona officials decided they must take the children in custody to Phoenix to continue the court hearings.

On Saturday morning, August 1st, the officers and matrons went to all the homes on the Arizona side of Short Creek. The mothers were told that the children were going to be taken to Phoenix and must be ready to leave in fifteen minutes. The bail had been paid for the men's release at Kingman, but the Sheriff would not release them, fearing trouble over the children being moved to Phoenix. The mothers said they would not allow the children to leave unless they could go with them, and due to the urgency of the situation, officials agreed.

The plan to fly the children to Phoenix fell through, so buses were scheduled. In the meantime, the women and children were forced to wait at the school house all day. It was an exhausted and unruly group that climbed on the five buses at 5:00 p.m. to begin the long trip, over 500 miles away.

Non-stop – without adequate food, water or rest stops for the forty-three mothers and their one hundred seventy-seven children – was an unspeakable hardship. Kidnaped from their homes in the solitude of remote Short Creek, they were forced into a crime-ridden city. During twenty months of captivity, seventeen more children were born to these mothers.

The men in Kingman were released from the county jail in the afternoon of Saturday, August 1, the same day their families were being taken to Phoenix. The young men did not arrive in Kingman with the vehicles (a truck with a touring car loaded on it) to bring the men home until late in the evening. After these men coming from Short Creek related what had happened at home, Leroy Johnson, taking the touring car, left for Phoenix, hoping to contact the women and children and search out an attorney to begin the long legal battle of bringing them back home. The other men loaded on the truck and began the long journey home, arriving in the early morning hours.

On Monday morning the fathers, with the help of the older boys that had been left at home, began the task of going around the community and cleaning up the abandoned houses that had been vacated so abruptly. The hasty departure had left food on the tables to spoil in the hot summer heat, dirty dishes, uncooked bread in pans, dirty clothes to be washed, and unmade beds. All the men from the Arizona side of town were invited to Fred Jessop's home on the Utah side, where they met each morning and night to not only eat their meals; they also all held hands and gathered in a circle prayer, asking their Father in Heaven to watch over and protect their loved ones, taken so far away. In these prayers they would also plead for the release of their wives and children, asking that the hearts of the Arizona Officials would be softened. These prayer meetings were faithfully attended by all members of the community, both from the Utah as well as the Arizona side for the twenty months the women and children were gone.

PLACING CHILDREN IN HOMES

In Phoenix, state officials began the process of relocating the children in homes throughout the state. The mothers were allowed to stay with their children who, being wards of the state, were placed on welfare for their subsistence. Since the mothers were under no restraint or arrest of any kind, the state would not pay for their keep. However, they were not at liberty to travel. If they were to leave their children, to even return home for a short visit, the state officials told them the children would be placed in foster homes, with intent to adopt them out to other parents. So they were just as much captives as the children.

The husbands were required to pay the state $30 a month for the support of each mother. This $30 per month was almost impossible to raise, so when each mother received it from the State, she would return it to Leroy Johnson, and he would use it to pay the State the next month. This created an almost unbearable hardship on the women and children struggling to survive. Kind people around them reached out a helping hand.

POLYGAMIST MEN RELEASED

On November 30, 1953, twenty-six of the Short Creek Polygamist men who had been arrested, appeared before Superior Court Judge Robert Tullar at Kingman, Arizona. In a plea bargain agreement they plead guilty to "Conspiracy to commit open and notorious cohabitation," a misdemeanor. On December 7, 1953, the twenty-six men were sentenced to one year suspended sentence and ordered to report to the Chief Probation Officer of Mohave County, Judge Charles Adorns, for probation. Judge Tullar ordered "That the bonds posted to assure the defendants appearance, be exonerated." The men were virtually free, while their wives and children were still held hostage. It would be more than another year from this time (December 1953) before the women and children would be allowed to return to their homes.

Because Carl Holm, Melvin Johnson, and Joseph S. Jessop were among the men who plead guilty to the misdemeanor, Judge Tuller removed them as trustees of the Short Creek School District, #14. Their replacements were Alfonzo Nyborg and Clifford Black of Short Creek, and David Ruesch of Hurricane, Utah.

School had started in Short Creek on August 31 with only eight Arizona students, the rest being in the custody of the State. On September 7th, twenty-seven students from the Utah side joined them.

With most of the woman and children gone, the community drew together. Each morning and each evening, they gathered for a community meal. Joining hands, they prayed for their loved ones absent, asking that they be protected.

The state of Arizona took a hard line. Mohave County School Superintendent, Mrs. Logsdon, told the Polygamists they could no longer use the school house for religious purposes, and that included funerals. When Joseph S. Jessop (eighty-four year-old grandfather to many of the people in Short Creek) died on September 1, 1953, his funeral was held in the front yard of Fred Jessop's house.

After this experience, the Polygamist Leaders concluded they would have to provide their own meeting house. They decided to dramatically renovate the chicken coops at Fred Jessop's home on the Utah side of town and create a small building for a meeting place. Also, they hoped that the Washington County School Board at St. George, Utah, would consent to allowing a public school be established in this same building. Utah seemed to be more accommodating to the people in Short Creek.

This work of remodeling began in September of 1953. Fred Jessop's home on the Utah side, which was used as a maternity clinic, had been known as "The Coop." The chicken coops were joined on to the house, with only a breeze-way between them. The work of remodeling began by removing the old roof of the coops and raising the walls about four feet. A new roof was then reconstructed, the building closed in and put into use before the winter weather set in.

Washington County School Board did indeed establish a school there by 1954 and the UEP-owned building was leased to the County for that purpose. Not only was the new building suitable for religious meetings, but also for dances and socials. With the rent income from the County, it would not be long until an addition would be built with more classrooms.

STATES LOOKING FOR PERMANENT SOLUTIONS

The State of Utah took a little different approach to solving the polygamy problem on the Utah side of Short Creek. They decided to test one case, putting it through the courts, reasoning that it would be less costly to the taxpayers. They chose the family of Vera (Johnson) Black, a plural wife of Leonard Black. Officers of the state picked up their seven children (the youngest was left in the care of his mother) on June 4, 1954, and placed them in foster care. A writ of Habeas Corpus was filed in the Supreme Court of the State of Utah. The State Supreme Court ruled in the favor of Vera Black and ordered that the children be returned to their parents, and in a matter of a few weeks they were returned.

The State did eventually win the case. An offer was made to Vera and Leonard Black that if they would sign a paper promising not to live polygamy, the children would remain in their custody. They refused the offer. On January 10, 1956, the children were picked up by officers from the State Welfare Department and placed in a foster home at Provo, Utah. This was very hard for Vera and Leonard Black to bear, not only losing their children but losing them at this time, because by then the women and children held in Arizona had been released and allowed to return home.

The next year, Vera and Leonard Black finally signed a statement agreeing to no longer live polygamy, making it possible for their children to come home.

In Arizona, the State Officials picked four test cases to try in court. The cases were each different in nature but covered the circumstances of the other cases. The goal of the State was to take the children from their natural parents and adopt them out to other families.

Meanwhile an attorney in Salt Lake City approached Council Member Guy Musser and informed him of an Arizona Statute that prohibited the State from adopting children out without the consent of their natural parents. When Leroy Johnson told their attorneys that such a law existed, they said they would check it out. Leroy implied to the people that he had received inspiration about this statute, never acknowledging that Guy Musser had been the one to tell him.

On March 3, 1955, Judge Henry S. Stevens of the Superior Court of Maricopa County ordered the children returned to their parents. After two long and difficult years, on March 21, 1955, the wives and children finally got to go home. And what a welcome they received. The community now had its women back in their homes, their kitchens filled with wonderful aromas, and children got to sleep in their own beds. The State appealed the Court's decision but never regained custody of the children. Thus ended Arizona's crusade against the Polygamists of Short Creek.

The whole episode of the Short Creek Raid gained national attention and became very unpopular in the state of Arizona. Public sentiment turned against Arizona Officials, and especially Governor Howard Pyle. It was not long until officials were regretting their actions. The Short Creek fiasco cost Governor Pyle his political career. He was never again elected to any public office in Arizona. He did, however, hold a position under President Eisenhower for a short time in the Federal Government at Washington D.C.

TOWN DISINTEGRATING FINANCIALLY

After the celebrations calmed down, everyone realized the community was in serious economic straits. The men had been working in the timber industry and for ranchers and fruit growers, but the Groups' focus had been disrupted for two years. Their money had gone to lawyers and to feed the mothers who remained with their children.

The wives and children of Leroy Johnson did not return to Short Creek, but remained in Phoenix for a time. He had been buying property in his own name, using tithing money paid to him by the people. He moved some of his family to the area around Manti, Utah, one of the places where he was buying property. Establishing himself there, he more or less began abandoning the people at Short Creek. The management of affairs fell on Richard Jessop, with Carl Holm and Fred Jessop assisting.

The Polygamists were not accustomed to providing for themselves. They had not been schooled in managing money or providing for their families. Those with multiple families were the hardest hit.

Nor could they pay the county taxes on the UEP property, which only amounted to about $3,000 a year. The tax burden fell on the people at Salt Lake who were aligned with the group at Short Creek. This burden became unbearable and they began complaining to their leaders. They felt that if the people at Short Creek could not even pay their own taxes, there was not much use to support such a place.

Food was scarce. In the late 1940s and the 1950s, the UEP would contract to buy the fruit from fruit farmers in Hurricane. This fruit would be picked and sorted by the young people, boys and girls, then it would be shipped and sold. The cull fruit would be hauled to Short Creek where the women would preserve it, putting it up in bottles or drying it. This was very hard work because there was a lot of cull fruit. Many times we would drive up to a home where two or three women were toiling to take care of the fruit we had brought the day before. We would beg them to take another ten bushels so we could get the truck unloaded. This fruit was a substantial part of the diet for the coming winter.

Those living in Short Creek were not only dirt poor, but also poor in spirit as they limped along for a year. About the only income to the UEP were the government checks received by the few widows living in the community, who turned their money over to the storehouse. Those in the leadership positions were unable, either by choice or circumstance, to provide any income to the group.

The Priesthood Council met and after much deliberation concluded that they would sell the property, leaving those living there to make their own way as best they could. But there was one member of the Council that did not want to give up on Short Creek. That member was J. Marion Hammon.

Marion Hammon, who had been sent to Short Creek in the early 1940s by Joseph Musser to be the general manager of the United Effort Plan, felt that he was still under the calling to see that the United Effort at Short Creek would succeed. He asked the other Brethren of the Council if they would allow him the opportunity to go back there and try to redeem the place. The other Council members finally agreed. He asked that they give him free reign and not interfere with how he would run things. Thinking there was not enough spirit left at Short Creek to accomplish any measure of success, they saw little risk and agreed.

6

Joseph Musser & Charles Zitting Pass Away

The year after the Short Creek raid, with the women and children still in Phoenix and surrounding areas, two prominent members of the Priesthood Council died within six months of each other.

On March 29, 1954, Joseph White Musser died at Salt Lake City. The Polygamist Group at Short Creek did not recognize him as the President of Priesthood due to his ordaining Rulon Allred and of his calling a new Priesthood Council. Charles Zitting had been the recognized Priesthood Leader among the people in Short Creek for the last three or four years. Musser's death had very little impact at Short Creek.

This is somewhat unjust, for history must give credit to whom and to where it is due. Had it not been for this man, "Saint Joseph White Musser," it is very likely there would never have been a Fundamentalist movement, or a Polygamist community at Colorado City today. Also, other Fundamentalist communities throughout the Mountain West would not exist. Joseph Musser was a dynamic person. He devoted the latter part of his life to establishing what he believed was the Gospel of Jesus Christ. It was because of such dedication that the Polygamists became so numerous and so well indoctrinated.

Joseph Musser was probably best known for his publishing of the *Truth* Magazine. He began publishing this monthly magazine in June of 1935. The *Truth* became the media used by the Priesthood Council to proclaim their doctrine among the people of the LDS Church. Along with the *Truth*, he also published numerous pamphlets and treatises, setting forth the doctrines of the Priesthood Group. It was Joseph Musser, along with Leslie Broadbent and John Barlow, who promoted Lorin Woolley (1929) into allowing them to write his story, of how he received the special calling to keep Plural Marriage alive after the LDS Church abandoned it in 1890. In 1935, after the First Presidency of the LDS Church publicly announced, "There is no authority on earth to perform Plural Marriages, either in the Church, or outside the Church," Joseph Musser responded and claimed that there was a higher authority than what the President of the LDS Church held, and it resided with the polygamists.

He published a pamphlet called "A Priesthood Issue," setting forth evidence that Joseph Smith had established a secret order of Priesthood called The Council of Friends. This Priesthood Order superseded any authority that the LDS Church President held. The Priesthood Group of Joseph Musser and his associates claimed to be of this higher order, thus placing them outside of the jurisdiction of the LDS Church Presidency. Of all the Priesthood Council Members, excepting for one small pamphlet put out with the help of Leslie Broadent in 1929, Joseph Musser is the only one who published any writings establishing the doctrines of the Polygamists. Without question, Joseph Musser is the most important person connected with the establishment of the modern day Polygamists. For this reason, it seems fitting to narrate a little of his history.

Joseph Musser was born in Salt Lake City on March 8, 1872, five years before Brigham Young died. At the age of twenty, he attended the placing of the Capstone on the Salt Lake Temple. From his journal, April 13, 1892: "I ascended the east middle tower of the Temple and touched the feet of the Golden Angel Moroni."

His formal school consisted of a "few years in the lower grades, never having attended high school or University." He did, however, work very hard at educating himself, learning shorthand and typing. He also studied extensively in law.

He and Rose Barquist were married June 29, 1892. Less than three years later, on January 27, 1895, he received a call signed by President Wilford Woodruff to serve a mission in the Southern states. He was set apart by Apostles Brigham Young Jr., Heber J. Grant, and John W. Taylor, then left for Alabama on April 13, 1895.

Joseph labored without purse or scrip. While on his mission his wife gave birth to their first son, Joseph Jr. on July 24, 1895. When the mission was completed, Joseph returned home and resumed his normal life. In the early part of the year 1900, on the threshold of a new century, his peaceful life was interrupted. In his own words, here is what happened.

"When the Wilford Woodruff Manifesto was adopted (October 1890), I was not married. I had been promised in the Name of The Lord, by my Stake President some days after the Manifesto was published, that I would enter The Law. I believed it and later while courting my young lady, I told her I expected to enter that law of marriage. That when the time came I would take it up with her and we would make the selection of other wives together. Although I was taking her out of a plural family, she took the matter coolly, but she was true to her promise on that occasion.

"In December 1899, after receiving my 'Second Blessings' (Joseph had received a written invitation from President Lorenzo Snow, 5th LDS President, to receive Higher Anointings, which was attended to in November 1899, in the Salt Lake Temple), a messenger came to me from President Snow, stating I had been selected to enter Plural Marriage, and to help keep the Principle alive. Apprizing my wife of the situation, we both entered into prayer for guidance. At this time I hadn't the slightest idea whom to approach. The Manifesto had been issued and word had gone out from Bishops and Stake Presidencies that a definite stop had been put to the practice. Those assuming to enter the Principle would be handled. I was placed in a peculiar situation. God's Prophet told me to accept the Law and keep it alive. His subordinates said if I did so they would cut me off the Church."

It was not until 1901 that Joseph married his second wife, Mary Hill. When he asked her father William Hill (a member of the Mill Creek Ward Bishopric) if he could marry Mary, her father told him it could not be done. In less than an hour Brother Hill returned and told him it was all right and he could go ahead and marry his daughter. Astonished at his change of heart, Joseph asked why he changed his mind. He answered that he had gone to apostles John Henry Smith and Mathias F. Cowley and put the question to them. They assured him it was all right and advised him to give his consent to the marriage. Mathias F. Cowley was the man who performed the marriage.

Joseph Musser married two more wives, bringing the number to four. His third wife was taken under the direction of President Joseph F. Smith (6th LDS President). His fourth was under the direction of Lorin Woolley in the 1930s. Apostles Mathias F. Cowley and John W. Taylor (a son of the prophet John Taylor) were later disfellowshipped from the LDS Church and dropped from the Council of The Twelve because of performing plural marriages after the Manifesto. Mathias F. Cowley was allowed back in the Church but never reinstated to The Council of The Twelve. John W. Taylor was excommunicated and died as a non-member of the Church.

On February 16, 1914, Joseph had an interview with Francis M. Lyman, President of the Quorum of The Twelve. At this time Joseph Musser was a member of the High Council of the Granite Stake of the LDS Church. Brother Lyman maintained it was a sin to enter into the relations of plural marriage since the Manifesto of President Woodruff. Joseph explained to him that he did nothing except through the council and ratification of the Members of his own Quorum. He was told he had no right to take counsel from members of the Quorum, but should have gone to the President of the Church. He was advised by President Lyman to resign his position in The High Council of Granite Stake. When Joseph related the circumstances of the interview to his File Leaders, the Stake Presidency, they advised him not to resign. He took their advice.

Joseph Musser became acquainted with Lorin Woolley in the 1920s. In his journal, he writes about an event that transpired with LDS Church Apostle Joseph F. Smith, prior to his meeting Lorin Woolley. From Joseph W. Musser Journal:

"In the year 1915 an Apostle (Joseph F. Smith) conferred upon me the sealing power of Elijah, with instructions to see that plural marriage shall not die out.... May 14, 1929, I was ordained a High Priest Apostle and a Patriarch to all the world by a High Priest Apostle (Lorin Woolley), and I was instructed to see that never a year passed that children were not born in the covenant of plural marriage. I was instructed to give patriarchal blessings to those applying for same and who were denied access to real patriarchs in the Church."

Then we find on page 20 of this same book, "When I was ordained a High Priest Apostle in May 1929, it was done in response to a revelation of the Lord to the President of the Priesthood (Lorin Woolley). Previous to this, however, I was given the Priesthood of Elijah with instructions, as I was informed from President Joseph F. Smith, to seal couples in celestial marriage (1915)."

Quoting further from this same journal: "I recall instructions given at the close of a prayer circle meeting held in the Salt Lake Temple in the early part of 1902. President Anthon H. Lund, a Counselor in the First Presidency was President of the Circle. We asked President Lund for a private audience after the close of the prayer. We made known to President Lund that children were being born to some of the Saints in the plural marriage relation and that they were not being recognized by the Church. We asked what should be done in such cases. His instructions came clear and emphatic.

"Brethren, you hold the Priesthood and stand at the head of your families. As your children are born you should give them a father's blessing and a name. When they reach the proper age for baptism, you should baptize them, confirm them members of the Church and confer the Holy Ghost in the usual manner. Be sure and keep the record and when the Church will receive it hand it in."

This short report on the early life of Joseph Musser is important in the history of the Polygamists. He was not a crackpot, but had been an active and faithful LDS Church member prior to his excommunication in March of 1921, and of his meeting Lorin Woolley. No doubt he would have excelled and gone far in the LDS Church had he accepted the changes that were necessary to insure its survival against the political pressures that were opposing its principles at this critical time in Church history. Instead, he chose to stand up for the principles he believed in and in so doing, ended up fighting the very source of his blessings. When the opportunity presented itself to carry on, in what he considered the Higher Principles, he was in a prime position to "Take the ball and run," thus changing not only his life, but the lives of a good many souls, both those living at the time and many more who were yet unborn. The effects of his efforts have, to this day, changed the history of the LDS Church and the Inter-mountain region, especially the states of Utah and Arizona.

The book entitled *Joseph W. Musser Journal* was compiled by him, using notes from his day to day journal and was written some years later and was published by his family sometime after 1952. This is not to be confused with his journal, which is a day to day account of his life and is quoted in earlier chapters.

With the passing of Joseph Musser, Charles Zitting officially became the next Council President for the Short Creek group. Rulon Allred became the leader of the Musser/Allred group at Salt Lake City. Since the Priesthood split, Charles Zitting had been acting as the leader for the Short Creek Group. When Musser died in March of 1954, Zitting moved into his leadership position without any opposition. His was to be a short rule.

Four months later, on July 14, 1954, Charles Zitting died. Though his position of President had been accepted by the group, it had been a strained relationship because of the influence that Leroy Johnson had over the people at Short Creek.

Charles Zitting was not a selfish man. He gave of his time and efforts freely. He was a considerate leader which enabled him to earn the respect of his followers. Had it not been that he was in the leadership position for such a short time, he no doubt would have been able to surpass the handicap of Leroy Johnson's efforts to undercut him.

Charles Fredrick Zitting was born on March 30, 1894. He married Minnie Affleck on September 15, 1920. Because of Charles' belief in plural marriage, the union did not last. They were divorced about six years later. Charles wasted no time in getting married again. He convinced two other girls to marry him about one year later. John Woolley performed the marriage, marrying one girl to him on August 13 and the other on August 30, 1927.

Because of this decision to marry more than one wife, he was excommunicated from the LDS Church in November of 1928. He was arrested several times in his life because of his belief and practice of plural marriage.

The longest time he spent in prison was during the polygamist crusade in 1944. He and fourteen others were sentenced to the Utah Penitentiary. All but four of these men signed a "manifesto" to gain parole after only spending a few months there. Charles was one of the men refusing to go against his conscience; by not signing, he remained in prison for the next thirty-one months before he was released. It was while he was in prison that he wrote his memoirs. It was in these memoirs that he tells of being called into the Priesthood Counsel, this event taking place in the spring of 1932.

He was ordained a Patriarch and Apostle of the Lord Jesus Christ by Joseph Leslie Broadbent, who acted under the direction of Lorin C. Woolley. Charles remained faithful to his belief in the validity of this calling until his death. He would make no concession of conscience for any reason and suffered because of it. The worst of these were put upon him after his death by men claiming certain things had happened that, in fact, they have no proof of. These men believe that by discrediting Charles Zitting, they can then change the history of the Fundamentalist movement.

He was accused long after his death of going against Council President John Y. Barlow, who felt all of his men in prison should have signed the agreement to get out of prison early. Thus, he was "removed from the Presidency for turning against the Head," by the sons of John Y. Barlow.

With the passing of Charles Zitting, there was a question among the Short Creek group as to who the next leader would be. The women and children were still being held by the state of Arizona and conditions in Short Creek were deteriorating.

The next legitimate leader in line was LeGrand Woolley. After him was Louis Kelsch. These two men were the last of the Council called by Lorin Woolley. But they both lived in Salt Lake City and were no longer associated with the group at Short Creek, because neither approved of organizing the polygamists.

As a formality, Leroy Johnson went to LeGrand Woolley and asked if he was going to assume the position of leadership over the people at Short Creek. LeGrand reminded him of the instructions of Lorin Woolley *not to colonize* and said he could not get involved. Leroy then went to Louis Kelsch with the same question. Kelsch asked Leroy if he had any revelation from God that he should lead the people. Leroy answered that he had not. Kelsch said that he likewise had received no revelation on the matter. Leroy then asked Kelsch if he had any objection to him taking over the leadership of the group. Kelsch said: "Roy, *if you have what you think you have,* you don't need my permission to go ahead."

Leroy Johnson then told the people at Short Creek that Louis Kelsch said he, Leroy, should go ahead and lead the people. Leroy was now the senior man on the Council, followed by Marion Hammon, Guy Musser, Rulon Jeffs, Richard Jessop, Carl Holm, and Alma Timpson.

Leroy was living in Phoenix when the two Council Members died, and the Short Creek women and children were still scattered around the state. By 1958, the situation in Short Creek was desperate and Marion Hammon asked for one last chance to save the population of approximately 800 people.

7

Saving Short Creek

Marion Hammon, having secured permission of the other Priesthood Council members to go to Short Creek to save whatever he could there, accepted this challenge with determination and set out with a vigor that was unparalleled by any efforts made at Short Creek up to this time.

In the summer of 1958 he showed up at a Priesthood meeting at the new meeting house recently completed behind the home of Fred Jessop. Priesthood meetings were scheduled on the first Monday of each month, beginning at 7:30 p.m. The brethren responsible for these meetings were Richard Jessop and Carl Holm. Neither ever arrived on time. Finally all the men learned to show up late.

Marion Hammon came to the meeting on time. No one was there. As he waited for the men to arrive, pacing the floor and looking at his watch, he became perturbed. Finally, an hour later, Council Member Richard Jessop and several men came in and Hammon, who was now in a very bad mood, stood up and opened the meeting. In scorching tones, he began to scold everyone, including Richard Jessop. Carl Holm had not yet arrived.

Hammon stated he would not tolerate tardiness in any degree. He was there to change things at Short Creek and he was going to start by demanding obedience and respect. He harangued the men for over an hour, but they didn't seem to mind. The feeling of the group was one of relief. They were pleased that someone seemed to care enough about them to try and help improve things in the community and the general spirit of the place. Marion Hammon was the right man to do just that.

He began first to hold meetings on time, Sunday meetings as well as Priesthood meetings. He did not dwell too much on spiritual doctrine in his Sunday talks, but talked more about how to improve things in the daily temporal lives of the people in the community.

The living conditions of the people were deplorable. Only a few houses in the community had running water (these were the houses on the old CCC line). None had inside bathrooms. The only electrical power in town was a small gasoline power plant at Fred Jessop's place and an old Cat diesel power plant on the Arizona side of the town that served about ten houses and was only run at night from dark until about 10:00 p.m.

There was no real telephone service. A few homes had some of the old crank type phones where a system of long and short rings was used to signal which person was being called, since all were on a party line. This phone line was only a local system without any outside connection. There was no high school in the community. There were no paved roads, either in the community or leading there from outside. The nearest town was Hurricane, Utah, about 30 miles of dirt road away.

The people were living in squalid conditions. They were proud, however, and resented the implications from Brother Hammon that they were poor in class as well as in material things. Getting them to change would be a challenge.

FINDING MONEY TO PAY DEBTS

To add to these problems, the United Effort Plan was in debt to several businesses, fruit growers and the like, in the surrounding communities. Realizing he needed some competent help to accomplish his task, Hammon turned to members of the Group in Salt Lake City that had both the experience and the ability to help him build his city. He would go to these men for the help he needed.

In order to change the image of the UEP, the debts had to be paid. He began by asking the male heads of families in both Salt Lake and Short Creek to raise thirty dollars for each member in their respective household. Several thousand dollars was soon raised. With this money, he then went to those the money was owed to and paid them off, thus creating good feelings and a new respect towards the UEP and the people at Short Creek from their outside neighbors.

This first effort of Marion Hammon to redeem Short Creek was very successful. It not only paid off the old lingering debts, but it also gave the people a renewed spirit and determination to move forward and do something to improve their circumstances.

He next established workdays. He would set aside a day, or days, when people would report to work on projects in the community. These days were every Saturday and any holiday that people could get off their regular work. This included not only the people at Short Creek but also the people from Salt Lake. The latter would leave Salt Lake on Friday nights and drive to Short Creek (referring to it as "going down south"), arriving there in the early morning hours. They would often get only a few hours sleep before showing up for work.

The projects at first included general cleanup work throughout the community: old eyesores such as abandoned vehicles and old farm equipment, old sheds and buildings that were no longer in use. These were moved or torn down. The fences throughout the area were repaired and new ones built as needed. These were worthwhile projects, but there were also other things needed.

The necessity of building houses was one of the most pressing. He went to people in Salt Lake who either owned their homes there or at least were buying their houses and had some equity. These people were asked to sell their houses, collect what equity they had and then go to Short Creek, using the money to build a new home there. They were promised by not only Hammon, but most of the Priesthood Council (including Leroy Johnson), that if they would do this, they would be given a lot to build on. The title to the property would remain in the name of the United Effort Plan. The purpose of the

UEP Trust was explained to them in somewhat the following generalities:

> The Brethren in the 1940s had set up the trust to hold title to the property for the security of their homes. Those building on the property would never receive a deed, the title remaining in the name of the trust. Anyone building homes would be allowed to live in them for so long as they chose, never being asked to leave them, understanding, however, that if they ever decided of their own accord to abandon their house, they would forfeit any claim of ownership.

The main purpose of the trust was to protect the homes and property from ever being taken for any reason. The people (not only from Salt Lake but also those from Short Creek) who would build homes, were told that they could rely on the Trust for all their security needs, such as life insurance, medical expenses, and also old age retirement benefits, that by contributing either time, money or property to the trust, they would be members of the United Effort Plan, becoming *co-owners in all the assets of the trust.*

The Brethren preached from the pulpit that the policy of the UEP was not to force anyone out, but that the promises of the men who established the gathering place at Short Creek was that "any who was not in harmony with the Priesthood would get discouraged and move out."

The members of the Short Creek group, those coming from Salt Lake as well as those already living there, looked to the United Effort Plan as a social order to assist them to achieve three major goals:

The first, to protect them against their enemies being able to confiscate their property (a threat made by Governor Pyle at the time of the 1953 Raid).

The second, to safeguard the property from any mortgage foreclosure.

The third, to help build up and revitalize the community.

They had full trust in their leaders, believing them to be honorable men, having no reason to suspect they would ever change the rules of the UEP as was explained to them at this time.

WARNING SIGNALS

There was only one small warning signal that would have caused any of them to doubt the honesty and integrity of these men.

A few of the people, who were asked to sell their houses in Salt Lake and move down south, asked to see the trust document. To their surprise, they were reprimanded severely for "showing distrust" in the leaders. It was intimated to them that the document was somewhat sacred and anyone wanting to see it was on the road to apostasy for mistrusting their word about what was in it.

Although the Trust document was filed in the county courthouses of both Mohave County at Kingman, Arizona, and Washington County at St. George, Utah, this information was not revealed to any of the members coming to Short Creek, so in their ignorance, these trusting people put the matter aside. Their eagerness to establish a place of refuge, where they, with their families, could live in peace until the millennium, far outweighed any omen of trouble that should have been foreseen.

This reasoning, along with the promises made over the pulpit, dispelled any doubts that may have foreshadowed their confidence in the venture. Having overcome these obstacles, the momentum of the work began to move forward with surprising success. The members moving to Short Creek thus felt confident they would forever be secure in the homes they were building there.

CHURCH HOUSES & TEMPLES NOT NEEDED

The United Effort Plan never claimed to be an ecclesiastical organization. There is no mention in the Trust Document of it being any kind of a religious Trust. The document specifically names the association as A Common Law Trust, leaving no doubt as to what the organizers intended.

The only reference to any ecclesiastical organization at Short Creek was referred to as The Priesthood Work. It was explained to the people in their religious meetings (from Leroy Johnson down through all the Council members) that "we are members of The Church of Jesus Christ of Latter-day Saints." All who joined the Fundamentalists, either as new members coming from the Mormon Church, or as children being baptized when turning eight years old (as is the Mormon custom), were all confirmed members of The Church of Jesus Christ of Latter-day Saints (the LDS Church did not recognize any of these confirmations and none of these people were ever placed on the LDS membership roles). Any members of the LDS Church moving to Short Creek would be called to a Church Court, tried for their membership and, if they would not denounce the Fundamentalists, would most certainly be excommunicated.

The Priesthood Council taught that the LDS Church was God's Church. God had not rejected it nor would He ever reject it. The Church was out of order because of giving up polygamy in 1890, but the time would come when "One Mighty and Strong" (D&C 85:7) would come and set the Church in order. They believed this One Mighty and Strong was to be Joseph Smith, and that when these events were to happen, the LDS Church leadership would be turned over to the Priesthood Council and the entire LDS Church would come under their jurisdiction.

The coming of these events were in the "near future" and there was no need to build any church houses because there would be plenty when the LDS Church was restored to the true Priesthood. They also taught that for these same reasons, there was no need to build Temples.

They made no effort to secretly go to any of the present day Temples of the LDS Church for they believed the Church did not have the true priesthood. The work of sealing marriages for eternity being done in the Temples was invalid and would all have to be done over. The only sealing work the polygamists performed was the marriage covenant and they claimed that a Temple was not necessary for performing this Ordinance: "It is the *authority* that validates the Ordinance, not the place." They not only claimed to be the only ones on earth having the authority to seal for time and all eternity, they also claimed to have the power to dictate who each girl was to marry.

CHILD BRIDES BEGIN

The practice of having the Priesthood place men and women together was first preached to the people in the late 1950s. Until this time, the policy of the Polygamists had been to go to one of the Brethren for permission to court and marry a girl for a new wife, the men having pretty much been allowed free rein to court whomever they chose.

By the mid-1950s this policy had become a major concern to the Priesthood Council. It created two problems. Any girl after reaching about thirteen years old (or child bearing age) would have a great number of suitors coming to her, all claiming to have had a revelation from God that she was to marry him, greatly confusing her young and tender mind. The other (and no doubt greater) problem was that the girls would invariably choose the younger men, making it almost impossible for the older Brethren to get new wives. The people were taught that only a member of the Priesthood Council could get revelation as to who a girl "belonged to" (should marry).

This situation brought the old clique factor into play. Each Council member would "place" the girls *within his clique* when they came of child bearing age, telling them who to marry.

If a man wanted to get a wife, he had to align himself with one of the Priesthood Council members, supporting him in his clique. This allowed nepotism to rule in who would get a wife and when (at what age) they would get married. A natural circumstance developed wherein the sons of the Council members would not only be the first (youngest) to be married, but also the ones judged worthy to become polygamists. In most cases they were the least qualified for the choice, creating many problems in their later lives when their fathers would die, leaving them to their own abilities to cope with the problems of the big families these polygamist marriages produced.

As to why the leaders thought thirteen-year-old girls were old enough to be married, perhaps they felt that LDS founder Joseph Smith and other early leaders had set the example.

LOVE UNNECESSARY & WOMEN INFERIOR

The Polygamists teach that love is not necessary before marriage. Women are inferior to men and must learn to school their feelings, yielding to the desires of their husband. The girls of the Colorado City Polygamists are considered as chattel, to be used by the leaders to reward the faithful men of the Group for their support of the Priesthood Work. And if a man is deemed unworthy, his wives and children are reassigned to another "more worthy" man.

I think the biggest challenge to women in the Polygamist society is their responsibility to have babies. Birth control was not allowed in any form. Women were taught by John Barlow's group that a woman should have as many children as she could. Fifteen to twenty for one woman was not uncommon. But Joseph Musser and Marion Hammon taught that women should only have a child about every three years. Hammon further taught that one wife should only have six children in her lifetime, and his wives only had six children each except one wife who had twins, therefore she had seven.

Very few women ever achieve any more than bearing as many children as possible, usually between fifteen or twenty. Most are expected to work, turning what money they earn over to their husband to use as he sees fit. A few become school teachers to work in the public schools, while others become nurses to work in hospitals of nearby communities. None are ever allowed to become professors, doctors, lawyers, or achieve other professional goals. Mostly they work at whatever unskilled jobs are available in the area.

An exception was "Aunt" Lydia Jessop, wife of Fred Jessop. The epitome of courage, she symbolized all that is good in a human being. Born in Fredonia, Arizona, on February 29, 1920, to Warren Elmer and Viola Spencer Johnson, she came to Short Creek in 1931 at the age of eleven. She married Fred in about 1935, as his first wife. Due to a childhood disease, Fred was sterile and Aunt Lydia never had any children of her own.

She made up for this misfortune by becoming a midwife and delivered thousands of babies for other mothers. Her children were everyone else's children and she was much loved by them all. She was also the "doctor" of the community for many years, setting broken bones, sewing up cuts, and nursing the sick through fever and other sicknesses. After a short battle with cancer in 1996, she passed away. If any person in the polygamist society deserves sainthood, it is Aunt Lydia.

TEENAGE BOYS PUT TO WORK FOR THE UEP

Next Marion Hammon organized a "missionary" program. Any boy just out of 8th grade (the highest grade available in Short Creek) or in that age group, was called on a Work Mission. These boys were asked to give two years of their time to financing and building up the United Effort Plan. In return for this service, they were told that after putting in their two years, they would be "given a wife and a lot on which they could build a house."

These boy missionaries would either be assigned to work on Priesthood projects to build the community or would be asked to seek paying jobs in outside communities, turning their entire paychecks over to Marion Hammon. The boy missionaries were not allowed to keep any of their earnings for their own support, but rather it was required of their parents to support them. Much of the building up of the Short Creek area can be attributed to these boys and their willingness to work, and to their parents who supported them.

There were two flaws. One was putting the burden on poor parents to support their young sons, and some had four or five boys serving at the same time. (Either the boys were close in age or they were from different mothers.) Once these boys were in the program, they would not be released in some instances for up to five years. Some would become discouraged, not knowing when they would ever be released, which usually came when a wife was available.

Second was that the sons of Priesthood leaders would get married before the boys from less prominent families. Such nepotism caused hard and bitter feelings among the boys and their parents. Any complaint made about this discrimination was met with harsh reaction from Hammon. He would publicly condemn and chastise the miscreants, thus discouraging any who dared question his actions.

ELECTRICITY & RUNNING WATER

One of the first projects Hammon chose for the missionaries was to get electrical power into the community. Garkane Power Company had recently installed a new hydroelectric generating plant at Boulder, Utah. Garkane was a small company and was looking for new customers because it was planning to expand its area of operation, anticipating acquiring a portion of the Government power that would be available when the Glen Canyon Dam would be completed. Hammon went to this company and negotiated a deal to get a power line into the community. Garkane Power had recently rebuilt a power line in Wayne County with new poles and wire. The company agreed that if Hammon would furnish the manpower to build a power line, they would supply the material, using the old poles and wire from the Wayne County project. This newly formed missionary program was used to supply the laborers to construct the new power line. The building of the power line was completed in 1959. Having electrical power in their homes greatly encouraged them, especially easing the burdens of the women.

At the same time the power line was being built, work was started on a pipeline to bring culinary water to the community from springs in Maxwell Canyon. The water rights to these springs were owned by the irrigation company that had been formed by the Lauritzens thirty or forty years earlier. Most of the Lauritzen families had moved by 1959, having sold their property to the UEP or people who had moved into the community and joined with the polygamists. For these reasons, it was a relatively easy task to get the water rights. The next step in building the pipeline was to raise money to buy the pipe.

Marion Hammon believed that the people should pay for improvements with their own money, not asking for government help, either in the form of loans or grants. He would often say from the pulpit: "There is nobody here but us chickens," meaning that it is our community and it is up to us to build it. He was afraid that if the Government were to help finance these civic projects, they would be able to dictate and control the town.

He asked every head of household to come up with more money. The people had not entirely paid off the last assessment, but this did not deter him from requesting more donations. The amount needed this time was $200 each. The money was raised, albeit a great hardship was put on the people to meet the assessment, because the people were living just a little above the poverty level.

Even though meeting these requests for donations would put families in hard straits, causing them to suffer, they felt they must meet any requirement placed upon them by the Priesthood. This was probably one of Marion Hammon's greatest faults, not knowing the true condition of the common people. He had no true comprehension of how poor the people really were. He always lived a much higher lifestyle than any of the lay members could even dream of, oft times chastising them in public meetings for their poverty.

An example is a Sunday Sermon where he scolded the people for not buying the high priced steak that was for sale at the community store. The steak had to be ground up into hamburger before the people would buy it. He said, "You people can't even appreciate a good cut of meat. We have to make hamburger out of it before you'll buy it." He never realized that they just couldn't afford to eat "a good cut of meat." They could barely afford to buy a little hamburger to use in soups and gravy.

The assessment for the pipe was also put on the Salt Lake members and, with their help, the money to buy the pipe and build a water tank was successfully raised. The pipe was brought into town and work on the project started. Most of the work on the pipeline was performed on work days; however, there were a few men that spent their full time on these projects, their temporal needs being supplied from the storehouse.

Two such men were Joe and Dan Jessop. Without their dedication, Marion Hammon's job would have been much more difficult. Had it not been for such men, these and others, he would not have accomplished his goals. Any success claimed by the leaders was really the success of people in the community. Their families have suffered poverty and privation to satisfy the callings the Priesthood placed on them. The doctrine of the Priesthood is this: "You must be willing to sacrifice everything you have, including your wives and family, to the up-building of the Work." Men like these deserve the highest credit.

Work on the pipeline moved along and was soon completed to a location just north of town, a distance just a little over a mile. The water storage tank was erected there. The task of putting in distribution lines was begun. This was a never ending project, but for the first time, running water would be available to every home in the valley. This, along with getting electricity into the community, was a real accomplishment for Marion Hammon toward redeeming Short Creek.

ELIZABETH BUILDS HER OWN HOUSE

Elizabeth (not her real name) and her family moved into the community in the 1960s. Her husband was unable to obtain work in nearby communities and had an offer to go to California to work in an aircraft factory. He only came home three or four times a year, thus leaving Elizabeth to take care of herself.

Spunky Elizabeth asked the leaders for a building lot, which they gave her. When she told them she was determined to build her own house, they chuckled among themselves.

In fact, Elizabeth constructed adobe, laid the foundation, poured the floor, and laid the adobes up, and put the roof on, doing the entire work almost entirely by herself. In the 1980s Elizabeth and her husband fell out of favor with community leaders and were asked to leave. She obtained a piece of property that belonged to one of her sons-in-law up the canyon above Hildale, and once again, started over. No one was surprised that she built another two-room house.

Sad to say, after she moved away from Colorado City, the community leaders bulldozed her first house to the ground. This was a policy of the leaders for anyone asked to leave. If their house was not a fancy house, it would be destroyed to eliminate evidence they had ever lived in the community. Elizabeth was a very hard-working, industrious person.

FRED JESSOP FINDS GOOD PAYING JOBS FOR MEMBERS

When Marion Hammon assumed the leading role of directing the affairs of the United Effort Plan at Short Creek, he displaced Fred Jessop. Not only was Fred no longer allowed to make the daily trips to town to buy supplies for the people, but his role of being the entertainment and activities director, along with controlling work projects, was taken from him.

In a sense, his wings were clipped, a hard blow to his ego. For the first time in his adult life, he got a job. Joining the Labor Union, he went to work on the Glen Canyon Dam construction site. His job consisted of riding around the dam site in a pick-up truck driven by a Teamster, to load or unload small items. According to the Union contracts, a Laborer could not drive on the site, likewise a Teamster could not load or unload the small items. Most of his working day was spent sitting in the dispatch shack, waiting to be called out.

While working on the dam project, he was able to win the favor of the Union Stewards and was instrumental in getting many of the men from Short Creek working there, taking advantage of the high wages being paid. His influence contributed much toward bringing in a lot of the money that built the community. He did, however, resent Marion taking his job from him. There would be bitter conflicts resulting from these resentments, especially in controlling the social affairs of the community.

The conflict between Marion and Fred intensified when Marion established a high school in the community, a high school that would ultimately dominate the social arena.

BUILDING A HIGH SCHOOL

In 1959, Arizona law did not require students to have a high school education. Mohave County had never provided any schooling above the eighth grade at Short Creek. In the early 1950s, there was an attempt made to establish correspondence courses through Phoenix Union High School for those wishing to acquire a high school diploma. The courses were limited at best and only the more tenacious and studious participants were able to achieve success. The Short Creek Raid of 1953 had put a stop to even this token effort.

Marion felt concern over the attitude the community members had toward formal education. Few of them showed any concern about the lack of their children's high school education. When a girl graduated from the eighth grade, she was considered old enough to marry and became fair game for the men (or boys) to court her. They believed the only education a girl needed was how to be a good housekeeper and mother. The boys coming out of eighth grade were expected to help on the UEP projects, or go to work earning money to support Fred Jessop's storehouse.

Marion concluded that a private high school must be built so the students could be taught the doctrines of the Priesthood along with academics. There was no available building in the community that could be used for the school, one must be built. Construction on the school building was begun in the spring of 1960.

The first obstacle to overcome was the question of building material. Hammon knew he could not ask the members of the group to donate more money, so he devised a way to construct the building from "out of the ground." He sent work crews (missionaries, as well as the crews on work days) to the rock quarries in the foothills. Here sandstone building blocks, to be used for the foundation, were hauled to the site picked for the new school, about 100 yards from where the old CCC camp had been east of the town. Other crews were put to work building adobes from the natural soil of the area. The adobe-making crews were made up primarily of the young people, future students of the school. By working long and hard hours, they accomplished the task and the adobes were built. Lumber for the roof was the next major hurdle to conquer.

SAWMILL & LUMBER

Back in the early 1950s, the UEP had purchased a small sawmill, setting it up just east of town, where the old CCC Camp had been. Then after the return of the women and children in early 1955, the sawmill at Short Creek was moved to a site just west of Mount Carmel, Utah, on the Muddy Creek. Timber was purchased from private land owners, and the milled lumber was sold to Whiting Brothers at Fredonia, Arizona (Kaibab Industries). It was not profitable, so the sawmill was moved back to Short Creek and set up again on the site at the old CCC Camp. It was this sawmill that Marion Hammon activated to obtain the lumber needed to build the new high school.

The first timber he obtained was from a small salvage sale on the Buckskin Mountain (Kaibab Forest). These logs were hauled to Short Creek and the sawmill was put into operation, using the missionary work force. One particular missionary, Andrew Bistline, a young man greatly talented along both technical and mechanical lines, was very dedicated to the Priesthood Work. He spent long and hard hours putting the sawmill in operation, dedicating his time and talents toward producing the lumber needed to build the high school.

Another person who later in 1963 would dedicate his time and talents to finishing the building of the high school, a step-by-step process that took almost ten years to complete, was Harold Blackmore. He was asked by Hammon to move to Short Creek to help in the renovation of the community. Living in Canada, he was associated with a group of Polygamists who followed the Priesthood Council at Colorado City. Because of his many talents in the building trade and his ability to procure building material, it was decided he would be an asset to the Priesthood Work.

Due to the dedication and hard work of such men as Andrew Bistline, Edson Jessop, and the missionaries, enough of the school building was completed that classes started by the fall of 1960. The name chosen for the high school was The Colorado City Academy and this institution grew to become the pride of the valley.

HOME INDUSTRY

Soon after the Colorado City Academy was completed, Merril Jessop took over the operation of the sawmill when Leroy instructed him that "the sawmill must run," so it could provide lumber for their homes. Merril soon discovered that the sawmill must be heavily subsidized from other UEP owned businesses that he was operating, the General Store and J & B Service Station. After negotiating a salvage timber sale with the Chief Ranger at Fredonia for timber on Mt. Trumbull, he began a modest logging and lumber effort. Missionaries provided most of the labor force, but it was necessary to have some management personnel. By paying very low wages, he was able to achieve a small measure of success in the operation.

Two of these men, Ray Jessop (Merril's brother) and Andrew Bistline, worked long hours for starvation wages to help out the Work. Ray, with the help of one or two of the missionaries, would drive his logging truck to Trumbull every day, load the truck, haul four to five thousand board feet of logs back home, and repeat the routine the next day. He faithfully hauled logs for a number of years. When the pile of logs got high enough in the sawmill yard, Andrew, with the help of a few missionaries, would crank up the mill and spend a few days, or weeks, and saw them into lumber.

Even though Merril subsidized the sawmill with funds earned from the other UEP projects and paid no wages of any consequence to the workers, it was still a failure. So he started a door mill company to manufacture cores for solid core doors and it was finally brought into successful production. The company grew and twenty people worked for Merril.

The Fates would have their due, however. On the night of April 9, 1971, the door mill burned to the ground, a loss of one million dollars in equipment and material. There was no insurance of any kind on the building or business, so everything was a total loss. The door mill was never put back into production and the sawmill was never used again at Colorado City. Merril Jessop pulled himself up by his bootstraps, and turned his efforts toward the rock, sand, and concrete business. In a few years he became very successful.

WELCOME, HILDALE

When Marion Hammon had returned to Short Creek in 1958, Fred Jessop could see the effect it would have on his long established managing position. In an effort to maintain a measure of control in the community, he devised a plan. He would legally establish a separate town for their people who were living on the Utah side of the valley. He named his new town Hildale and began the process of incorporation. Washington County Commissioners had to approve the incorporation, which put the final incorporation at about 1968. He did not wait for the incorporation to be completed before he began operating as a town.

Fred would dictate who would be on the Hildale Town Council, thus assuring that none of Marion's clique would have any role of managing His Town. Fred was able to do this because of the influence he had with Leroy Johnson, and because he only allowed one name on the ballot. Fred's most prominent supporters were his nephews, the sons of John Y. and Martha Jessop (Fred's sister) Barlow. Fred appointed himself the Town Clerk, and as such, he had the Council vote unanimous on each measure he would put before them. All he had to do was tell them "this is what Uncle Roy wants."

With Fred Jessop establishing a new name for the Utah side of town, Marion Hammon decided it would be wise to change the name of the Arizona side as well. Short Creek was changed to Colorado City in 1961 soon after the high school was opened. He concluded that because of polygamy and the notoriety of the 1953 Raid, the name Short Creek was a stigma. He supposed that if the name were changed, the feelings of the people from the outside communities would change towards the polygamists.

These feelings did change over the next few years, but it was more because of the changes made by the people in Colorado City, rather than the changing of the name itself. The polygamists earned a reputation of being a hardworking and honest people, and the neighboring communities came to respect their ability to perform in their contracts made with them and the quality of work. The young men that came from the community, and especially from The Colorado City Academy, were always in demand by outside employers. The reputation these young men established was known for miles around. This is what changed the stigma of Short Creek from one of disrepute to Colorado City's reputation of being an honorable one.

STORING WHEAT FOR HARD TIMES

It has always been a Mormon philosophy to store food, especially wheat. In the 1960s Marion Hammon put the responsibility on the women to raise money to buy wheat and store it for hard times. They took this responsibility seriously and organized themselves to raise the money. They sponsored plays for a small admission fee, sponsored bake sales, made quilts and auctioned them off, and thus raised several thousand dollars. Several tons of wheat were purchased and stored in granaries, but it was not protected against weevils and after a few years had to be fed to the pigs. These women continued to raise money, just giving it to Hammon and he spent it for whatever he wanted.

DAIRY, HIGHWAY & TELEPHONES

Marion Hammon was responsible for other civic improvements in the community. He established a new dairy, building a new barn with modern equipment such as milking machines and sanitary facilities to properly handle and take care of the milk. The old barn, one that had been built in the early 1930s by Isaac Carling, was an eyesore in the center of town. This was one of the first buildings torn down when the renovation of the community began.

A new paved highway was constructed from Hurricane to Colorado City, and completed in 1962. The highway was not completed on to Fredonia until 1965, but having a paved road into the community made a tremendous impact on the people living there.

Another improvement by Marion Hammon was getting telephone service into the community. Louis Barlow was the person who did the negotiation and ground work to accomplish this achievement, but he was acting under Hammon's directive to do so.

South Central Utah Telephone Association, a user-owned cooperative with the main office based at Escalante, Utah, agreed to provide telephone service to Colorado City if enough subscribers would join the association. There was no problem getting the number of potential users to sign the membership pledge. The membership initiation dues were forty dollars per member, to be paid at the rate of five dollars a month, added to the phone bill after hookup service. This made it relatively easy for the users to obtain service. A telephone line was built from Hurricane to Colorado City and the first telephone, a single toll station in front of Louis Barlow's house, was put into operation in April of 1964. An automated telephone exchange building was constructed on the south side of the Creek and work began on running underground lines to all the homes in the community.

Telephones were a luxury to the people of Colorado City. They had not missed them before having them, but one thing the polygamists are notorious for is their gift of gab. In the first few years after telephone service was available to them, a high percentage would have their service disconnected due to unpaid bills. This was a discipline problem that was hard for them to cope with. Important Elders such as Orvil Johnson (Leroy's son) were the worst of the offenders. Any small excuse to talk long distance would, in their own minds, boost their ego, convincing themselves that it was all for the good of the Work.

The telephone company did not feel that their intentions of helping the Work was reason enough to excuse people from having to pay their bill. When their phones were cut off, these important people, never having been responsible for paying their own way in the past, having been accustomed to riding on the backs of the more conscientious UEP members, would become very indignant when expected to pay their own bills. Nevertheless, the telephone company was no respecter of persons and, if the bill was not paid, the service was discontinued.

The polygamists have learned that any outside controlled utilities such as telephone and electrical service must be paid for, or they will be disconnected. The same is not true for utilities controlled by the companies within the community. Such services as water, sewer, and garbage collection are not paid for as conscientiously, because they know these services will not be cut as quickly. Water bills into the thousands of dollars are never paid by some of the high ranking members and service is never discontinued to them, putting the burden on the lay members to carry them. Members who do not pay their bills are the elite of society, affording trips and tours to exotic lands and places.

DEVELOPING FARMS AND HOME INDUSTRY

Marion Hammon encouraged the polygamists to establish as much home industry as possible. The first place to begin was to bring the farm lands of the community into production. The biggest drawback was the lack of irrigation water for the fields that lay barren. Hammon reasoned that if the water could be put in a pipeline, it would not only irrigate more farmland but could also be pressurized to utilize a sprinkler system. The first step to accomplish this would be to obtain pipe for the project. In the fall of 1964, he stood before the people in a meeting at Hildale and asked for a donation of $500 from each man to pay for the pipe. Most responded and the money was raised.

The Mercury Project, where the testing by the Atomic Energy Commission was carried out near Las Vegas, Nevada, was closing down and there were several miles of 10" steel pipe that had been used as gas lines. The government put the pipe up for bid at a salvage sale and Marion was the successful bidder. It was still underground and had to be dug up, cut into forty foot lengths, and hauled from the area.

This task fell to Joe Jessop and a crew of missionaries. The work of salvaging this pipe, moving it to Colorado City, digging the trench from Water Canyon, welding the pipe together and burying the pipe, was a major undertaking. Joe was capable of the challenge and, in a little over a year, the job was completed. This successful herculean project of Marion Hammon is further evidence of the dedication and willingness he was able to inspire in the people who honored him in his calling of building a community where they could enjoy security and self-sufficiency.

ACCEPTING GOVERNMENT MONEY

After the pipeline from Water Canyon was completed, work was begun on the construction of two large reservoirs east of Colorado City, near the mountain. These reservoirs were built under the supervision of the Soil Conservation Service, the costs being reimbursed by the government when the projects were completed. Marion Hammon was against taking money from the government to pay for UEP improvements, and Leroy Johnson felt the same way. Fred Jessop disagreed, saying, "We are entitled to all the government will give us, for they owe it to us."

Fred reported to the men in Priesthood meeting one morning that the Government was going to give him money to build a new road from the highway (U-59) into Hildale (Utah Avenue). Leroy got up and told the men, "If we take money from the government, we will lose control of the town. If the government puts money into a community or project, they can come in and dictate how the community is run." Fred was not willing to follow the counsel of either Leroy or Marion. He wanted his town set up to succeed, whatever it took. So he took the Government money and built the new road. This step was the first and it eventually led to scandalous abuse of the government help systems. (By the 1980s more than fifty percent of his group would be on either food stamps or WIC, Women, Infants and Children program).

ACQUIRING FARM LANDS

Once the irrigation system was completed, the next step was to bring the farm lands into worthwhile production. Out of all the Polygamists at Short Creek, about the only person who had been successful at farming was Bill Cooke, but by the mid-1960s his age ruled him out. It was necessary to go outside the community to find someone with the experience to make a success of the endeavor. In Hammon's search among the Priesthood's followers, he settled on Parley Harker.

In 1950 the Federal Government had opened up the Escalante Desert, just west of Cedar City, for Desert Entry (Desert Entry was an act that allowed farmers to Homestead designated areas, bringing the land into production). Parley Harker had moved from Lewisville, Idaho, about this time, taking out a claim on a parcel of the land offered in the Escalante Valley. He was a brother in-law to Newel Steed and after a few years of his moving to Southern Utah, he became converted to polygamy. Parley Harker was a very successful farmer and in the ten years since leaving Idaho, he became quite prosperous and was well respected in the Beryl area. The farming operation was turned over to Parley in 1963. He spent much of his time (and his own money) establishing a successful farming operation, leaving his own farm at Beryl to the management of his oldest son Merril, who was able to do a very good job of running the place.

Hammon did something out of character; he turned the project over to Parley to manage as he decided. This was the one thing that made it possible for Parley to succeed, being able to make all the decisions necessary to run the operation. The biggest mistake made by the leaders of the Polygamists is that of not allowing their followers the freedom necessary to run the stewardships that are placed upon them. The leaders always want to make the decisions, using the excuse that only they can get the revelation necessary to make the projects successful. Parley had the equipment and the expertise necessary to put the farm lands at Colorado City into successful production, but the soil was run down and needed fertilizer. When he went to Hammon with the problem of where to obtain inexpensive fertilizer, Hammon met the challenge – he would use chicken manure.

There was a chicken farm in LaVerkin (near Hurricane) owned by Mr. E. J. Graff. On this farm was a huge pile of chicken manure that had accumulated over the years. Hammon negotiated a deal with Mr. Graff to not only buy the manure pile, but to clean the coops for the next several years to come, hauling it to Colorado City and spreading it on the fields. This turned out to be a successful and worthwhile project, building up the soil sufficient to produce abundant crops.

For the first time in the history of the United Effort Plan, crops were successfully grown in Short Creek, one of its main goals since its inception. This became possible for two primary reasons: Hammon's missionary program produced the money and the labor necessary to carry out the program, and he turned the project over to the competent management of Parley Harker to run the operation as he saw fit.

A SUCCESSFUL COMMUNITY

Things were looking up for the polygamists. Towards the end of the 1960s, the dreams of their founders were finally being realized. A united effort among the members was proving a success. Several new and modern homes had been built, including one for Leroy Johnson. Electrical power and telephone service had been brought into the community. A new paved highway was completed from Hurricane. A culinary water system was in operation. A modern dairy was established. The farming projects were economically producing crops, both for the community and even such produce as hay was being sold outside the town. These improvements had all been accomplished with the work and money contributed by UEP members (both in and out of the missionary program). And the credit for the rebuilding of Colorado City and the UEP must be given to Marion Hammon.

Through the efforts of Council Member Alma Timpson, a plan began that would bring a sewing plant into the community in the late 1960s. Barco Inc. in Southern California would supply employment for about eighty people in town. Providing employment for their members was something the leaders had dreamed about for years and this seemed to be an opportunity.

But in every society, there is always an element that will attempt to seize power and control of any new enterprise that is expected to create a power base or to make money. As soon as it was realized that a money making institution was to be established in their midst, the sons of John Y. Barlow began planning how to get control of it.

8

Hammon vs. The Barlows

In the early 1960s Marion Hammon had organized the Planning Board Committee. This committee was to meet with him once a week and help with the decision making of running the community and the UEP. Hammon knew what he wanted to accomplish and felt he had the experience and talent to make it happen. Therefore he tended to surround himself with people who would simply follow his decisions without question. He also organized the Colorado City Area Development Association and began to use this Association to conduct the business he felt would help the United Effort Plan.

When Hammon had returned to Short Creek in 1958 to see if he could save the community, he understood he had been given free reign by the Council and Leroy Johnson to do whatever he thought best. By setting up and using the CCADA, he was able to make certain business decisions without consulting other UEP Trustees. For example, he negotiated a purchase contract on The Hirschi Property, several hundred acres of land about six miles west of Colorado City. Since the UEP preferred donated land to be free and clear, Marion decided to handle the purchase of the Hirschi Property under the CCADA. Then when it was paid for, he would donate it to the UEP. With this in mind, he called for donations of money from the people to make the payments of $10,000 a year.

It was through these two organizations that all the decisions of running the community were made. This became a sore spot for some of the men who previously had been making these decisions and they would not fully accept Hammon's control. Fred Jessop was one of the most prominent among this group. He would appear to follow Hammon's direction when in his presence, but then would go about undermining what he did not agree with, always going through Leroy Johnson so as to move with credibility.

With the organization of the Colorado City Academy high school, Marion Hammon through its auspices was pretty much in control of all the social activities of the community. This had been one of Fred's responsibilities before Hammon took over the management of the UEP. Before the establishment of the Academy, these social activities had consisted primarily of a dance every other Friday night, a movie on the alternate Fridays, and a celebration on the 4th and 24th of July each year. Fred would usually stage a play production every year or so, using the same scripts over and over. There were only two scripts that he would approve, not only in his productions, but also in the public schools: "Windmills of Holland" and "Little Women." The people were getting a little tired of these two plays, to say the least. The socials of the Academy were a welcomed relief to most of the community members.

Every fall the Academy students would go to the Harker Farm near Beryl, Utah, and help in the potato harvest in the Escalante Valley. The money they earned would go toward running the Academy. These harvest projects would last for two weeks and when the students returned home, Marion would have a Harvest Ball. The whole community would participate in these celebrations and they were the highlight of the summer's end. Fred decided to use the authority of Hildale Town to compete with Marion and the Academy.

In order to diminish the impact of the Harvest Ball, Fred began having a Hildale Town Fair every fall, staged a week or so before the Harvest Ball of the Academy. These Fairs would last about three days and were lavishly staged, using local talent to provide entertainment. They were well supported by the people and did indeed diminish the impact of the Harvest Ball, thus accomplishing Fred's designs. The Hildale/Colorado City Fair was put on every year for the next fifteen or twenty years, becoming quite popular among the entertainment-starved Polygamists, especially the younger people.

GUARDING THE GIRLS

One of the biggest mistakes the Polygamist Leaders make is neglecting to provide activities and entertainment for the young people of the society. The policy of the Priesthood is to separate the boys and girls and this is the main reason that so few social activities are allowed. This policy has been the cause of many problems for the young people, especially the boys at Colorado City.

Since this mating policy of the Priesthood (that of placing the girls with their marriage partners) created problems for the young boys and girls who become attracted to each other, it became necessary to establish a monitoring system to protect the girls from becoming involved with a boy. In the 1960s the leaders became so concerned that it was necessary to take steps to curb any out of line associations between the young people. Their first line of defense was to place a peace officer in charge of keeping the problem in check.

After the families of the Polygamists had been returned to their homes following the 1953 Raid, the County Officials at Kingman deemed it no longer necessary to keep a County Deputy Sheriff on the Arizona Strip. This meant there was no civil law enforcement authority in Colorado City. The Priesthood, however, concluded it was necessary to establish some kind of Peace Officer status. To accomplish this they created a fictitious entity called The Colorado City Law Enforcement Agency.

This agency had no recognized civil authority whatsoever and was only established so the Polygamist leaders could better control their young members. Sam Barlow (son of John Y. Barlow) was picked to be the enforcement officer. He was supplied with a badge to give the illusion that he had peace officer status, when in reality, he had no legal authority at all until about eight years later.

Sam's paramount duty as a Peace Officer was to make sure that the boys would not associate with the girls. At his discretion, he would run the undesirable boys out of town, forcing them to go to the neighboring communities to fend for themselves as best they could. He was encouraged and supported by Leroy in this action.

The birth ratio of boys to girls among the Polygamists is the same as it is anywhere else in the world, pretty much one boy to one girl. If one man is to have even two wives, then some boy in the society must not get married, and the doctrine of the Polygamists is that a man must have at least three wives to reach the highest degree of heaven. The perceived importance of a man goes up by the number of wives he has, thus the ratio of wives to a man is important; those in leadership positions have wives numbering into the tens. This causes a dilemma for the Polygamist Leaders, what to do with the surplus of boys.

It is only natural for young boys and girls to be attracted to each other. Most girls relate more to boys near their own age, rather than to a man ten to thirty years older (the extreme is a seventeen-year-old girl marrying a ninety-five-year-old man). In later years these young people have learned how to beat the system. If a boy and a girl decide they want to get married, they simply have sex with each other, then go to the Prophet and confess their sin. He tells them to have a civil marriage, wait a year, come back to see him, and if he feels they have repented, they can get rebaptized and he will seal them to each other.

It becomes paramount then to keep the boys and girls separated at all costs; only under very strict supervision are they allowed to associate with one another. Since this is not always possible, it became necessary to establish a Goon Squad / Teenage Chastity Patrol, with Sam Barlow at its head. His primary police duties in the next fifteen to twenty years evolved to that of running the surplus boys out of town, making it possible for the "worthy" men to live the Law of Celestial Marriage by adding more wives.

He was able to do this by trumping up some criminal charge against the boy he would select to eliminate from the society. He would then harass the offender (under his peace officer status) until finally he would leave (some of these young boys were as young as thirteen years old).

This high handed and immoral conduct by Sam Barlow and the Polygamist Leaders began in the 1960s and reached its peak in the late 1970s and 1980s. How Sam Barlow was able to worm his way into such a position as to be the Judge, Jury, and Executioner is worthy of explanation.

SAMUEL STEVENS BARLOW

Samuel Stevens Barlow was born at Short Creek on February 18, 1937, the sixth living son of John Y. Barlow and Martha Jessop (fourth wife). Sam's mother died when he was only six years old. His father had recently married a new wife (a fifteen-year-old girl whose widowed mother had just moved from Idaho after joining the Work) and the responsibility of taking care of Sam and his eleven siblings (of which three were older than she was) fell on the shoulders of this new wife. About this time Sam's father took him on his knee one day and told him, "You were named after Samuel of old (Biblical Prophet) and the day will come when you will be a great Prophet like him."

This event was a significant occurrence to Sam and he would reiterate it to his associates throughout his life. In his adolescent years he would attempt to rule over his peers. This only resulted in him becoming despised by his contemporaries, none of them placing any trust in him. Consequently he became a loner. He resorted to becoming a "Snitch," always sneaking around, trying to get the goods on his friends, so he could run to one of the Brethren and report what evils he had uncovered. This, of course, only lessened his credibility with those he associated with.

Sam's first role as a policeman was while he was in the 7th grade of the Short Creek School, where his older brother Louis was the principal. Louis Barlow was hired as the principal of the Short Creek School in 1949 and taught the 7th and 8th grades. He told the students one morning that he did not want a school policeman, because he didn't like the idea of having to have a policeman bully the kids. He did, however, think it was necessary to have some kind of police presence on the school grounds, not to bully the kids, but rather to protect them. He chose his younger brother, Sam, to be this policeman and called him the Chief Protector.

As the Chief Protector, Sam was really in his element. The very thing that Louis had warned against, a Police Bully, was what he turned out to be. He would not confront any of the students he felt were in violation of the rules, but rather would just go to Louis with exaggerated stories of wrongdoing by the students he had singled out for breaking the rules.

Thus he would punish those who refused to show him the proper respect he felt he was entitled to. He learned at this young age to take some small fact and embellish the story with his own imagination to convince Louis that some great crime had been committed by the poor unsuspecting victim of his scheme. He also learned to use religion to accomplish his designs, convincing Louis that the boy he was reporting on was guilty of some immoral conduct such as masturbation, a most grievous sin among the Polygamists, or worse yet "looking on some girl, to lust after her," thus being guilty of lewdness. Some of Sam's accusations toward these boys have followed them throughout their lives, making it very hard for them to gain the confidence of the Polygamist Leaders.

After leaving school and as he grew older, Sam carried on in this role of being the Chief Protector of the community. Instead of reporting to Louis though, he would report to those of the Brethren who would listen to him, primarily Leroy Johnson, Richard Jessop, Carl Holm, and in the 1960s, Marion Hammon. None of his peers ever took him seriously, never suspecting that he had any more credibility with the Brethren than he had among them. It was a big surprise to many of his victims, when out of the blue, they would be severely scolded by one of the leaders for some infraction of conduct that they, in most cases, knew nothing about.

It was this man, Sam Barlow, who was chosen by the Priesthood to be the Peace Officer in the polygamist society in the early 1960s.

In the 1960s there was a group of Polygamists living in Western Canada that aligned themselves with the Group at Colorado City. The leadership of the Canadian Group was assigned to Ray Blackmore, a man the Priesthood Council had confidence in. His nephew Harold Blackmore was actually more competent than Ray, when it came to making crucial decisions. This caused a severe controversy among the Saints at Canada. It became so bad that the Brethren determined to do something to solve the problem.

Harold, an industrious person, owned a nice tract of land near Lister, B.C. that was much coveted by the United Effort Plan Leaders. A scheme was devised to get Harold out of Canada and at the same time get his property. In discussing the situation with Louis Barlow, Leroy Johnson asked him about acquiring Harold's property for the UEP. Louis thought this would be possible and was told, "If there is any way you can get the property, I want you to do it, no matter what you have to do." To accomplish this, Louis solicited the help of Jack Knudson.

In the mid-1950s Jack Knudson worked as a stockbroker in Salt Lake City. He had learned how to manipulate the stock market by acquiring stock certificates of new companies while in their infancies, then promoting the stocks of these companies to his clients. This would cause an artificial inflation in the stocks of the company and he would then sell his own shares, flooding the market, which would then cause the stocks to fall. He reasoned that he could start his own companies for the sole purpose of promoting the stocks, not really intending that the company itself make money. (He was eventually caught by the Securities Commission and his Broker's license temporarily suspended.)

One of the companies he had formed for this purpose was a real estate company named National Land Corporation. The company was formed with a stock value of $1.00 per share. It took him about three years to pump the value up to $12.00 a share, at which time he began dumping his stock. The company soon became almost non-existent due to this stock maneuver. Then Jack Knudson formed a new company, using the assets of National Land, and converted the National Land stock to stock in the new company, thus eliminating National Land altogether.

Louis Barlow was involved with Knudson in the National Land scheme and profited greatly financially. After the National Land Fiasco, Jack Knudson's stockbroker's license was suspended. Along with this suspension, Knudson was put on a five year probation, prohibiting him from dealing in any kind of stock transaction. He moved from Salt Lake to Colorado City and began teaching in the newly formed Colorado City Academy. It was soon after Knudson began teaching that Leroy Johnson directed Louis Barlow to get the Blackmore property for the UEP. Louis and Jack came up with the following plan.

Louis would convince Harold to put his property into a land development corporation. They would then sell stock in the company to raise the money to build a hunting lodge that Harold would manage, providing employment for a few of the polygamists in Canada. The Priesthood would then ask Harold to go down to Colorado City to help with building homes for the people there. While Harold was in Colorado City, Louis and Jack would convey the property to the UEP, moving some faithful members onto the place, thereby preventing Harold from moving back on the property.

It was suggested to Marion Hammon that he approach Harold Blackmore and ask if he would come to Colorado City and help with the building of homes. Whether Hammon had any idea of the plans of Louis Barlow and Jack Knudson is unlikely. In a deposition taken in July of 1988, Harold explains in detail what happened. A reading of the deposition makes it clear that the UEP had every intention of moving Harold Blackmore out of the way of his Uncle Ray in Bountiful, Canada, and of obtaining his land at the same time. It was a very slick operation. It was about three years before Harold realized what had happened. In the meantime Harold was working hard to help those in Short Creek with their building needs.

To help build houses for the people of the Group, he devised a plan to finance the building of these houses and he discussed it with Marion Hammon and received tentative approval. The plan was to work as follows: Twenty-four men (families) were to begin paying $200 a month into a fund to build a house for each of them. Harold, by using the high school boys and a few of the missionaries, would construct these houses at the rate of one per month. It would be determined by lot who would get the houses in the order they were completed. One man would get his the first month, while the last man would get his at the end of two years. After paying $200 per month, each man would have a home built and paid for. This plan seemed all right to Hammon, except he decided that he would be the one to collect the money.

Only one man (Dan Barlow) paid his $200 every month. At the end of the two years, Dan Barlow went to Hammon and asked, "Where's my house?" Though Hammon had collected Dan's $200 every month for the last two years, there was no house built nor did Hammon have any of the money Dan had paid him. Hammon got up in Sunday Meeting and told the people that they had to build a house for Dan Barlow. Enough of them responded that a house was built for Dan, but due to Hammon's management of the money collected for this enterprise, the plan was a failure and turned out to be just one of many bitter disappointments for Harold.

When Harold came to Colorado City, he had several good ideas to help the people there to improve their circumstances, but he met resistance from Hammon on almost everything he tried to do. Hammon was reluctant to allow anybody free reign in the community. He would have to pass final judgement on anything and everything that Harold wanted to do. At the end of the three year period Harold was so distraught that he began to study the scriptures to determine just what allegiance he owed to this Priesthood Council. It didn't take long for him to convince himself that it was not a Priesthood Council ordained by God, but rather it was Priestcraft. He determined he would be better off to leave the Group.

In the three years that he was in Colorado City, Harold had built a house for himself. He went to Hammon and offered that if he could get $6,000 for this house he would move out of the Polygamist Community. Hammon accepted his offer. The money was raised and Harold moved to LaVerkin, Utah, where in the years to follow, he became very successful in the building trade, becoming quite wealthy. The Priesthood thought they were rid of him, but he was to cause them trouble again in the mid-1970s when Leroy Johnson, president of the UEP, stole the house of James Blackmore (Harold's son).

JOB OPPORTUNITIES FOR WOMEN

In about 1964, the elementary school in Colorado City was moved to a location better suited for expansion. The UEP donated the property and moved one of the buildings from the old location. Over the next few years, with the help of the students and with the UEP donating some material, a new building was constructed, with Alvin Barlow supervising the adobe building in the summer months. The lumber for the roof was again sawed on the sawmill, with Andrew Bistline donating most of his time.

In 1968 the public school in Hildale was combined with the school in Colorado City, to free the building at Hildale to temporally house a sewing plant being moved into the community to provide employment for some of the Polygamist women.

Alma Timpson had been contacted by a representative from the Barco Sewing Co. of California. The owners of Barco were interested in establishing a sewing plant in Colorado City if the United Effort Plan would furnish a building. Timpson reported this to the Priesthood Council and everyone was in favor of accepting Barco's offer. Since Marion Hammon was the Manager of the UEP projects at Colorado City, he began speculating on how to raise the money to construct the needed building.

He first proposed setting aside an acre or so from trust property that could be mortgaged to a bank, thus borrowing the money for the building. He presented this idea in a General Priesthood Meeting to all members one Sunday morning. When Fred Jessop heard this, he immediately opposed the idea. He did not oppose building a building for the sewing plant, but rather opposed mortgaging the property. (It turned out that he was not so much against mortgaging the property as he was of Hammon having control of the sewing plant.)

Fred Jessop, along with some of his Barlow nephews (Louis, Joe, and Dan Barlow), gathered at Leroy's place immediately after this meeting. These conspirators pointed out to Leroy that mortgaging the property was not the thing to do. They asked him to let them come up with a way to raise the money to construct the building, thus allowing them control of operating the sewing plant.

An association was formed by the conspirators to expedite the project. They named it the Colorado City Improvement Association. Among the board members were Fred Jessop, Merril Jessop, Truman Barlow, Dan Barlow, and Bill (William) Shapley. The United Effort Plan leased a small tract of land (about five acres) to the Colorado City Improvement Association (CCIA). This lease was granted by Leroy Johnson, who acted solely on his own initiative, never bringing it up in any UEP Board Meeting.

With the twenty year lease, Fred Jessop (CCIA) went to the bank in Cedar City and asked for a construction loan to put up the building. The bank granted the loan, accepting the lease as collateral. When Leroy informed Marion of these developments, he and Alma Timpson made no objections. They were both naive enough to believe that it didn't matter whether they or Fred built the building, so long as employment for the people was provided. Marion felt a little rebuffed that Leroy had not bothered to include him in the decision making of such a major transaction.

The Barco sewing plant at Colorado City opened in the fall of 1970, in the former Hildale Meeting / School House behind Fred Jessop's home. Dan Barlow was appointed manager. This opportunity for some of the women of the community to work was a welcome thing indeed. Until now there had been very little employment in the area for the Polygamists to support themselves.

The new building (on the Arizona side of town) to house the plant was soon completed and eventually about eighty people, mostly women, were gainfully employed there. The payments on the construction loan were $800 per month, but the rent received from Barco was only $400. This deficit had to be made up every month.

Fred went to the women who were working in the sewing plant and asked if they would contribute part of their wages to him to make these payments. Almost all of the women were willing to help out and each gave Fred $4.00 per week. This was subsidy enough for him to make the payments.

None of the money paid to Fred by these employees was ever accounted for. The employees were never reimbursed for it nor were they given any credit for it on the books of the UEP. Their sweat equity went into the Colorado City Improvement Association, owned and controlled by Fred Jessop. In truth, their equity belongs to the United Effort Plan Trust (of which most of these workers were beneficiaries), the registered property owner of the land on which the building is standing. Barco continued to pay the $400 rent for many years after the building was paid for, and none of it was ever given back to the working women who helped pay for the building.

HAMMON'S SCHOOL LUNCH PROGRAM DROPPED

When the Colorado City Academy opened, a homemaking class had become part of the curriculum. Part of the homemaking class included teaching the girls to cook. Marion Hammon thought it would be a good idea to have the high school girls at the Academy prepare a noon meal for the elementary school students as part of this class. The meals were prepared at the Academy (these meals usually consisted of a serving of soup or stew with the students providing their own eating utensils and a slice of bread from home), then at noon the kettles were taken down to the elementary school where it was served to the students in their classrooms. This procedure worked pretty well, the only real problem was that some of the parents would have preferred their children come home for lunch, especially those living close to the school.

Hammon would not allow this option, but rather decreed that all children must remain at school to eat the lunch prepared by the Academy students. After this program had been in effect for three or four years, Hammon decided to also provide breakfast for the school children. He was concerned that a number of the Polygamist children were not getting proper nourishment because so many of their mothers would not get up in the morning in time to prepare a proper breakfast for their children. Hammon's assessment of this situation was correct. Some of the parents were very remiss in providing enough for the youngsters to eat. It was not with malice that he wanted to feed the children, but rather out of pity for the children themselves, to assure them good health. He planned to go ahead with this program in about 1969.

Marion Hammon got up in a General Priesthood meeting one Sunday morning and announced his intention of implementing breakfast into his School Lunch Program. After telling the men all the benefits, he turned the time to Leroy as was the custom (each of the Leading Brethren present at the meetings were given an opportunity to talk to the men in these meetings before they would separate to their respective classes). Leroy got up and immediately began to criticize Hammon's plan. He said, "This thing of furnishing meals for the children at school is a trick of the Devil." He told them that the children should not only eat their breakfast at home but should also go home for lunch. He was unmerciful to Hammon, and the school lunch program was discontinued. Alvin Barlow, principal of the elementary school, chose to go along with Leroy.

The school lunch break was extended from one hour to one and a half each day. School buses were provided, not only to pick the children up in the morning, but also take them home for lunch at noon. Alvin required that all children ride the buses home to lunch, even if they lived only a block from the school. Not only was it necessary to hire more bus drivers, but also more buses had to be purchased by the small school district. This greatly increased the cost of running the school, money that could have been put to better use, such as paying the teachers a wage comparable to other schools in the area.

STRATEGY TO UNSEAT MARION HAMMON

In 1968 the sons of John Barlow actively planned and began implementing an underground movement to discredit Marion Hammon's reputation and good standing in the community. And for good reason. Because there had always been enmity between the sons of John Barlow and anyone who did not actively support Barlows's One Man Doctrine, the Barlow Boys were beginning to feel a little uneasy over the situation of Hammon being the next man in the line of seniority of the Priesthood Council after Leroy Johnson. After all, Leroy was now eighty years old and Marion was sixty; it was only natural to assume that Leroy would die before Marion.

This became a matter of deep concern for the Barlows. If Hammon were allowed to take over the UEP it would put them in great straits–not only their positions of power within the community, but also their way of life. They knew that as long as Leroy controlled the Trust, they could be assured of never losing the silver spoon to which they were accustomed. They also knew that if Marion became President of the Trust, he would expect them to earn their own way in life, the same as the other UEP members were doing.

In secret meetings they began plotting how they could keep Marion from ever gaining control of the UEP. They planned to somehow destroy the confidence between him and Leroy Johnson. If they could destroy the bond that held the Priesthood Council together, then they could come between Leroy and Marion, and from there it would only be a matter of time until Marion was out of the picture, and the Barlows would finally gain control of the United Effort Plan.

One of their first bold efforts was to take control of the Barco sewing venture. By keeping this money-making industry out of the United Effort Plan, thus out of reach of Marion Hammon, they were able to exercise control over not only who worked at the sewing plant, but where the money went that was earned there. They also knew that in order to accomplish their goals, their maternal uncle, Fred Jessop, would have to be included in the conspiracy. Fred had been in the Work from its inception and was one person that Leroy had confidence in. If the time ever came that Leroy would have to make a choice between placing his loyalty with Marion Hammon or Fred Jessop, they knew that he would choose Fred. They had become very close friends during their struggles in the 1940s and their families were related.

By now Marion Hammon realized he had serious problems with the Barlows, but he believed that the bond between himself and Leroy and the covenants they had made in their Council Meetings would be stronger than any seeds of discord the Barlows could sow between them. There were more members of the Council who believed the same as Marion in relation to doctrine, than believed in what the Barlows advocated. Leroy went back and forth in what he seemed to believe.

Marion Hammon never thought he could lose his position in the Priesthood Council, so never worried too much about the undercurrent of unrest that the Barlows were stirring up among the Group members concerning him. He just went on with his work of building up the city and the Kingdom for the Priesthood. He was being called "a sick old guy" by Louis Barlow, and Joe Barlow was telling people that Uncle Marion "has always been a problem child of the Priesthood." With these little fiery darts, the work of destroying a man's character was begun.

9

The Barlow Takeover

On April 27, 1972, Carl Holm died in Salt Lake City of congestive heart failure at age fifty-five. As the next to last member that John Barlow had called to his priesthood council, his passing came as a shock to the Polygamists. He was the youngest member of the Council and it was expected that he would some day be the Priesthood President. Before his untimely death, he was choosing to side with the Barlows on the One Man Doctrine. With his passing, the Barlows lost their edge in the balance of power in the Priesthood Council. His death left the Council with three members against the One Man Doctrine, two in favor and one undecided. The undecided member was Rulon Jeffs.

Because of his early teaching not to turn against those whom the Lord had chosen, it was a real trial for Rulon when Leroy Johnson began supporting the Barlows in their claims of the One Man Doctrine. Rulon was very close to Guy Musser (Joseph's son), also a member of the Council and very much against the Barlow doctrine. When the Barlows began the campaign to destroy Marion Hammon's credibility among the Polygamists, Guy came to his defense with public support. This put him in the Barlow line of fire just like Marion Hammon. Jeffs began to understand the dilemma he was facing; he could go with his teachings and conscience, or he could choose the political course and be safe. The decision he must make was a hard one, whether to go with his conscience or with the Barlow claim that only one man held the keys, and should make all the final decisions. He chose to follow the one man rule.

The Barlows, along with their maternal uncle, Fred Jessop, fully intended to keep the UEP from ever falling into the hands of Marion Hammon. If Hammon were ever allowed to achieve the position of President of Priesthood (as he surely would according to the order of succession set up by Lorin Woolley), he would also gain control of the United Effort Plan. The Barlows knew this would mark the end of their power and that of Fred Jessop. To prevent this from happening. the people would have to be told things about the religious history of the polygamists that were untrue.

Fred Jessop and his Barlow nephews believed "The Work" belonged to the "Chosen Seed," the lineage of John Y. Barlow. The Keys of the Priesthood must be protected from falling into the hands of any outsiders and Marion Hammon was definitely an outsider. Hammon's credibility had to be destroyed and that is what they conspired to do. First they began whispering it about that Marion was not willing to do what Uncle Roy asked him to do. They would hatch up incidences where it would appear that Hammon was not willing to support Leroy. Their biggest cannon was the controversy over the One Man Doctrine, which everyone knew Hammon did not agree on.

If the Barlows were going to gain control of the United Effort Plan, they would have to promote Leroy as the only man who could make decisions in regards to the management of the Trust, effectively making him a king. And this is what they set about to do. All they would have to do to get the people to believe their false doctrine would be to tell them that it was what Leroy was teaching.

In his mid-eighties, Leroy was emotionally committed to the Barlows and Fred Jessop. Their early days of struggle together in the 1940s were cemented in Leroy's heart and mind. As he grew older and suffered with health problems, he necessarily relied more and more on those he trusted. And whatever these men told him, he believed. So the One Man Doctrine that had been at issue for many years became a topic they talked more and more about to him, persuasively, quoting scriptures, reminding him of his loyalty and promises to John Barlow.

In meetings every Monday with Leroy at the Sugar Loaf Café in Cedar City, attended mostly by Barlow supporters, they would discuss and criticize the things that Marion Hammon and Alma Timpson had said the day before. These meetings at the Sugar Loaf became legion, for it was here that the Doctrine of the One Man Authority was taught to those who were allowed to participate in the gatherings. There would be from ten to thirty people there.

Aging Leroy would always insist that he pay the bill for the meals, which would run into the hundreds of dollars. The Barlows were very aware of those in the entourage who would later slip up to Leroy and give him at least as much money as his portion of the bill. Those who were dilatory in paying their share would be in danger of being whispered about later.

It was in these meetings at the Sugar Loaf that the Barlows were able to do their greatest damage in manipulating the truth and destroying the Priesthood Work. Not only were they able to gain many converts to their doctrine, they were also able little by little to warp and mold the mind of Leroy Johnson.

MARION HAMMON FINALLY SEES THE DANGER

Marion Hammon began to see what the Barlows were up to. As the animosity against him grew, he became hurt over what was happening. He had genuinely put his all into the up-building of the Priesthood Work and now his name was being dragged through the dirt and respect for him was fading. He began looking for another place where he could go and continue living the true principles of the Gospel. He reasoned that there must be other disillusioned people who could see what was happening and would be happy to move with him to create a new United Order based on correct doctrine.

Marion had been farming and ranching on UEP property with the help of his sons. This included the farm near Beryl, Utah, and a cattle ranch at Hatch, Utah, several hundred acres in size. These two properties were free and clear, having been paid for with time and money donated by UEP members. Marion decided to ask Leroy for the deeds to these properties, and it is unclear what reason he gave. One day in 1971, Leroy told the Boys gathered at the Sugar Loaf Café in Cedar City, "Brother Hammon came to me and demanded the deeds to the Hatch and Beryl properties. The Lord told me that if I gave him the deeds he would lose the property, but He (the Lord) told me to go ahead and give them to him."

Leroy did indeed give the deeds of these properties to Hammon. They were signed by Leroy as UEP President, and Rulon Jeffs as UEP Secretary. This transaction was executed without ever holding a United Effort Plan Board meeting and without a resolution by the Board of Trustees authorizing such a major transfer of UEP assets. As a matter of fact, the only Board members that even knew of the transaction were Leroy, Rulon, and Marion. Such maneuvering has the earmarks of the Barlows encouraging Leroy to buy Marion out of the United Effort Plan.

Marion Hammon was originally from Idaho and knew people there. As soon as he had the deeds of these properties, he began looking for a place in Idaho where he could establish himself. He reasoned that by going back to Idaho, it would be easier to live a United Order because farming would be more successful than in the semi-arid conditions of Southern Utah and Northern Arizona.

Hammon's success in Idaho would depend on two major factors: finding a good farm and getting competent help to move there with him. To find the good farm, he went to Jack Knudson, the same man who had robbed Harold Blackmore of his property in Canada for the UEP.

It just so happened that Knudson had a farm that was for sale. In his land swapping deals, he had acquired a farm near Blackfoot, Idaho, and he had been trying to sell it for some time. This seemed to be an opportunity for them both; Knudson could sell something he did not want and Hammon could get a farm.

The Blackfoot farm was not one of premium value. Having been reclaimed from the midst of a lava bed, there were almost as many acres of rock (islands in the portion that was being farmed) as there were acres of arable land. At the time, prime farm land in the Blackfoot area was selling for about $400 per acre, but Knudson was not inclined to give Hammon any kind of a special deal. He had chosen the Barlow side in their One Man Doctrine controversy, so he decided to ask $800 per acre for his inferior farm.

There can be no dispute that he inflated the price for this reason. He probably expected he would have to negotiate the price down some, but knew he had a fish on the line and was going to get all he could. Hammon could have bought the farm for less had he attempted a lower offer, but instead, he agreed to pay the exorbitant amount.

As a down payment Hammon gave Knudson the Hatch Ranch (which was probably worth more in actual value than the Blackfoot farm) and what equity there was in the Hirschi property at the Gap west of Colorado City. Knudson would carry the contract, allowing Hammon to pay him off over 20 years. Jack Knudson really cleaned up. He not only dumped the place in Blackfoot, but after selling the Hatch Ranch he made more money than he gave for the Idaho farm. He had the property in the Gap as a bonus.

MARION HAMMON PLANS A NEW UNITED ORDER IN IDAHO

Marion Hammon began his exodus to Idaho in 1972. This was a major undertaking in his life and he had no intention of ever coming back to Colorado City. He planned to move all of his family to Idaho as soon as he could make arrangements for them.

He felt an urgency to establish himself outside of the dominion of those who had betrayed him. He justified what he was doing, not because he thought he had anything coming for his services, but rather he believed that he was setting up a refuge where the faithful people could go after the Barlows had completely destroyed the United Effort Plan. His problems began when none of the Polygamists would see it the same way; most of them thought he was just getting out and taking what he could grab as he went. One person Marion hoped would go with him was Edson Jessop.

Edson Jessop had come to Short Creek with his father Lyman (a brother to Richard and Fred Jessop) in the early 1940s. A young man at the time, he became a very zealous supporter of the Priesthood work. He was the same caliber of person as were his cousins, Joe and Dan Jessop. Much of the success of building up Short Creek in the early years can be attributed to Edson Jessop.

When Marion Hammon had returned in 1958 to save the United Effort Plan, he depended a great deal on Edson and his ability and trade as a carpenter. Edson became very close to Hammon, emanating many of his characteristics, becoming a protege to him. For these reasons Marion felt certain that Edson would go with him to Idaho and help with his new United Order. When Edson was approached by Hammon and asked to go to Idaho, it became one of the biggest trials he had ever faced. It upset him greatly to think that the Priesthood would ask him to leave his beloved valley, which he had been taught for most of his adult life was where the Promised Land was being established by the Priesthood of God.

Like his uncle, Richard Jessop, he had been taught that all of the men in the Council held the same authority, that if any one of them asked you to do something it was the same as if God Himself was asking you. He spent many sleepless nights contemplating what he should do. He finally decided to go against all that he had ever been taught, go to another one of the Brethren, explain his dilemma, and seek different counsel.

He went to Leroy Johnson to have him confirm what Marion was asking him to do, or to tell him he didn't have to go to Idaho. He explained that he did not feel very good about leaving Colorado City and running off to Idaho to establish a new Order. He explained his love for the valley, the mountains, and the goals of the former leaders he had dedicated his life to support. He was not aware of the split that was developing between the members of the Priesthood Council and supposed that Hammon had cleared everything with the other Council Members. Imagine his surprise when Leroy told him he did not need to go to Idaho.

Edson Jessop's refusal to go was a great blow to Marion Hammon. Of all the Polygamists, he supposed that Edson would be one he could count on. Then Hammon discovered that not even one of the Colorado City Polygamists would go with him and help with his plan. For this reason, more than any other, his dream would result in failure.

Marion Hammon had never had any real experience in successful farming. All farming projects he had been involved in had been heavily subsidized by other sources of financial support, such as tithing or money from the missionary program. He had also been able to call on such people as Parley Harker for competent advice and even physical help when needed.

In Idaho, he had neither the subsidizing money nor the competent help. The only people he was able to take with him were some of his sons, none of which had the ability to successfully run the farm. Some of these sons were able to obtain work in the nearby communities as drywall laborers, which did help to subsidize the project to a small extent, but even this venture brought sorrow to Marion Hammon and his family when one of his young sons was killed in an automobile accident on the way to work one morning near Blackfoot, Idaho. This was a terrible blow to Marion and from this time on things in Idaho went downhill. He leased part of the farm to a local farmer of Japanese decent, who was quite successful in raising potatoes. Hammon attempted to induce the man to come to work for him and manage the whole farm, but was unsuccessful.

After the third year of trying to run the farm in Idaho, Hammon could see there was no chance he would ever be successful. In severe dejection, he went to Leroy and offered to turn the farm into the United Effort Plan. He supposed that if the UEP owned the farm, then Leroy would send him both competent help and financial support, but Leroy refused. Leroy had assumed that by giving him the UEP farms at Hatch and Beryl, Marion would be out of the picture forever. With this rejection Marion was really in trouble. All he could do was look for a way to dispose of the farm and move back to Colorado City.

He put the farm up for sale and had to raise $20,000 dollars to put with it. In the three and a half years that he had made payments to Jack Knudson, along with the down payment made when he bought the farm, he still had to come up with $20,000 to get out from under the contract with Knudson.

It was about 1976 when Marion Hammon returned to Colorado City, hoping he would carry on there as he had before. He found, however, that very few people respected him. The Barlows had been very busy while he was going back and forth to Idaho.

His family had remained at Colorado City during these four years and he would return most Sundays, to remain active in preaching to the people in Sunday meetings. With the stress of the situation, he suffered a heart attack and underwent a five bypass operation. Serious infection set in and he would never fully recover. He did manage to outlive Leroy and recuperated enough to come back to church in the early 1980s, when the controversy over the One Man Doctrine reached its height. Marion Hammon would yet play a key role in Colorado City.

Jim Blackmore was told to relinquish his home to the UEP, a house he had built in the late 1960s. After completing a mission for the Priesthood, he had built his house on UEP property, as was the custom. When his father Harold Blackmore left Colorado City in anger and moved to LaVerkin, Jim had begun working with him in the home construction business. Jim built an additional home in LaVerkin and had temporally moved there while helping his father build houses.

Brother-in-law Marcus Jessop had moved from Salt Lake City to Colorado City and needed a place to live, so Jim allowed him to live in his house. In 1976 when Jim was ready to move back to Colorado City, he asked Marcus to vacate the house. Jim didn't think it would be a problem since Marcus had built a new house and was ready to move into it. Then Leroy stepped in and told Marcus to stay in Jim's house and to not let him have it back. This stunned Jim. He had maintained good relations with the Polygamists at Colorado City. He had faithfully attended church, paid his tithing to Leroy, and given allegiance to their religious teachings. When he asked Leroy why he was out of favor, he was simply told that because he was Harold's son, he was no longer welcome. In frustration he went to his father and they decided to file a lawsuit to see if Jim could regain occupancy of his house.

This lawsuit put a real scare into the polygamists. Leroy would get up in meetings and plead with the people for money to help fight it. He would always collect money, because the people were told that if the UEP lost the lawsuit, they would all lose their homes (a scare tactic to generate the money they requested). It did not take Harold and Jim Blackmore long to see that they would not get justice from the courts unless they had thousands of dollars to pay the lawyers. They decided to drop the lawsuit. Before they dropped it, however, they had their attorney require that the UEP file a list of all its *beneficiaries* in the county court house in Kingman, Arizona, in accordance with a law that had recently been enacted by the Arizona Legislature. The law states in effect: "A trustee (of a blind trust) shall name the beneficiaries of such trust and their addresses; …and file the names in the public records in the court house of the county in which the property is located." Fred Jessop made up the list of all members of the United Effort Plan who were living in Colorado City in 1976 and filed it in the Court House at Kingman, Arizona.

Because of the threat of the Blackmore lawsuit, the UEP Trustees realized the importance of implementing the means to protect themselves from any such threats in the future. A document was drawn up and *all UEP members were required to sign it*. It acknowledged that as members of the UEP, if they ever decided to move from their homes, they would not attempt to legally claim any equity in them, thus protecting the UEP from lawsuits. The trusting members, in signing the document, looked at it quite differently. They believed it to be a guarantee that *they could never be asked to leave their homes*; but they would lose their equity if they decided, on their own initiative, to leave these homes. At the time this occurred, almost all the UEP members were satisfied with the management of the UEP and could see no problems ahead. Most all of them willingly signed it.

The stealing of Jim Blackmore's house was the first act of this kind by the Polygamist leaders. In the past, when people who had donated property to the UEP became dissatisfied with the poor management of their assets, the Polygamist Leaders had always made an effort to appease the situation. In some cases deeds of property were given back to the dissatisfied members or leases on property or equipment were granted, but none had ever been asked to give up the homes they had built. The past policy of the Polygamist Leaders had always been "if someone apostatized, they will get discouraged and leave." This policy had worked well because those who became dissatisfied had eventually done just that, picked up and moved.

But when the UEP had paid Harold Blackmore for his place in the 1960s, Leroy Johnson made the statement: "This will be the last time we will ever pay an apostate for his home." Perhaps with some coaching from the Barlows, Leroy had decided to become a harsher leader than were his predecessors. He was now willing to force any member out of the society if he believed that person was out of harmony with him in any degree.

This was a dramatic change in the policy and purpose of what the United Effort Plan had been set up to be used for by its founders. From this time on, the feelings and the spirit of the Polygamist Society at Colorado City began to change from a carefree atmosphere of freedom and joy, to one of fear and oppression.

REVELATION FROM GOD OR SATAN?

On October 23, 1978, Priesthood Council member Richard S. Jessop died. The death of Jessop gave the Barlows a free and open road towards their goal of taking over the UEP. Richard had been their biggest obstacle up to this time because they could not completely sway Leroy's mind on Priesthood history so long as Richard Jessop was alive. He was a living testimony of what the history was, having personally lived through it.

Richard Jessop was the only member of John Barlow's Council that had known Lorin Woolley in any degree of intimacy. In the early 1930s, during the years of the Great Depression, he had spent many hours talking with Woolley. The only other Council member that even knew him at all, probably ever met him, was Guy Musser, son of Joseph Musser. Leroy Johnson met John Woolley once but had never met Lorin Woolley.

Richard Jessop would often tell about his experiences of being schooled under Lorin Woolley. In these sermons he would always emphasize the Priesthood lineage in the order of seniority of the Presidents, those who had held the keys to Priesthood down through the Polygamists' history. Often, after Richard had finished his talks, Leroy would get up in the meeting and, in agreement, confirm the truth of Jessop's statements. Richard Jessop was never challenged on his testimony of the Polygamist lineage of Priesthood authority, either by Leroy or any of the Barlows. With Richard Jessop gone, the campaign began in earnest to change the history of the line of authority so the doctrine of a One Man Rule would become the new "truth." Their only obstacle now was Marion Hammon.

To eliminate Marion Hammon from the leadership position of the Priesthood Council, they would have to destroy the credibility of all of the earlier Polygamist's Leaders whose teachings contradicted John Barlow's belief and claim of only one man on earth at a time holding the Keys of the Priesthood, and thus the authority to make whatever decisions he wanted.

In the 1950s Guy Musser had put together a collection of ten photographs depicting the Presidents of Priesthood according to the Polygamist's teachings: Joseph Smith, Brigham Young, John Taylor, Wilford Woodruff, John Woolley, Lorin Woolley, Leslie Broadbent, John Y. Barlow, Joseph Musser, and Charles Zitting. All devout Polygamists purchased a set of these photographs and proudly displayed them on their living room walls. By the end of the 1970s any of the Polygamists who were accepting the Barlows' One Man Doctrine had removed from their walls the photographs of Wilford Woodruff, Leslie Broadbent, Joseph Musser, and Charles Zitting, posthumously stripping these men of their Priesthood Authority.

The following is the correct Polygamist line of Priesthood authority, and the names in parenthesis are those eliminated by the Barlows:

Joseph Smith, Brigham Young, John Taylor, (Wilford Woodruff) John Woolley, Lorin Woolley, (Leslie Broadbent), John Barlow, (Joseph Musser), (Charles Zitting), Leroy Johnson, (Marion Hammon), (Alma Timpson) and Rulon Jeffs.

Next the Barlows were finally able to convince aging Leroy that the 1880 Revelation given to Wilford Woodruff was really two revelations. The first part was from The Lord, that there was to be a senior man by order of ordination, who would lead the group; the second half was from Satan, that they would make decisions together.

Six months after Richard Jessop died, Leroy presented this theory to the remaining members of the Priesthood Council in one of their regular meetings at Salt Lake City in the spring of 1979. Present were Leroy Johnson, Marion Hammon, Guy Musser, Rulon Jeffs, and Alma Timpson. After Leroy presented his astonishing interpretation of this revelation, Alma Timpson picked up the Three In One (a book containing the Book of Mormon, Doctrine & Covenants, and the Pearl of Great Price, the standard LDS scriptures) and asked: "Can we discuss this, Brother Johnson?"

Leroy became very upset, saying; "Do you want a sign, brother Timpson, like Korihor of old?"

Alma Timpson, closing the book, simply replied: "No, Brother Johnson, I don't need a sign." Leroy's reference here to "Korihor of old" no doubt was to intimidate Timpson. Korihor was a character in the Book of Mormon who asked for a sign from Alma (religious leader) and was struck dumb because he did not believe what was told him by this Alma (Book of Mormon, Alma 30: 43-50). The implication was that if Timpson did not accept Leroy's doctrine on the 1880 Revelation, he too would be struck dumb.

This was one of the last times the Priesthood Council met in a regular Council meeting. Rulon Jeffs was the only one of the Council who accepted Leroy's philosophy regarding the 1880 revelation. This left the Council split. Leroy Johnson and Rulon Jeffs in agreement with the Barlows' One Man Doctrine. Marion Hammon, Guy Musser, and Alma Timpson against it.

These three men could not go against their earlier teaching that all the Brethren in the Council held the same Authority. Rulon Jeffs chose to side with Leroy and the Barlows. It appears that this was a political decision he chose rather than a doctrinal one. Shortly after the Council meeting wherein Leroy made his stand, Rulon, in a Junior School of The Prophets meeting at Colorado City, got up and, in a halting address to those attending the meeting, told them that the second part of the 1880 Revelation to Wilford Woodruff was from the Lower Regions. This firmly assured his position with the Barlow Cabal.

Soon after this, Leroy Johnson became sick with the Shingles. This left the conducting of the Short Creek meetings and the affairs of the Polygamists in the hands of Marion Hammon as the next senior member of the Priesthood Council. These next few years became years of turmoil. Hammon, along with Guy Musser and Alma Timpson, labored to convince the people that because of Leroy's age (ninety-one in 1979) and his sickness, he was vulnerable to be swayed by unscrupulous men in their greed and desire for power.

The unquestioning love the people had for Uncle Roy blinded them to these warnings. Because of his anxiety over the issue, Marion Hammon became very sick again and was unable to go out among the people for the next two or three years.

Guy Musser, the next senior member of the Council, spent his time in Salt Lake City while Timpson was in charge at Colorado City. This arrangement was not at all satisfactory with the Barlows and they did everything they could to discredit what these two Brethren tried to teach the people. By 1980, the split was creating many hostile feelings in the community, not only in the day to day mingling of the people but more particularly in their religious meetings. The Sunday teachings of those called on to talk to the people became a loud and often ugly debating match.

Many quit attending Sunday meetings rather than endure the bitter disputes between the opposing factions.

10

Evicting The Sinners

Marion Hammon had established the Colorado City Academy High School in the1960s, and shortly thereafter the Mohave County Community College established a branch at Colorado City. Classes were held in the Academy building and Cyril Bradshaw, the principal of the Academy, was also chosen as the administrator for the College. The Community College, using the teachers in the local schools as instructors, offered much needed classes for the residents of the area.

Because the Academy was a product of Marion Hammon's effort to rebuild Colorado City, having it succeed was a thorn in the sides of the Barlows and Fred Jessop. And the time would come when they would be willing to sacrifice the Academy to rid themselves of Hammon.

As religious doctrine disagreements were intensifying, the recreation-starved people of Colorado City enjoyed plays performed by both the Academy and the College. The college had a drama class taught by a young lady who had majored in that field and recently had moved to Colorado City to teach in the elementary school. The young lady was an excellent teacher, but her ideas and training were markedly different than those of conservative Fred Jessop. Fred had been accustomed to having things his own way for twenty years or more and did not appreciate a young upstart (not only a female but one who was under the direction of the Academy) changing the status quo. She was ignorant of this situation, however, and threw herself into her work with the enthusiasm of youth.

"Harvey," the first play of any consequence, was put on by the Academy. It was cast in the Round and used no props, a very innovative thing for the Polygamists to do. An unqualified success, the play was the first of many productions to come (along with the Harvest Balls), either sponsored by the Academy or the Community College. In 1972, another play "Naughty Marietta" was enjoyed very much by everyone and, the last night it was presented, it received a standing ovation. Fred was very disgruntled over its positive reception and left the building grumbling that such programs should not be allowed among the Saints.

In the fall of 1977 Fred's annual Town Fair was probably the biggest and best that was produced up to that time. Fred had delegated people to set up booths and provide something that could be sold to the people. Food, crafts and recreational programs were presented, where for a small fee ($1.00) people could sit and be entertained.

Later in this same year the Community College sponsored a Christmas program, which was a very big success. It was called "Holiday Special" and included a segment copied from the "Hee Haw" television show. Fred Jessop had two criticisms against this program. The first was that the Polygamists don't believe in celebrating Christmas on December 25; they celebrate April 6 as the day the Savior was born. The second was the type of music that was presented by the cast; it was too worldly, and the Hee Haw segment made a satirical jab at Fred himself, a real no-no.

In 1978 the Community College put on the play "The Mikado." In this story, an emperor of Japan is worshiped by the people as God. His very word must be obeyed as if God himself spoke. The moral of the play was that the Emperor was only human and was subject to making mistakes. When the people finally learned this, then they were able to prosper, not being held back by superstitions. This production was well presented and much enjoyed by the people. Again Fred had a problem with the play. In his mind there was too much insinuation (though not intended) as to Fred being this "Lord High Pu-Ba." Yes, there were those in the community who compared him with the Mikado all right, but those producing the play had no such motives. Fred still took offence and vowed that such insinuating parodies *must forever cease*. The academy *must* be closed down, and its leader, Marion Hammon, removed from the community. This became an obsession with Fred Jessop.

Leroy Johnson was still living in the big Hildale home that Marion had arranged to be built some years before. Because he was still ill and no longer able to attend any of the religious meetings, the Barlows would bring stories to him about what the other Council members were teaching the people. They did not stop with Leroy, but continued to spread their doctrine to people in the community. Anyone defending Hammon and Timpson was also brought into the line of fire. The Barlows would start stories against them of sexual improprieties and other sordid tales. The problem escalated and finally in order to address the situation, Marion Hammon attempted to bring the perpetrators of these deeds to an accounting.

On April 23, 1978, Marion Hammon gave a sermon in a Sunday public meeting and said to the Barlows: "You cannot try me without a hearing. You are going around telling the people (and President Johnson) that I am teaching things that I am *not* teaching. If you have an accusation against me, then there is a proper way to handle it; call a High Council meeting and present the evidence and let it be handled the proper way."

When the Barlows reported this meeting to Leroy, they told him that Marion had said in Church today "nobody can call him to an accounting but he could call Leroy to an accounting if he so chose." Such was their accuracy in reporting things to Leroy.

While Leroy was confined to his sick bed, it became necessary to give him narcotic pain killing drugs. At the height of his suffering he was receiving a shot of Demerol every two hours. While under the effect of these hallucinating drugs, he began seeing "visions" and receiving "revelations." These manifestations were along the lines of the end of the world and the destruction of all the wicked people, *especially those members of the Polygamists who were opposing him and his doctrines*. There were many bizarre stories coming from him as to what was going to transpire in the world. These ranged from natural catastrophes to the *slaughtering* of the "wicked" people living in the community. Many of the Polygamists, because of their traditions and superstitions, believed these weird "Prophecies" and began living in a state of fear. The dissidents knew they were considered "wicked" and that the Barlows had hidden away a stash of guns somewhere in the town. And Leroy told Sam Barlow to clean up the town.

SAM FINDS "WICKEDNESS"

Chief Protector Sam believed he was the perfect person to begin looking for "wickedness." His first victim was a woman with eight young children. The young woman had been a second wife to a man of questionable morals. His first wife had died due to a brain tumor and soon after her death, the husband was convicted of child molestation of his own minor daughters and was sentenced to serve time in the Arizona State Prison. A short time after this, the surviving wife became a target of Sam's cleanup campaign. He judged her immoral, accusing her of being involved in sexual activities with men of the community. There was never any direct accusations made to her, nor was there any kind of proof that such was the truth; this did not matter. Sam simply told Leroy that she was doing immoral things. Leroy never called her in to confront her with the accusations, but told Sam she had to leave the community.

Earlier Sam Barlow had enlisted a group of zealous supporters to assist him in his "duties" of policing the Polygamists. These men were organized into a vigilante group of law enforcers that were nothing more than a "Goon Squad" to harass the young people and any who they felt were not living their lives according to the standards of the Priesthood. These Goons were becoming very bold in going throughout the community and beating up on the young boys they felt were not worthy to live there, forcing them to leave town. It was this Goon Squad that Sam used to force the young mother from her home and the community.

The woman, needing to support her children, had accepted an offer of employment from a sympathetic friend in Salt Lake City, so she temporally moved there. When the time came for her children to start school for the year, she went to Leroy Johnson and asked his advice on what she should do about enrolling her children in school. He told her to enroll them in a school in Salt Lake City since she was working there. She would travel to Colorado City about once a month to check on her house and keep her ties with the community. She fully intended to move back once she had earned enough money to pay for some improvements on her home.

On October 22, 1982, after returning to Salt Lake from Colorado City, where the day before she had attended meetings there and paid Leroy her tithing for the month, she received a telephone call from a friend telling her that men had broken into her house and were taking possession of it and moving her belongings out. She immediately left for Colorado City.

Arriving just after midnight, she found the lock on the front door had been changed.

Entering through the back, she stumbled upon several men in sleeping bags on the floor of the front room, which had been stripped of her belongings. She began screaming at them to get out of her house.

The men scrambled from their bedrolls and called for "backup" assistance on hand held two-way radios. They began to harass her as to what she was doing there.

She said, "I live here and I want you guys to get out."

Nephi Barlow, a brother of Deputy Sheriff Sam Barlow, ordered her out of the house, informing her it was no longer hers. He told her she couldn't take any of the furnishings, nor could she go in or out of the house without his permission.

It became a standoff. She refused to leave and the intruders said they were waiting for Sam Barlow to come before they would leave. She went outside, brought her children in to put them to bed, and discovered another shock; their bedrooms had been stripped of the beds. She went into her own bedroom and, discovering that her bed was still there, took the baby and went to bed. The other children huddled around the fireplace where they spent the remainder of the night. At one point, Jerry Jessop asked why she didn't just go home?

She replied, "I am home."

Sam Barlow never showed up. He realized that it would be a civil rights violation if he were to openly take Leroy's side in the issue. He did, however, act as a go-between for the woman and Leroy. The next day he told her she was being evicted because she was behind in paying his brother, Truman Barlow, taxes he had levied against her house (he would never tell her the real reason why she was being kicked out of her home and the town).

She went to Marion Hammon, seeking advice and help. When she informed him of the tax issue, he gave her $3,000 (the amount Sam told her was owing) to give to Truman. She gave the money to Truman, which he took, but she was not allowed to have her house back.

Two weeks after she had been kicked out (she was allowed by kind friends to stay with them) Sam Barlow officially through the mail gave her an "eviction notice." It stated she was to remove all her personal belongings within two weeks and was never to enter the premises again. With her Prophet Leroy against her, she felt she had no choice but to comply. She did indeed leave the community, enduring many trials and hardships, making her way in the world on her own. One of Truman Barlow's recently married sons, who had one wife and no children, was "given" the large house. It had been built and paid for by the evicted woman's husband before he was sent to prison and was valued at $150,000.

Leroy never conferred with any of the other UEP Trustees or the other members of the Priesthood Council.

THE SEARCH GOES ON

This was only the beginning of the evictions that were to come to those whom Sam Barlow felt were not worthy to live in the community. After this successful eviction, Sam Barlow began searching for others whose "immorality" would make them suitable candidates for the same treatment. He was lucky, for it seems that a man had molested one of his daughters several years earlier. Sam somehow discovered that this crime had taken place and he set about to remove the "blot" from the society of the Saints.

In order to have him arrested and convicted, Sam would need an injured party as a complainant. The alleged victim of incest, his daughter, had grown to maturity and moved to Salt Lake City some ten years earlier. This did not deter Sam. He went to Salt Lake and began harassing the girl to sign a complaint against her father. She did not want anything to do with the matter. Sam was persistent. He convinced the girl that in order to help her father, she needed to sign the complaint so as to allow Sam to arrest him and get him into treatment for his own sake, to help him overcome his "problems."

The daughter reluctantly signed Sam's complaint. The fact that Sam Barlow was acting completely outside of his jurisdiction by going to the girl in Salt Lake City, without working through the local law enforcement agencies there, did not even cross his mind. He was doing it for the "good of the work" and any actions on his part would be justified, regardless of the legal questions.

Armed with the complaint, Sam went back to Colorado City. He contacted the man, who was working in the Las Vegas area for a time, and convinced him to meet. They did and Sam persuaded him to be arrested and taken to jail in Kingman, the Mohave County Seat.

Sam never had any intention of doing anything to "help" the man as he had alleged to his daughter. He succeeded in having the bail set so high that it was impossible for the man's family to bail him out. When his wives (of which he had two) went to Leroy for advice and help, he simply told them that he would not be bailed out and must be sent to the state prison. This was a real shock to them. They had known of his conduct with his daughter, but had been willing to forgive him, and were going on with their lives. Now their world was crashing down around them.

After about ten days in the county jail, he was brought before the judge for a preliminary hearing. In about five minutes time the judge learned that the "crime" was over seven years old, which was the statute of limitations on the offence. He scolded Sam severely and dismissed the case. The man and his family were ecstatic; but little did they know that their real problems had just begun. Sam was furious. He was not going to allow anyone to make a fool of him.

The arrest occurred January 1983. Two months later Steve Bailey, a newly hired deputy of the Mohave County Sheriff's department, delivered a Notice to Vacate to the family, giving them thirty days to move.

Their home was one of the more expensive of the community. He had spent several thousands of dollars on the material alone and had never dreamed that he could ever be forced to give it up and move from the community that he had spent most of his life helping to build up. This was such a shock to his family that one of his wives suffered a nervous breakdown and was hospitalized, where she prematurely gave birth to a child she was carrying. She would never completely recover from the trauma of this experience and died a few years later from a brain tumor.

The man pleaded with Leroy about his situation, hoping he would relent on his decision to have him evicted. Leroy showed no mercy, saying he would have to move out, but if he would change his ways, he *might* be allowed to move back into the community sometime in the future. With a broken heart, a wife and premature baby in the hospital, the man prepared to move. On the thirteenth of March, he moved his large family to Phoenix, where he began the struggle of surviving under the hardships that Sam Barlow and Leroy Johnson had forced upon him and his family.

TEENAGE BOYS VICTIMS OF THE GOON SQUAD

The Goon Squad organized in the 1960s to "spiritually" police the community took on another duty in the 1970s when Ervil LeBaron of Mexico began making threats against any of the Polygamist Groups that would not acknowledge him as the rightful successor to Joseph Smith, granting him their full allegiance. Threats reached their peak with the assassination of Rulon Allred, leader of the Polygamist Group set up by Joseph Musser. A contingent of the Goon Squad was designated as a Night Patrol to guard against any suspicious intruders.

Guards sat at the roads coming into town, where everyone entering could be screened. The intruders would then be followed by one of these Patrol vehicles. If just being followed would not intimidate them enough that they would drive out of town in the next few minutes, they would then be stopped and checked out by these self-appointed "policemen."

Then in the 1980s, the Teenage Chastity Patrol / Goon Squad / Night Patrol became more openly aggressive within the Group and was used by Sam to clean up the town, not only of sinners, but also of excess boys.

A particular contingent of Sam's handpicked Goon Squad was headed by Jerry Jessop, and included some of the most "self-righteous" young men, including: Stanley Jessop, Nephi Barlow, J. L. Jessop, Joe Timpson and any others they would call upon as more were needed for backup.

This group became a fear and a scourge among the boys of the community. Without warning, they would gang up on any who they judged was "out of line," fiercely beating them up. The offences of the boys were such things as wearing long hair, talking to a girl on the street or just not supporting the Priesthood. They became so bold as to storm into the homes of the boys in the middle of the night, pulling the boys from their beds and beating them up in front of their parents, who, in most cases were helpless to stop them.

ULTIMATE POWER OVER FAMILIES

To understand the power Sam and his Goon Squad had over the people of the community, several things must be explained. Any one of the factors involved might not seem like too much of a power grip, but when added up it then becomes clear how it worked.

The first control Sam had over the people was that the homes they had built were located on property that was titled in the name of the United Effort Plan. Although all who had built these homes were listed beneficiaries of the Trust, some had been forced to leave the community. This was becoming a real threat to members of the community who were daring to stand up against the high-handed acts of Sam and his Gestapo-like Goon Squad.

To take a stand against Sam was the same as taking a stand against Leroy Johnson. Sam had become his right-hand man in such matters and it was easy for Sam to get Leroy to endorse any decision he might make regarding what action should be taken. To stay in Leroy's good graces, no one dared displease Sam Barlow.

In the event one of their sons was singled out by Sam as one who should leave the community, the father was placed in a dilemma; he must believe Sam, standing against his own son and not even allowing the boy to tell his side of the story of whether or not he was guilty of any "crime," allowing him to be driven from the society. Or if he chose to side with his son, allowing him to tell his side of the story, then he was placing himself and his family in jeopardy of being evicted from their home and cast out of the community. Most of these family heads were polygamists with a very large family, making it almost impossible for them to go out into other communities and completely start over. Most would just swallow their pride and allow their sons to be sacrificed, consoling themselves with the reasoning that whatever the "Prophet" asked of them was right.

Sam Barlow, a Mohave County Deputy Sheriff, was the only law enforcement authority in the Colorado City area. Any complaints taken to him by the parents of the boys were simply "shelved" and the only action taken was against the boys themselves, if they refused to leave when they were warned by the vigilantes. Sam would build some kind of charges against the boys that would range from "amorously enticing a girl" to throwing eggs at his Night Patrol.

Another factor governing the non-action of the parents was polygamy itself. All polygamists believe that in order to reach the highest degree of heaven, they must live polygamy. Whether a man would get additional wives depended upon whether or not one of the Council members would allow him to do so.

In most cases it was Leroy himself who reserved the right to decide who was "worthy" to get wives. If a man was to offend him, it virtually cut off any chances of him ever becoming a polygamist. Since courting was not allowed, because all girls were "told" who they should marry, it was almost impossible for any man to go out and get a wife without Leroy's approval.

But, in truth, if any of the Polygamists were to give an honest answer as to why they desired to enter polygamy, it would not be to gain this highest degree in heaven, but rather it was to gain the "status" of being a polygamist. In Colorado City, those who are not polygamists are looked down on as though they are not quite as good as those who are. A non-polygamist cannot "preside" over a polygamist. This does not apply to ecclesiastical positions only, but is carried throughout all aspects of the society, whether it is in the work place, the schools, or in the town governments. The school principal, the town mayor, or even a foreman on a work project has to be a polygamist.

Another advantage for those who remain in Sam's favor are the benefits they receive from the storehouse. If Fred Jessop, who controls the storehouse, judges a person "worthy," he not only gives them commodities, but does not require them to pay their water bills, sewer bills, or health care bills. Also, Fred Jessop controls the person who is County Representative for the Arizona State Medical Assistance Program in the Colorado City area. He decides who is "worthy" to receive these benefits. Few polygamists have any kind of health care insurance, so they are dependent on staying in the good graces of Fred.

Along with all these factors is the stigma of being castigated in the community if you are an "apostate." If you turn against the Priesthood, the whole society turns against you, doing anything in their power to cause you to "get discouraged and leave." This stigma carries through from the parents to their children and it becomes very hard on the children of the "offenders" (apostates) in the schools where the other children will bring all kinds of persecution upon them.

The parents of these innocent children, when going to the school superintendent, Alvin Barlow, never got any justice from him. He would do whatever he could to "discourage them" from remaining in the community. Thus, the lives and health of people in the community are held hostage.

After a beating, some of these boys would be given warnings to leave the community with the threat that they would receive more of the same if they failed to do so. Along with the beatings, Jerry Jessop and his henchmen began dirty little tricks such as slicing tires on the cars and All Terrain Vehicles of any who they felt should be harassed out of town. This was not limited to the young boys of the community, but was also being carried out against adults who were judged as "apostates."

CHALLENGING THE GESTAPO-LIKE GOOD SQUAD

Five men in the community decided to do something about the atrocities. They had come to realize that Leroy's Priesthood Work was in fact a cult and the sooner the people could understand this, the sooner they would be free from the illegal, unrighteous terrorism of such men as Sam Barlow.

In an effort to put a stop to the beatings, they contacted the Mohave County Sheriff's Department at Kingman, asking for a representative of the Sheriff to meet with them to hear their complaints. Ironically, this request had to be made through Sam Barlow. In a confrontation with one of the five men (Ben Bistline), wherein he accused Sam Barlow to his face of running a Gestapo, Sam, in righteous indignation, offered to set up an appointment with one of his superiors in the sheriff's department.

On the morning of March 8, 1983, Sam called Ben Bistline and one of the other five men and said that a Lieutenant from the sheriff's department was in his office and, if they so desired, they could come over and talk with him. The two men went to the office, where Sam, after making the introductions, excused himself and left the office, secure in his mind that these men would feel too intimidated to reveal anything that would cause him loss of credibility. He was partially right. The second man became very nervous and, after a few minutes of talking with the Lieutenant, excused himself and left. The other man (Ben Bistline) was not intimidated and proceeded to relate to Lieutenant Crouse some of the problems the polygamists were facing due to the policies of Sam Barlow. At first Lieutenant Crouse seemed uninterested, passing it off as only a personality clash between Ben and Sam, who had grown up together in the community.

When the beatings by the Goon Squad were related to him, he began to take interest. After asking a few questions, he said, "If such beatings are going on, then we will get them stopped." The beatings were indeed stopped.

When confronted by Lieutenant Crouse, Sam denied knowing anything about them. Lieutenant Crouse forcefully told him that if they were not stopped there would be some intervention from Kingman on the matter.

Sam Barlow, right in character, blamed the whole matter on Jerry Jessop. He went to Leroy, explaining that he, Sam, had known nothing about it, putting the whole blame on Jerry, telling him about how the Sheriff's Office was going to get involved if the beatings were not stopped. This caused a panic for Leroy; if there was anything he didn't want, it was to have outside law enforcement in the community. Leroy summoned Jerry and, acting as if he had no knowledge of the Goon Squad, Leroy lowered the boom on the unsuspecting man.

ANOTHER EVICTION, ENTITLED "NOTICE TO VACATE"

Sam's next victim to evict was Andrew Bistline, the same man who had spent so much of his younger life up-building the Kingdom. Andrew had spent twenty years working on projects for the Priesthood Work for which he had received little or no wages and very little thanks. He was the one who had renovated the sawmill to cut the lumber for the Academy building and many other buildings in the community; and he had spent many hours working for Merril Jessop to get the door mill working.

By 1983 Andrew was becoming disillusioned with how things were being conducted by Priesthood leaders. He was dissatisfied with the inequity and partiality meted out. He began studying the scriptures and came to the conclusion that their claims of authority and their changes in doctrine were a contradiction to what his conscience told him was correct. He decided it was time to move away. Purchasing a very run-down house in Fredonia, a neighboring community, he began renovating it for his wife and ten children. He planned to take a year to make all the necessary remodeling changes, so it would be habitable. Meanwhile, his children would stay in school in Colorado City for another year.

During this time, he began drinking with friends who felt as he did about the leadership. On one of these occasions, he had faced a confrontation with Sam that would result in eviction from his home in Colorado City.

On the evening of February 21, 1982, Andrew and another man were returning home from a drinking party at the home of Mayo Stubbs. They were intoxicated and their car was being driven by Mayo's daughter. She was an inexperienced driver and slid off the road into the snow. J. L. Jessop and his stepbrother Stanley Jessop came along, but when asked to help, they refused, then drove back and forth harassing them and making sarcastic remarks.

When Andrew finally got home he contacted Deputy Sheriff Sam Barlow to complain about the boys' harassment. Sam Barlow drove up near Andrew's house and stopped someone for speeding. Andrew saw him and asked him to do something about J. L. and Stanley's harassing him, which Sam refused to do. Andrew then called Sam "a chicken shit son-of-a-bitch," which resulted in Sam giving Andrew a ticket, saying that nobody was going to get away with "insulting my mother." Andrew paid a $250 fine. The fine levied against Andrew was not satisfactory punishment to please Sam. He decided that in order to properly discipline Andrew, he must have him banished from the community. After all, he had Leroy's directive to "clean up the town." He began watching to find an excuse that would justify such action. One year later on the 24th of July 1983, he obtained the evidence he would need.

Fred Jessop staged a Pioneer Day celebration at the Hildale Community Park in Maxwell Canyon. An attendee found an audio cassette tape lying in the parking lot and turned it over to Sam. This tape was an important discovery for Sam. It contained recordings of a camp-out party where some of Andrew Bistline's boys were present. The tape revealed things said by his boys that were not complimentary to Uncle Roy or Sam.

After spending two weeks analyzing the tape, which included calling in the brothers of Andrew (and several other people of the community) to listen to it, Sam went to Leroy to report his findings and interpretation of "what the tape really said." He put his own interpretation on things, such as: "cedar berries" to mean "marijuana," and "cactus" to mean hard drugs such as cocaine. With such imaginary evidence, he convinced Leroy that the boys were not only involved in using narcotic drugs, but also the distribution. Since he had no real evidence that his accusation was fact, he could not arrest them. The only solution of ridding the town of the evil was to have their father, Andrew, evicted from his home. Leroy gave Sam the go-ahead.

Sam Barlow contacted Steve Bailey, the new Deputy of the Arizona Strip area, telling Bailey to meet him in Kingman. They went to the Sheriff's office where Sam presented a document to the clerk to be officially stamped. He then paid her $50 and gave the document to Steve Bailey, telling him to serve it on Andrew Bistline in Colorado City.

Andrew was working at a uranium mine on the Arizona Strip about fifty miles south of Colorado City. He would stay the week at the mine, coming home on weekends, then he would go to Fredonia to do renovation work on the home he had purchased. On August 10, 1983, while he was at the mine, Steve Bailey served the "notice to vacate" on his wife, Irene.

Andrew and his family scrambled to move by the thirty day deadline, albeit under severe hardship. They moved into the house at Fredonia before it was completed, with plastic covering the windows, a light grade of felt tar paper on the roof, and no electricity. The only conveniences were a water faucet in the front yard and an outhouse in the back. The United Effort Plan had driven him from a comfortable home that he himself had built with material he paid for, a home furnished with all of the modern conveniences, to the home in Fredonia that had almost nothing. It forced great hardship upon his wife and children.

It should be noted that these evictions (entitled "notice to vacate") were being authorized by *only two* of the four living UEP Trustees, Leroy Johnson and Rulon Jeffs. The other Trustees, Marion Hammon and Alma Timpson, were never informed by Johnson and Jeffs. Because the four Trustees were split as to what UEP policy was, Johnson and Jeffs felt they could make whatever decisions they wished without consulting either Hammon or Timpson. The fifth Trustee, Guy Musser, had died on July 11, 1983, at Salt Lake City.

ATTORNEY CAUTIONS LEROY JOHNSON

Soon after Andrew Bistline's eviction, Leroy was warned by his attorney that he was putting himself in legal jeopardy by evicting recognized beneficiaries. Since Andrew Bistline was listed on an "Affidavit of Discloser," filed in the Mohave County Court House in Kingman, Arizona, in October of 1976 by the Trustees of the United Effort Plan, there was no question as to whether or not he was a beneficiary. Because of this warning, Leroy met with Fred Jessop and the Barlows to discuss strategies for legally evicting beneficiaries.

It was arbitrarily concluded that a new list be drawn up, removing any and all of those members of the United Effort Plan who "might need to be evicted" and filing it in the Court House to replace the list filed in 1976. This new list was filed in Kingman in November of 1983.

Sam Barlow pulled off one more eviction in 1983. On or about December 1, 1983, Sam, without a search warrant, entered and searched the home of Dwight Nyborg looking for "evidence" against him.

Dwight was unmarried and living alone in a small two room house that he had built, paying for the material with his own money. He had served a two year mission for the UEP and was "given a building lot and a wife" in compensation for his faithfulness. The wife did not choose to remain married to him and left the community a few days after the arranged marriage. Dwight remained, hoping to be able to receive another wife to replace the one that left. Sam Barlow decided Dwight was a menace to the community and began a witch hunt to find evidence to have him expelled. He found what he decided he needed while going through Dwight's personal property at his home. It was a body building magazine with pictures mostly of mens' bodies, but there was one picture that showed a woman's bare breast. This was all he needed.

Sam went to Leroy, telling him that Dwight was taking juveniles into his home and showing them lewd and pornographic material, and showed him the Body Building magazine for proof. Leroy gave his permission to have Dwight evicted.

In Dwight's case there was no written eviction notice issued. Sam merely told him that Uncle Roy wanted him to leave, which Dwight complied with, moving to Phoenix with a broken heart.

Along with these efforts to clean up the town by evicting the undesirables, the Barlows stayed busy at their work of programming the mind of Leroy Johnson against Hammon and Timpson. They were having so much success, the Brethren no longer met in their Council Meetings. It was impossible for Hammon or Timpson to even meet with Leroy because the Barlows would not allow anyone to have private access to him.

In the late fall of 1983 in a Sunday meeting, Alma Timpson was getting after the Barlows for wearing out Leroy. He accused them of pestering him so much that it was destroying his health. After haranguing them for some time, he said: "Keep your ungodly presence from Uncle Roy's midst." At this, Dan Barlow stood up and said: "That's a lie."

Such open defiance surprised Timpson. He stood speechless, staring at Dan. In an instant Truman Barlow stood up, quietly staring at Timpson. Then almost everyone in the building stood up. In a few moments Timpson regained his composure, and said, "If that's the way you want it, then dismiss yourselves at home." He then walked out of the building.

The year 1983 ended on this note. The Barlows had effectively broken up the Priesthood Council and Sam had successfully evicted four families from their homes and the community. The next step toward reaching their goal would be to strip Marion Hammon of his "Priesthood." Accusations would be made against Marion Hammon and Alma Timpson to further discredit them.

SEXUAL ABUSES AGAINST THE GIRLS

Chief Protector of the community Sam Barlow began looking for sex offences in the lives of those he was trying to eradicate from the community. There were many rumors and accusations made against several men, who would not support Sam in his "calling," and especially any who vocally disagreed with the actions of Leroy Johnson in his support of the One Man Rule.

These accusations even included Marion Hammon and Alma Timpson. Hammon was accused of incestuous acts with his own daughters. Timpson was accused of using narcotic drugs to increase the sexual passions of his wives. These accusations were entirely false, with no evidence of any kind ever shown. But there were some men and boys who were guilty of sexual abuse. These would include men making sexual assaults on their own daughters, boys enticing and even forcing sexual intercourse on their younger sisters, and there were some instances of young unmarried men being involved in sexual conduct with young wives of older men (All of the Priesthood Council members had married young teenage girls).

Some of these girls were trapped in a dead-end situation with no hope of any fulfillment of life's joys. In such hopeless conditions, it was relatively easy for some young Lothario to come into their lives and take advantage of the situation.

Throughout the 1980s and into the 1990s there were about eight men of the Polygamist Community that Sam sent to prison on sexual charges. These were men who were "out of harmony" with him and Uncle Roy. They were vigorously pursued by Sam and in about half of the cases the men only plead guilty because they didn't have the money to hire an attorney to properly defend themselves on charges that were highly exaggerated.

On the other side of the coin, there were over twice that many men (and boys, sons of the Barlows) who were guilty of the same offences (accused by their own daughters), who did no prison time at all except for the two or three days spent in a county jail waiting for bail to be raised. They were either Barlows, the sons of Barlows, or relations to Leroy, or in some cases a man had given Leroy a large sum of money, some as much as $5,000. These men were provided with reputable attorneys paid for by the UEP and plea bargains with very light sentences. There is evidence that Sam would even go into the Sheriff's offices of the county involved and remove critical evidence such as reports he himself had filed, after Leroy would inform him that he was to get the particular person "off."

In some of these cases no arrests were made. One in particular involved a son of Sam Barlow himself. The young man had become sexually involved with a younger wife of one of the older men of the community. This affair went on for a while before it was discovered. The girl was older than the man (who was not a minor), so Sam simply blamed the whole affair on her saying: "In all my experience of law enforcement, this is the first time I have found the blame in a sexual offence to be the fault of the girl." The girl was ordered to leave the community while the punishment for Sam Barlow's son was an advancement in the Priesthood. About one month later he was ordained an Elder in the Melchizedek Priesthood.

The saddest part is that the lives of the people who were "out of harmony" were, in some cases, totally destroyed. One of the young men Sam sent to prison committed suicide. Fred Jessop would not even allow the boy's mother to bring his body home, but rather had the State cremate his remains, disposing of them in any way they chose. Other men lost their wives and families, for no other reason than being "out of harmony."

There was never any effort made by the community leaders to "rehabilitate" any of these offenders. The attitude can be pretty well summed up in this statement of Sam Barlow: "These men are Non-Persons, they never existed."

BARLOWS WANT A GOVERNMENT FUNDED HIGH SCHOOL

Some of the polygamists, including the Barlows, pulled their children out of high school at the Colorado City Academy to protest Marion Hammon. In their battle to gain complete control over the polygamists, they needed to force Hammon to leave the community, and that would shut down the Academy.

A year earlier the state had authorized the town to add ninth grade to their public school, and the Barlows knew that the following year the state planned to mandate that all students attend school through the 12th grade or until age eighteen. So they needed a high school in place to take over the students from the Academy. Everyone knew that teachers at the Academy were poorly paid. If the Academy were shut down, the teachers could work for the public high school and be paid better salaries.

So the Barlows decided to pursue legislation to get a public high school funded by the state. One requirement was that the school have 200 students. Even though most of the high school students were attending the Colorado City Academy, they were confident that in one more year, the Academy would be history.

Dan Barlow, a Colorado City School District Board Member, and Alvin Barlow, Colorado City School Superintendent, through the district Representative of the Arizona House of Representatives, sponsored House Bill 2238 into the Arizona legislature, which passed in January of 1984. This proposed Bill, if it won in the election in November, would allow the Colorado City School District to form a new High School District, and exempt them from assessed valuation requirement. The House and Senate made this exception and approved the bill. Governor Bruce Babbitt then signed it on May 4, 1984. If it won in the election, their new "parochial" high school would be funded by Arizona taxpayers.

THE POLYGAMIST COMMUNITY SPLITS

To finalize their assault on the character and lives of Marion Hammon and Alma Timpson, the Barlows would need Leroy to come back to church and personally tell the people that these men were "out of line" and that he was now going to take over and set things straight. Two months after the defiant "stand up" church experience against Alma Timpson, Leroy Johnson did indeed come back and stood in the pulpit to talk to the people.

On February 12, 1984, Leroy told the people that it had been six years since he had been able to talk to them, that he was not pleased with what the other Brethren had been teaching while he had been sick with the shingles. In this sermon, he said: "I was struck down in the early part of 1979. I had been called upon by some of my brethren to have the word of God changed in our Doctrine & Covenants, and this I objected to. Shortly after that, I was branded as a fallen prophet. I want to say a few words to these men who sit here on the stand today."

He turned to face J. Marion Hammon and Alma A. Timpson. "The Lord gave you men five and a half years to change your thinking on this principle of having one man holding the sealing powers in the earth at a time, and you have made a miserable mess of it by coming here and preaching over this pulpit that I was about to die because of my attitude towards the principle." Turning back to the audience he continued to speak.

"I know there are people here today who don't believe in me. They feel I have forfeited all my privileges to the Melchizedek Priesthood, (but) I am not afraid to speak. There is only one man at a time, and that is the way it has been throughout all the history of God's dealings with people, both in this world and the world before this one, and the world before that one. Only one man at a time holds the keys and power of the sealing power, and those who act during his administration are only acting under a delegated authority. That is what I told these men.

"I am coming back now. I am going to take my place, my position at the pulpit…. He (God) is going to come and visit this earth with great judgments. They have already started. He said 'In My house shall it begin.' It began with this council – six years ago this coming April. This Priesthood Council was broken up. Since then, we have suffered the death, first of Brother Richard Seth Jessop, and then Brother Guy H. Musser. So there are only four of us left. For about three and a half years, neither I nor Brother Rulon Jeffs were allowed to speak to the people. Why? Because I was stricken down and I couldn't speak, but I am speaking today. They (Hammon, Musser, and Timpson) would not allow Brother Jeffs to speak because he sustained me (in declaring the 1880 Revelation change)…. From now on, there will be nobody in the Priesthood Council only those who sustain the words of the Prophet Joseph Smith. There is only one man at a time that holds the keys of the sealing power while he lives."

With this sermon of February 12, 1984, he removed Hammon and Timpson from the Priesthood Council and told them they could no longer sit on the stand and address the people.

It was a sad day for many of the Polygamists. They believed beloved Uncle Roy had been badly deceived by a few men. They had assumed that God was at the helm and such a thing could never happen. Hammon and Timpson were probably the saddest of all. They believed their life's work was for naught. To see the "Keys wrested from the Priesthood" was almost beyond bearing.

The Barlow Boys were ecstatic. All their plans and hard work had finally paid off, and they were now in the position of power they had wanted for years. And because all faithful polygamists had been taught to humbly accept whatever the "prophet" said as divine law, they counted on the defrocked Hammon and Timpson to offer no resistance.

Men from left: unknown, Joe Jessop, Fred Jessop and Leroy Johnson with some of their wives.

Aerial view of Colorado City and Hildale in the 1970s.

Both photos show the LSJ Metting House under construction.

Fred Jessop leads the Pioneer Day (July 24) Parade.

Pioneer Day Parade Float.

Pioneer Day Parade Float.

Pioneer Day entrepreneurial effort.

Pioneer Day Parade Float.

Pioneer Day Parade Float.

Typical polygamist family.

Polygamist family trip to Lake Powell. They are not allowed to wear swimsuits.

Warren Jeffs in his late 30s. He is presently 48 years old.

11

A Town Divided

Marion Hammon and Alma Timpson were stunned. After decades of service to the community, Leroy Johnson had publically removed them from the Priesthood Council. After the initial shock, they spent several weeks trying to decide what to do. How could they remain in the community, given all that had happened?

Soon after that fateful Sunday meeting, several people went to see Hammon and Timpson to appeal to them not to abandon the people who still wanted the truth to be taught, the same truth that Wilford Woodruff had taught, the same truth the Doctrine & Covenants taught, that decisions must be made as a Priesthood Group, and not by one man. And they wanted to rid the community of the strange doctrine of worshiping a Man.

Hammon and Timpson gave it a great deal of thought and prayer. As several months passed they finally decided to meet with the people who wanted changes, both in the religious doctrine and in how it ruled the people.

On the night of May 13, 1984, three months after they had been dismissed by Leroy Johnson, Marion Hammon and Alma Timpson held the first Priesthood Meeting of what has come to be called the Second Ward. It was held at the home of Alma Timpson. News had spread about the meeting and openly lurking outside were two men writing down license plate numbers of the men inside. This gestapo tactic was meant to intimidate any man bold enough to openly support Hammon and Timpson.

These men still felt allegiance to Uncle Roy. They believed because of his old age and incapacitated condition, he had been swayed by the aspiring men surrounding him, and was not responsible for the action he had taken against Hammon and Timpson. Surely things would eventually be straightened out, they fervently hoped, thinking that if they would stand by the principles taught by the Priesthood Council, that eventually all would be made right.

But as the weeks passed, it became clear that Hammon and Timpson were permanently dismissed. Bitter feelings grew between the people of the two groups. Leroy said he wanted to just wash his hands of those who would not place their allegiance with him, letting them go their own way. But the Barlows wanted the "apostates" to move away, leaving everything behind, including any interest or control in any businesses, buildings, or property under their jurisdiction. All their plans and strategies were designed to force non-compliant men out of the community so they had complete control.

But Hammon and Timpson not only did not leave, they soon gained a group of followers urging them to stay and start a new group. And then the Barlows learned that Hammon and Timpson's Second Ward was holding religious meetings in the Academy building. They were furious.

In a strategy session, Leroy and the Barlows discussed the fact that the land on which the Academy was built belonged to the UEP, just like the homes of members of the community. Therefore they could "evict" the occupants. To have a building on their land used by an Apostate Group could not be tolerated. And they needed the Academy to close its doors so they would have the requisite number of students for their proposed new public high school. They quickly concluded that if Leroy would withdraw from the Board of Trustees of the Academy, it would somehow cripple the institution and it would have to close.

COLORADO CITY ACADEMY GETS NEW LEADERS

As luck would have it, a couple of weeks later on May 30, 1984, Marion Hammon called a meeting of the Board of Directors of the Colorado City Academy to discuss and plan what to do about the school. The meeting was held in Salt Lake City with the four remaining board members of the Academy: Leroy Johnson, J. Marion Hammon, Rulon T. Jeffs, and Alma A. Timpson (the original Board of Directors were the seven members of the Priesthood Council, of which three had died). Also attending was Cyril Bradshaw, Principal of the Academy. At the beginning of the meeting Hammon asked Leroy what he wanted to do about the school. Leroy hastily said, "I don't want anything more to do with it. I resign from the Board." At this, Jeffs spoke up and said, "I resign also."

Hammon then asked Leroy who he wanted to put on the Board to replace them. Leroy responded, "You only need one man," and pointing to Cyril Bradshaw, continued, "you can put Brother Bradshaw on." With that the meeting was over.

Cyril wrote up the minutes and two amendments to the Articles of Incorporation of the Colorado City Academy. The first amendment changed the life of the corporation from 25 years to perpetuity. The second amendment changed the number of trustees from seven to three: J. Marion Hammon, President; Alma A. Timpson, Member; and Cyril Bradshaw as Secretary. He filed the documents with the Arizona Corporation Commission, and then received a phone call from Rulon Jeffs telling him that he and Leroy had changed their minds and didn't want their resignations to stand.

It is clear what happened. The Barlows suddenly realized they had made a mistake. If Second Ward was moving ahead with their plans to be a separate group, they would have complete control of the Academy buildings. Such could not be allowed because it would adversely affect their plans for a publicly funded high school. Immediately they began telling people that Cyril had forged Leroy's signature of resignation. Of course, there was no written resignation ever in existence, only the minutes of the meeting where Leroy and Jeffs said they resigned.

To cover themselves, the Barlows had their attorney write a letter to the Corporation

Commission, telling them to not accept any documents that might come from Cyril Bradshaw. In the letter Mr. Ditsch states: "It is our understanding that a purported amendment to the Articles of Incorporation of Colorado City Academy has been submitted to your office…my clients constitute two of the four members of the corporation and were not notified of any meeting to vote on the amendment; therefore, it would appear that said amendment was not properly adopted.…"

When Cyril Bradshaw was contacted by the Corporation Commission, he called Leroy in Salt Lake City and recorded the telephone conversation, so he would have a record. The call was received by Mildred Barlow Johnson (one of Leroy's wives):

I (Cyril) asked to speak with President Johnson and he answered. I identified myself. He asked how I was doing. I answered that I was doing fine and asked how he was doing. He said "OK."

I then said, "I'd like to talk to you sometime about the Academy, if that's acceptable to you." He replied, "I've nothing to do with the Academy any more. I'm out of that."

Cyril: "President Jeffs gave me to understand that you wanted back in, so I–"

Leroy: "If you want to – if you run that Academy it will be separate from us – from our people."

Cyril: "All right, sir."

Leroy: "Under the direction – you've been operating under the direction of Brother Hammon and that's where you're going to be. If you want to go – be under my direction you're going to be there, so you can take your choice now."

Cyril: "All right, sir."

Next Rulon Jeffs called the Arizona Corporation Commission and told them not to accept the filed documents. When the Commission called Cyril Bradshaw and asked what to do, Cyril told the lady to ignore Jeffs call because he was acting without authorization, which she did.

Rulon Jeffs held an interesting position. He was now next in line after Leroy on the Council, he was the CPA who handled the Trust, he was the secretary of the UEP, and he had a large home in Salt Lake City where local meetings were held. Before Guy Musser died he would not allow Rulon to talk to the people even in his own home, because of his position on the 1880 Wilford Woodruff Revelation. Also, although the polygamists generally do not use tobacco, they do use alcohol and some to excess.

LEROY WARNS THE SLAUGHTER WILL SOON BEGIN

With Marion Hammon and Alma Timpson out of the way, and LeGrande Woolley and Louis Kelsch not interested, Leroy Johnson was the only council member in power in Colorado City. The deceased Richard Jessop had been a calming influence on Leroy, and with him gone, Leroy began to do some strange things.

The First Ward holds a priesthood meeting once a month on the second Sunday, where all male members over twelve years old attend. In the August 12, 1984, meeting Leroy stood before the congregation of about 400 men and called three men to the stand: Orval Johnson (Leroy's son), Joe Barlow, and David Zitting. Leroy said, "We are going to ordain these men Patriarchs. If there are any in the building who do not agree with what we are doing, then you can just leave." He then proceeded to perform the ordinations.

None of the candidates had been advised in advance this would occur and they were given no choice in the matter. Some in the audience disagreed with Leroy's tactics, but did not get up and leave. They did, however, stop going to his Priesthood Meetings. They knew the true character of Orval Johnson and Joe Barlow and believed them both to be immoral and dishonest.

The next week, on the 19th of August, 1984, Leroy made an alarming statement: "In two weeks the slaughter will begin. We are building coffins for the good people, but we will just dig a hole with a backhoe to put the wicked ones in." After the meeting a group of men went over to his house and anointed their cars and ATV's with consecrated olive oil, and then blessed them for protection. The dissidents began to discuss with one another the rampant rumors of a secret cache of guns and feared what might be in the works.

MARION HAMMON BLACKMAILED

Eleven days later, on August 31, Leroy called a Board Meeting of the UEP Trustees to meet at his home in Salt Lake City. This was the first meeting of this kind ever being called since 1946, because all UEP Business had been handled during Priesthood Council Meetings where all the Council Members were also UEP Trustees.

When Hammon and Timpson arrived at Leroy's home, they were surprised when a group of men met them at the door and informed them that Timpson could not attend the meeting because he was not, nor had he ever been, a Trustee of the United Effort Plan. Imagine the surprise to these two men. After thirty-five years of Timpson acting as a Trustee, all the documents filed in the Court Houses of the respective Counties declaring him a trustee, all the Priesthood Council Meetings where he took part in the decision-making processes of the UEP, and all the times it had been declared from the stand in public meetings that "all the Council members" were UEP Trustees, then at this late date the Barlows decided he was *not* a Trustee because his name was not on the original document filed in 1942.

Such arbitrary, self ruling reasoning had been practiced for a long time by men who knew they held people hostage. Looking at each other for a few moments and with no words spoken, Hammon and Timpson understood the situation. Timpson turned and left while Hammon went on in.

Present at this meeting were Leroy S. Johnson, Rulon T. Jeffs, J. Marion Hammon, and Warren S. Jeffs (Rulon's son). Leroy began the meeting by saying: "Brother Hammon, I called this meeting of the trustees of the United Effort Plan. The purpose of this meeting is to remove one of our members from the board of trustees, which is yourself.... We'll give you the opportunity to resign if you'd like. If not, we'll present it on the merits of the case."

Jeffs, speaking to Hammon said: "I have a form here prepared if you wish to resign. Or if you decline that, we will go into the merits of the case.... There's been no meeting of the board to appoint any more (trustees). But through the years, affairs of the United Effort Plan were discussed in Council Meetings." Jeffs went on to say that the *only* UEP business discussed in the Council Meetings was about property being transferred out of the trust.

Hammon asked: "Weren't they involved in receiving property?"

Jeffs: "No. Just transferred out."

Hammon: "What was transferred out?'

Jeffs: "Much was to you."

Hammon: "I don't ever remember any going out."

Leroy: "What about the Hatch property?"

Jeffs: "And the Beryl property."

Hammon: "Well, that wasn't in my possession long."

Jeffs: "It was used to pay your debts."

Jeffs then mentioned the Hirshi Ranch and the particulars of Marion Hammon controlling that property.

Jeffs: "I have all income tax records on which these transactions were reported."

Hammon: "That may be so. I haven't any records."

After some discussion about how their lawyer had counseled them that they could put Hammon in prison if they wanted, because of him losing UEP Property, it came down to Jeffs telling Hammon:

"I have a form of resignation if you want to sign it."

Hammon turned to Leroy, whose eyes were on the floor, and said: "And I thought we were brethren." Members of the Priesthood Council had covenanted before God long ago with one another that they would never take each other to a civil court, or use lawyers to settle differences they may have between each other.

Turning back to Jeffs he took the form of resignation and with much disgust said:

"I'd like to see it. I don't want to sign with my eyes shut."

After some discussion of being exempt of any liability on Hammon's part, he signed the document. He then said: "Well, it took thirty years to get here and just thirty minutes to leave. That puts an end to that. We had high hopes for this thing. We sat in there with Joseph (Musser) and John (Barlow).... There's been lots of conversation over matters. Some things had foundation in truth, but a lot was falsehood...the Lord must handle all men."

Blackmailing Hammon into resigning from the UEP Board of Directors under threat of prosecution was only a bluff. If there had ever been any court action on the matter, it would have been shown that it was Leroy Johnson and Rulon Jeffs who "lost" the property when they signed the deeds over to Marion Hammon, with no specific written instructions as to why they "gave" it to him.

The meeting ended. Hammon met Timpson before his return home and told him he too had been dismissed. When Hammon arrived in Colorado City, he met with his family and friends and told them that he and Timpson were both off the Board of Trustees of the UEP.

All of these men still held a secret hope that somehow the Lord would cause Leroy to come to his senses. Now they realized it would never happen. Fear and apprehension increased over the recent evictions. Many felt they had lost what little protection they had in the "balance of power" in the United Effort Plan. Now the Barlows could indiscriminately take away a home from anyone they wanted to run out of town.

BARLOWS STRATEGY TO SHUT DOWN THE ACADEMY

There were a few surprises in store for the Barlows. As they proceeded with plans to obtain their new public high school funded by the state of Arizona, they also waited for the "lease" on the Colorado City Academy UEP-owned land to run out. They needed the students and they needed the teachers. And they had other plans for the Academy buildings.

What they didn't know or remember was that the property on which the Academy buildings were built had been leased to the Academy with a "Warranty Deed" for the 20 acres of land, and that Deed was controlled not by the UEP, but by the Academy Board of Directors.

The Barlows wouldn't do their homework and learn about this until six months later on January 29, 1985, when the Academy Board decided to give former teachers Jack Knudson and Claude Cawley the deeds to their homes, located on the same acreage with the High School. The Board wanted these men to be responsible for paying their own taxes. When Jack Knudson received his deed, he immediately went to Leroy to find out what was going on, and he handed Leroy the deed. It is an understatement to say "that really kicked the lid off."

Meanwhile the election of November 6, 1984, went bad for the Barlows. The proposed new High School District at Colorado City was defeated at the polls because of a newspaper advertisement the Dissidents placed in a Kingman, Arizona, newspaper the day before the election.

The Barlows would not give up. In spite of the cost to the community, they planned a special election for March 1985.

SECRET CAVERN WITH GUNS

During all this, some of these Dissidents began mailing out anonymous letters to selected community residents. One of the letters told of a cache of guns that had been purchased by Louis Barlow and stored in a manmade cavern in the hill above Fred Jessop's home.

Those putting out the letter had done their homework well. The man who had sold the guns to Louis (in Los Angeles) told them that Louis had bought 100 SAM 180 semiautomatic .22 caliber rifles and hundreds of thousands of rounds of ammunition, and that the guns were stored in the manmade cavern behind Fred Jessop's house. He even sent them a list of the serial numbers. When the letter hit the streets, Sam hurried to the Washington County Sheriff at St. George and demanded that an investigation be launched to find out who was putting out the letters. He, of course, denied that there was a cache of guns stored in the cavern.

When those putting out the letter learned that Sam was "making a federal case" out of the issue, they went to the Sheriff and told him who was responsible for the letter. The Sheriff became very concerned about whether or not there were guns in the cavern and decided an investigation was in order. He did not reveal to Sam who put out the letter, but rather began asking Sam about the guns being in the cavern. One day when he was questioning Sam about them, Sam asked: "Do you want to come out and inspect the cavern to see if the guns are there?" The Sheriff just said "no," he didn't need to do that.

The next morning he showed up at Sam's office in Colorado City and told him he was there to inspect the cavern. This greatly unnerved Sam. It threw him completely off guard. He had supposed that when the Sheriff declined his offer to show him the cavern, he was not going to pursue the matter any farther. He began stammering, saying something about there were only two men who had keys to the cavern and they were both out of town. This did not satisfy the Sheriff. He wanted to go into the cavern and the more excuses Sam made, the more determined he became. Someone in Sam's office spoke up, not realizing that Sam was stalling, and told him that one of the boys who helped Fred in the storehouse had a key to the cavern. This destroyed Sam's alibi and there was nothing he could do but take the Sheriff and his Deputy to the cavern. The young man was located and did indeed have a key to the cavern. The group then made their way up to the cavern on the hillside.

The cavern is constructed with a corridor leading about fifty feet back into the mountain. There are rooms leading off from this corridor which are used for storing foodstuff and other necessities that would be needed in case of a survival situation. The first corridor leading to the right after entering the cavern leads into a room about forty feet in diameter. After entering this room one finds that it has been divided by a partition made of one-half inch iron bars. There is a gate in this partition leading into this part of the room. On the far side of this divided side of the room is a metal vault door with a combination lock. Behind this vault door is a room of about ten feet in diameter that was intended for storing the records of the polygamists. When the group accompanying the Sheriff reached the cavern, the young man with the keys opened the padlock on the gate at the entrance. He then led them to the room with the iron bar partition, which also had a chain with a padlock on it.

While he was unlocking the gate, the deputy who was with the sheriff looked through the bars and across the room to the vault on the other side. He observed that the vault door was not locked, but was opened about two feet wide. To his amazement, the young man who unlocked the gate immediately walked across the room and slammed the vault door shut. This action, needless to say, surprised the Sheriff and when he asked to see behind the vault door was told by Sam that Fred and his brother Virgil were the only ones in the community who knew the combination and they were both out of town. This flippancy on Sam's part greatly annoyed him, but he was now convinced that there were guns behind the vault door. He decided to contact the Alcohol, Tobacco and Firearms (ATF) agency to ask their assistance in the investigation of the situation.

The ATF sent an agent down from Salt Lake City to work with one of the Sheriff's deputies on the case and they spent about six months trying to uncover the facts in the matter. This investigation was a problem for the officers because they were unable to get Sam to cooperate with them. He would never come clean and tell them the truth. This was frustrating because local officers will always cooperate with federal officials unless they themselves have something to hide. It was concluded early on in the case that Sam did indeed have something to hide.

ATF FINISHES INVESTIGATION

After the six months investigation this is what they found out:

Louis Barlow had purchased 100 guns, but one had been kept by the man delivering them. The remaining 99 guns matched the serial numbers supplied to the Dissidents. When the ATF tracked down these guns, it was found that Louis had purchased them to put in survival kits he was promoting to sell to those who believed that "Doomsday" was soon to come. This particular venture was a complete failure and Louis eventually sold most of the guns back to the dealer he bought them from at a one hundred dollar loss on each gun. These guns were never stored in the cavern, but were shipped directly to Salt Lake City to a dealer that Louis was working with on the survival kits.

But there were an additional 50 guns in the same shipment that were never accounted for. These 50 guns were unloaded at Las Vegas from the companion shipment of 100 guns that were shipped from Los Angeles to Salt Lake. It was these 50 unaccounted for guns that, in all probability, were the ones that Sam was hiding in the cavern. There are two witnesses (young missionary boys) who unloaded the guns from the vehicle and put them in the cavern, who confirmed that the guns were there.

It seems that after six months of investigation, the ATF just became tired of the whole deal and decided to drop it. After all, the guns were legal guns and owning them was not a crime.

One thing was accomplished that benefitted the community. The Washington County Sheriff withdrew his authorization from Sam to act in any law enforcement capacity in the County and the State of Utah. He did this because he believed Sam was lying to him and he realized that if Sam ever had to make a choice between the civil law and his religious authorities, his loyalties would be with his ecclesiastical leaders rather than with the sheriff's department. For this reason, the Sheriff felt he could no longer trust him. This was the beginning of Sam losing his credibility as a reliable peace officer among the surrounding communities.

SAM BARLOW REMOVED

Sam Barlow had more troubles coming. In the fall of 1984, the man Fred Jessop supported for the Mohave County Sheriff lost the election. Joe Bonzelet, an unknown among the polygamists, won the election by a margin of about nine votes county wide. This was a very close race and the incumbent demanded that the votes be recounted, not once, but several times. The issue was finally settled and Mohave County had a new sheriff.

Unsure of his position, Sam Barlow went to Kingman. He arrogantly informed the new sheriff that in the past it had been the policy of newly elected County Officials to leave intact any of the appointees on the Arizona Strip. This, of course, included him as the Deputy Sheriff.

Sheriff Bonzelet was unimpressed. He disliked Sam's arrogance from their very first meeting. He asked Sam what benefit it would be to the Sheriff's Department to keep him on as deputy. Sam's reply, "We can give you 350 votes in any future election."

The Sheriff said, "I won without you. I don't need your votes."

Sam's attempt to politically "buy" the Sheriff with the votes of the polygamists only convinced him to no longer keep Sam as a deputy. Sam Barlow had been a full time deputy for about twelve years and it was not a simple matter to dismiss him. However, Sheriff Bonzelet came up with a plan that he felt would work. The deputies of the Mohave County Sheriff's Department were paid an hourly rate for the time they put in for the department. Any overtime hours (over 40 hours per week) were to be paid at the rate of time-and-a-half. The policy of the Sheriff's Department had been to not pay for this overtime, but rather let it accrue over the years, calling it "comp-time." The idea being to allow the deputies to use it when they needed occasional time off, yet still be paid. But some of the deputies accumulated far more comp-time than they could ever use.

By 1985, the payment of this comp-time to the deputies was a very heated issue. They were asking for a cash settlement from the county because their retirement was coming up. Sam was about eight years short of retirement, but when other deputies began demanding their comp-time payments, he thought he could collect for his, which had accrued to about 4,000 hours and amounted to a cash payment of about $70,000.

Unfortunately for tax paying citizens in the state, Sam Barlow's comp-time accrued from overtime hours "enforcing religious policy" among the young people of the community, and not in legitimate law enforcement duties.

When Sam Barlow approached Sheriff Bonzelet to ask to be paid for his comp-time, the sheriff told him the only way he could get paid was if he resigned from the department. He told Sam that if he would write a letter of resignation he would present it to the County Supervisors and ask that they pay him off. Sam proposed the idea that he could resign, collect his payment, and then go back to work for the Sheriff's Department for another eight years, then he would be eligible for the state's public safety retirement money. The Sheriff agreed that such a plan would be entirely legal and it could work, if all parties agreed to it. He was careful not to actually agree to the plan.

Sam Barlow wrote his letter of resignation. The Sheriff took the matter before the County Board of Supervisors and, after some heated debates, it was agreed to pay Sam off.

Six months later on May 15, 1985, Sam Barlow was paid almost $70,000 for his 4,000 hours of compensatory time, sick leave, and accrued vacation time. It is interesting to note here that the other deputies who had first asked to be paid for their compensatory time did not collect when Sam Barlow did. This caused some bitter feelings among those involved and there would be some lawsuits filed in an attempt to collect this money, using Sam Barlow's case as a precedent.

Sam was very pleased about his good fortune. A few months after he collected the money, he went back to the sheriff and told him he was ready to go back to work. The sheriff told him that he did not have a job for him and was not about to hire him back. This was a big shock to Sam. He thought that a deal had been made for him to come back to work. He threatened a lawsuit, but the sheriff stood his ground. Sam went back to Colorado City and no lawsuit was ever filed.

Sam's dismissal from the Arizona Sheriff's Department marked a milestone in the history of the polygamists at Colorado City. The young man who took his place as deputy was more careful than Sam had been about using civil authority to enforce ecclesiastical rules on the young people of the community.

HOMEOWNERS SEEK LEGAL ADVICE

Due to the increasingly aggressive actions of the UEP Trustees, a meeting was called by those who feared for their future. It was decided that an attorney should be contacted to determine what protections might be available. On October 3, 1984, a delegation met with Clay Huntsman, an attorney in St. George. They discussed the possibility of him handling negotiations between the UEP trustees and the dissidents, and asked what the retainer might be.

After this meeting of inquiry, two of the delegation went on to Kingman to search documents that Jeffs had filed. There were three documents: 1) the amended affidavit of disclosure, where the names of the beneficiaries of the United Effort Plan had been changed on November 12, 1983; 2) a second amended affidavit of disclosure dated September 5, 1984; and 3) a third amended affidavit of disclosure dated September 24, 1984. The second affidavit of disclosure stated that the original affidavit of disclosure filed in 1976 was in error wherein it listed Guy Musser, Richard Jessop, and Alma Timpson as trustees of the United Effort Plan. The third amended affidavit of disclosure stated that J. Marion Hammon had resigned as a trustee of the United Effort Plan and Fred Jessop had been appointed to replace him.

The Amended Affidavit of Disclosure had deleted over a hundred people as beneficiaries. One hundred and fifteen of the beneficiaries on the 1976 list were removed, while eighteen new names were added. Of the sixteen new names, six were Barlows, sons of the sons of John Y. Barlow, two were sons of a daughter of John Y. Barlow. Three of the names removed were of people who had been evicted. Fifteen of the names removed were of deceased members. And ten of the names removed were of women (widows). *The new list contained no names of women.*

This action of Leroy Johnson, Fred Jessop, and the Barlows had been conducted in total secrecy and it remained so for almost a year.

Half a dozen shocked men met again with Clay Huntsman on November 30 to discuss their options. He was given the thousand dollar retainer and agreed to write a letter to Rulon Jeffs, Secretary of the UEP, asking that they be "given" the deeds to the homes built on UEP property. The letter surprised the Barlows. They didn't think anyone had the courage to ask for their deeds. A hurried trip to Phoenix and a meeting with their attorney Charles Ditsch was immediately executed.

About forty of the Barlows and their supporters met with Ditsch on December 4, 1984. Leroy Johnson was in the meeting in his wheelchair dozing most of the time. It was Sam and Dan Barlow who did most of the talking. Sam was doing most of the dictating to the attorney as to what he should write in the return letter to Mr. Huntsman.

It was decided in this meeting that before they would answer Mr. Huntsman's letter, they should ask him for the names of those requesting their deeds. The names were provided: Andrew Bistline, Ben Bistline, Don Cox, Marko Dutson, David Stubbs, Cora Fischer, Mike Pipkin, and Jerry Williams. As soon as these names were revealed, a hate campaign was started against them. It began with Rulon Jeffs' announcement in a meeting on January 20, 1985, at Salt Lake City, about those asking for their deeds. Next Fred Jessop in a short paragraph in *The Twin City Courier*, a little one-page newspaper he printed about twice a month, stated:

> "Blessings lost sight of in these days has caused some to become embittered against the hands through which our community's solidarity has been made; and, like all others who have forsaken faith, they have resorted to the outside enemy help, for hoped for comfort. . . ."

Then, on February 10, 1985, Fred Jessop read a letter to the congregation in Sunday Meeting from Charles Ditsch, the UEP attorney, to Clayton Huntsman.

Fred gave the following short sermon before reading the letter:

". . . . But in the latter days, nearing the winding up scene of the great work of the Lord, the Prophet has been inspired to set up a system that would last, that would succeed. Now this system that will succeed eliminates men, but not the system. . . . And in as much as he has been challenged and threatened with courts of law. . .we have to use the tools unconverted people can be dealt with. So Uncle Roy has engaged the services and blessed the man, Charles Ditsch, to represent him through the law. And he's asked for this letter to be read.

"Now those opposing and challenging Uncle Roy have engaged the services of one Clayton Huntsman of St. George, through which they allege that they will break the United Effort. So this is the letter that Mr. Ditsch has sent to Mr. Huntsman."

Dear Clay:

. . . .My clients have had their way of life, their freedom and their families attacked before. United Effort Plan has helped them survive those attacks. It is not now their purpose or intent to take steps which will lead to the eventual dissolution of the United Effort Plan which is such an integral part of the life and values of a majority of the Colorado City residents.

Other than the two people who abandoned or were soon to abandon the residences they occupied, none of your clients have been asked to leave the homes they live in. This is not to say that they will not be asked to leave if they conduct themselves in a manner which is prejudicial to the spirit of the United Effort Plan, however, the same applies to all other residents of the United Effort Plan land whether or not they are on any list.

If your clients are intent upon causing a legal confrontation which will bring untold misery and suffering to the community because of the close relationship between many of the families living there, my clients will resist such actions for as long as it takes to protect and preserve their way of life. There will be no spoils for the victor in such a battle; however, my clients are convinced that they will prevail however painful the victory. Nonetheless, they are convinced, as are the vast majority of the people in the community, that a painful battle is far less painful than to consent to the destruction of the community and life they have worked for so hard and so long.

Very truly yours,   (Signed) Charles A. Ditsch

After Fred read the letter, Leroy Johnson spoke to the people from his wheelchair. His speech was halting and he paused several times to collect his thoughts before going on, excerpts of which follow:

"I feel very humble, my brothers and sisters, in trying to say something to you and I pray that the Lord will put in my mouth the words that He wants me to say. . . .

"They can take it or leave it. It was given to us by the Lord for a protection for his people, his saints and I'm not afraid to speak in defense of it, because every man who has taken up his arms against the United Effort Plan and against this work that I profess to be the head of, they're fighting against God, not me and they'd better look out because if they push it any farther God will lay a heavy hand on their shoulder, and I'm not afraid to say it, because I have the Spirit of God upon me and He's dictating my words at the present time. And they better take it. They'd better not push me any farther toward the wall, until I can get on my feet and get my people behind me and get the non-believers out of this place. I want them to get discouraged and leave right away, every one."

After this sermon, everyone in First Ward believed their homes had been under personal attack by those who hired Clay Huntsman. But hearing the letter from an "authority" such as Charles Ditsch gave them the illusion of certain victory. Their attitude in the community became one of righteous arrogance.

Meanwhile, those who finally discovered the new list mailed an open letter to all of the disenfranchised members.

"Many of us were invited into the community to help build this community and consecrated our time and talents toward that end, supposing that our efforts would be beneficial in helping establish the Kingdom of God. All that we brought with us was invested in the United Effort, by improving the lot that was assigned to us, by furnishing materials and labor in the various public works projects that the Priesthood sponsored, etc. Many of us consecrated lands and other valuable considerations to this same cause, fully considering that our consecration (which was expected by the trustees of the United Effort Plan) would resound to our good. . . . This amended document also amends the list of beneficiaries. The right column on the list denotes these "updated" beneficiaries. Please note that over 115 of the original beneficiaries have been deleted from the original list, and some others added. To which camp have you been assigned?"

NEW HIGH SCHOOL WINS THE VOTE

On March 5, 1985, the special election was held in Mohave County to form the new High School district, and it won. "Colorado City High School District No. 2" would have to remain in existence for one year. After that, it would be combined with the Elementary District, being called "Colorado City Unified District No. 14." Now all they needed to do was somehow regain control of the Academy.

USING LEROY TO MAKE MONEY

On March 4, 1985, a new grocery store was opened in Colorado City, after years of effort.

When the practice of living the United Order was changed from the members receiving their commodities from the storehouse to the issuing of script with which to purchase their necessities, a store was in operation at Short Creek. Originally called Short Creek Supply, it was operated by David Broadbent and he had changed the name to Dave's Mercantile. David Broadbent was a good business man, but he lacked capital to expand. When Hammon came back to the community in 1958, he removed David Broadbent and replaced him with a promoter, someone who could hustle credit to more abundantly stock the store.

Merril Jessop did a good job and the name was changed to General Supply. About this same time Truman Barlow took over the management of the service station just across the road from the store building. It was called J&B Service, where he sold gasoline and other automotive services.

Merril and Truman were first cousins, had grown up together and were very close friends. They operated these businesses pretty much as though they were one. The first mistake they made was allowing credit to the people. By the middle of the 1960s these businesses were so bad off that almost all the polygamist money was going outside the community. Marion Hammon, who was still in charge of running the affairs of at that time, could see a new program must be initiated.

They needed a new building, because the old building was too small for the expected growth of the community. To raise this money, the General Supply was changed to a co-operative. People were "invited" to buy $500 memberships in the Co-op; and at the end of the year, they would be "given" a dividend on any profit made. The plan succeeded in raising enough money to construct the store, but it was never completed. The General Co-op stopped in the late 1960s, because all the UEP projects were in a stalemate condition with the battle for control between Hammon and the Barlows.

In 1984, after Hammon lost his influence in the community, the Barlows again promoted the selling of memberships in the Co-op to raise money to complete the building and stock it with commodities. To help the project along, at one of their money raising rallies, they wheeled ninety-seven year old Leroy onto a platform in the parking lot of the new building, and with a forklift raised the platform into the air. They took turns standing on the platform with him, telling people in the crowd below that Uncle Roy wanted them to buy more memberships.

Of course, they were successful in raising the money they needed and on March 4, 1985, the new store was completed. On opening day they took in $52,000. The operation was turned over to Joe Barlow to manage, but he went broke in less than one year. Another plea was put to the people for money to bail him out and restock the store. It only took another year for him to go broke again. The management was then turned over to Art Blackmore, who made it a successful venture.

LEGAL ACTION TO GET THE ACADEMY

The Barlows began making threats and promising lawsuits if the property was not turned back over to the UEP. In a Sunday Meeting on June 9, 1985, Leroy said, "If Claude Cawley does not have his deed on my desk by Monday morning, he will be served a summons in a lawsuit on Wednesday." Immediately, Claude Cawley, who was given his deed by Marion Hammon, caved in under Leroy's threat and gave his deed back to the UEP. After the meeting, the Barlows left for Phoenix to see their lawyer to find out what could be done about getting the twenty acres back from the Academy.

MAIL FRAUD

Meanwhile, Fred Jessop was doing his part. The postmistress was holding up some of the first class mail. An affidavit was made by a teenage girl, who was living in the home of Fred

Jessop at the time, that the postmistress (one of Fred Jessop's wives) would bring several letters home each night and Fred would steam them open, read them, then have her take them back to the post office the next day where they could be delivered to their rightful owners. In a deposition of Fred Jessop in 1989, he testified that his wife had, indeed, been dismissed from working for the postal department for opening first class mail.

12

The Battle To Win

On August 2, 1985, Leroy Johnson and Rulon Jeffs filed a lawsuit in Arizona Superior Court, Maricopa County (Phoenix) against J. M. Hammon, Alma Timpson, and Cyril Bradshaw. The purpose of the lawsuit was to regain control of the Colorado City Academy.

This lawsuit claimed that the actions of the Board of Directors of the Academy taken in May of 1984 had been illegal because Leroy and Jeffs had not received a ten day notice that such action as their resigning was to take place in the meeting. The fact is that the meeting was not called to consider the resignation of these two members. The meeting was called to consider what to do about the coming school year in regards to the Academy operating.

Charles Ditsch, attorney for the United Effort Plan, claimed the amendments entered by Colorado City Academy with the Corporation Commission were "forged" by Cyril Bradshaw.

The matter never went to trial, because Hammon and Timpson would honor their covenants before God to never use the civil courts to settle differences among members of the Priesthood Council. If it had gone to trial, there is little doubt that it could have been proven that the Plaintiffs were not telling the truth.

In the settlement, the Defendants were to totally vacate the premises. No guilt of any wrongdoing on the part of the Defendants was acknowledged. This agreement was then signed by the parties involved and moves were made to carry it out. The premises were vacated and the Defendants took all the furnishings, storing it at one of their places of residence outside of the community.

On the night of September 10, the day that the Academy ceased to exist, some distraught students feeling bitter about losing their school, went to the premises and broke all the windows in the buildings. The Barlows goal of reclaiming all the students for their new publicly funded high school had succeeded.

ACADEMY DESTROYED

What would come later was devastating to students of the Academy and their parents.

In a Sunday talk several years later on May 1, 1988, Rulon Jeffs told his congregation "the Colorado City Academy was built by Apostates and all evidence of its existence must be destroyed." Fred Jessop followed by saying that the building must be torn down in order to "obey the Prophet." Plans were made for the following day.

The teachers and students of the new public high school were told there would be no school on Monday, so they could participate. They would provide a substantial work force for Fred to achieve his objective. Some of the teachers and many of the students in the public high school had spent much of their young lives attending the Colorado City Academy; many of them went about the task of "destroying it" with heavy hearts and tears in their eyes. One of the teachers, who had received his high school education at the Academy, finally had to leave, unable to endure what was happening.

In his justification of destroying the buildings of the Academy, Fred Jessop used the excuse that the buildings would no longer meet the fire code of the city and must be razed. This was not the truth, because the buildings were made of adobe and were virtually fireproof. All the halls were eight feet wide and the emergency exits were adequate. Even if the buildings were no longer needed for educational purposes, they could have been easily adapted to apartments, to be used for young couples as living quarters, especially since there had always been such a great need for homes in the community.

Such unnecessary destruction, of not only tangible property, but also of historical and cultural wealth, is one of the greatest detriments that a cult imposes on its members.

SECOND WARD BUILDS A CHURCH & SCHOOL

After losing the Academy, where they had been holding their church meetings, the Second Ward began meeting in Alma Timpson's home. Some of the Barlows began making threats that they were not going to allow them to hold religious meetings in homes built on UEP property. It became apparent that Second Ward had to build their own building, not only to have a place to worship, but to continue on with The Colorado City Academy. Many parents wanted their children in the Academy and not in the new high school with curriculum controlled by First Ward.

Realizing they would not be able to have a school for the 1985-86 school year, their goal was to have it in operation by 1987. This seemed an almost insurmountable task. Property would have to be obtained and a suitable building erected in only one year's time.

Master organizer Hammon stood up in a Sunday meeting held in the Timpson home and appointed a committee of four men to look for property in the area. He said, "Go buy some property where we can build a building that NO DAMN MAN CAN TAKE AWAY FROM US."

The committee began looking in the Cane Beds area to the south of Colorado City. One parcel about eight miles to the southeast seemed good, so they began negotiations. Just when they thought they could raise money for a down payment, Jack Knudson went to the owners and bought it out from under them. Jack didn't want the property, nor did the United Effort Plan. They simply wanted to keep Second Ward from getting it. Jack Knudson immediately sold the property to a firm in Idaho.

Next they began negotiating with Hilda Perkins, a widow who lived in Cane Beds, who owned about 1,000 acres adjoining the UEP on the south of Colorado City, but it was in the Cane Beds area proper. While these negotiations where going on, Sam Barlow went to see Mrs. Perkins. Taking her to dinner in St. George and using all his charm, he tried to dissuade her from selling her property to the Hammon and Timpson Group; he even offered her more money if she would sell it to the UEP. His scheme failed and she proceeded with the agreement she had made with Second Ward.

The Second Ward Group formed a land holding trust to hold title to the property. Unlike the United Effort Plan Trust, the new trust was organized only for the purpose of holding the property in trust until it could be deeded to those who would build homes on it.

They named it Deseret Land and Trust Company, and it was governed by a member board of trustees. Each trustee was to serve a three year term, after which he would be subject to an election by the members of the trust. The trust would serve no other purpose than to govern the disposition of the land. No claims or attempt was made to live a United Order. The money to buy the property would be raised by people putting money into the trust for that purpose. For every $1,500 paid, a member would be guaranteed one acre of land, and at some future time he would receive a deed. These people had learned from hard experience how to properly develop and implement their plans.

The price was $330,000 for the land, to be paid for over a three year period. Half of the money was to be paid up front with a clear title for one third of the property. The remainder was to be paid for in two more annual installments in equal amounts. Another third of the property would be titled to the trust at the end of the first year, the remaining property would be released at the end of the second year.

Money was raised for the down payment and the one third portion of land chosen for the clear title was on the extreme west portion of the property. This was the most suitable for agriculture purposes, so they could start a farming operation. The location chosen for the church/school building, however, was on the extreme eastern end of the property, and ground breaking for the building started right away.

Throughout the winter months of 1985-86, work on the Second Ward meeting house moved along quickly. They were holding their meetings at the Timpson home and, though some instances of harassment occurred, the winter passed with relative peace.

COLORADO CITY INCORPORATES

Meanwhile an effort was made by the Barlows to incorporate Colorado City. After the necessary elections and preliminary steps were taken care of, the Mohave County Board of Supervisors granted their petition to incorporate, with the actual incorporation taking place on September 17, 1985.

This was a major move for the polygamists. It gave them the advantage of receiving government money to make improvements in the community. It would allow them to have their own police force, something that they felt they needed because, since Sam's dismissal as County Deputy, they no longer had control of law enforcement in the area.

A Town Council was "appointed" with Dan Barlow as the mayor. Leon Johnson, who had been acting as part-time marshal for Hildale, was hired as Colorado City Marshal to work for both cities, his salary being split between the two municipalities. Sam Barlow was not involved in law enforcement, but questionable events would come about to put him back in the position.

THREAT OF VIOLENCE BY THE LEBARONS

In the spring Sam Barlow presented a letter he said he had received from a Leo LeBaron, threatening the life of Leroy Johnson if "he did not repent and join forces with Leo LeBaron." The letter was received in about March of 1986. It set a time limit for sometime in April for Leroy to "repent," or he would be assassinated.

> "On August 16, 1984, a warning was given the fundamentalist Mormons, that God would destroy you all suddenly if you did not answer to the call of repentance. You have chosen to mock God and his Most Awesome Patriarch, Ervil LeBaron. A new Patriarch, Leo LeBaron, will now carry out the order given by the Most Awesome Patriarch Ervil. There are those living in your community guilty of sins that can only be forgiven through the ordinance of Blood Atonement.

> "Do not suppose that God will not carry out his commandments, as given by his legitimate Prophet. His work of retribution will be carried out upon those not willing to repent and follow this true Prophet and Patriarch. This last warning is given to you. It is your duty to spread this warning among your people. Repent, or be destroyed by the sword of the Lord!!!

> "If no evidence of sincere repentance is observed by the 1st of April, 1986, this work of redemption will begin, starting at the head, even with your false Prophet, Leroy Johnson.
> "This work will be done by the 'Avengers for The Church of The Lamb'."

Sam turned the letter over to the Washington County Sheriff at St. George (Leroy Johnson lived in Utah) and asked for his help. The first conclusion the Sheriff considered was that Leo LeBaron was indeed Leo Evonick, a former disciple of polygamist Ervil LeBaron, the man who had Rulon Allred killed some fifteen years earlier. (Ervil had just died a few years earlier in the Utah State Prison and Evonick was claiming to be his successor). Sam had produced some letters that had been written earlier by Evonick where he had signed his name as Leo LeBaron. For these reasons the threat was taken seriously.

As a result, the newly incorporated town of Colorado City hired Sam as a deputy marshal to assist the Sheriff in the protection of Leroy. This was a slap in the face for those who had worked so hard to get Sam out of law enforcement.

Sam Barlow's first action was to invite television reporters in to cover this alleged threat by Evonick. He claimed it would be harder to carry out an assassination under the scrutiny of news cameras. He also volunteered to the sheriff that the polygamists did indeed have the guns that he had denied having just a short time before. Sam offered to arm selected members of the community to assist the sheriff in protecting their leader, but the sheriff declined his offer. This admission of Sam Barlow, however, destroyed any remaining credibility that he had with the sheriff.

All but one of the roads into town were barricaded off and sheriff deputies monitored everyone coming and going on this one opened road. For about a week, tension in the community ran high, the situation hitting national news. This caused much publicity for the polygamists, something they had always shunned, but when they felt they were in some kind of danger they were willing to call on "their outside enemies for hoped for comfort."

After a week of this excitement, Leo Evonick, the person being blamed for it all, contacted the Washington County Sheriff and denied having anything to do with the threat. After some investigation by the authorities, it was concluded that Evonick was innocent of any wrongdoing in the matter. He felt that Washington County had harmed his reputation and filed a libel lawsuit against the County. This lawsuit was never brought to trial.

About six months after the incident, he disappeared without any trace, and nothing has been solved on the case. The authorities investigating his disappearance concluded that one of the other LeBaron rival groups was responsible for his vanishing. This led the sheriff of Washington County to believe that the whole thing had been a hoax, with the finger of blame being pointed toward Sam Barlow himself.

Many believed he had created a situation where he would be called back to his position in law enforcement. Whatever the truth was, Sam Barlow had been hired by the newly incorporated town of Colorado City. The matter quietly faded away, leaving the sheriff highly embarrassed over the whole fiasco.

Once again Sam was the Chief Protector of the community. Immediately he restarted his religious campaign of "cleaning up the town" of wayward boys, both in Hildale and Colorado City.

SAM BARLOW BACK IN BUSINESS

Once again, citizens became concerned about Sam Barlow. They wanted to know who hired him and what he was being paid. They went to Hildale Mayor David Zitting and asked for a copy of the minutes where Sam allegedly had been hired by the Hildale Town Council.

The minutes from the Hildale town meetings were never produced, so the citizens contacted Lorin Webb, a reporter for *The Spectrum*, a St. George newspaper. He had to wait two hours for Fred Jessop to send the requested minutes to the town hall where Webb was allowed to read them. They did not contain anything about Sam Barlow being hired as a policeman by Hildale.

A written request was made to Colorado City for a copy of their minutes regarding Sam

Barlow. After much stalling, the minutes were produced. Sam Barlow's working in Hildale was addressed in the minutes of Colorado City. It was agreed that he would be allowed to act in Hildale as part of an interagency agreement between the two towns. There were no particulars about how much, if any, of his salary was to be paid by Hildale, only that he was allowed to "play cop."

The issue of Sam being certified in Utah to work as a peace office was then taken to the Utah State Police Academy (P.O.S.T) and it was only a short time until he was denied certification in Utah, due to his being a polygamist. Next they went to the state of Arizona.

A petition was drawn up with over 300 signatures to have Sam decertified in Arizona. The petition was sent to the Arizona Law Enforcement Officer Advisory Council (ALEOAC) at Tucson, Arizona.

Excerpts of the petition:

". . .Sam Barlow is a poor influence on the youth in the community, in that in his interrogations of the youth he always brings the conversation around to 'sex,' asking the party about his (or her) sex experience. If a young man were to admit to any sex activity, he would promptly be arrested and incarcerated or harassed until he left town. If he had a home, he would be evicted, the eviction being enforced by Sam Barlow.

"Please consider our petition to review certification of Samuel S. Barlow, and revoke his certification in Arizona."

Sent with the petition were affidavits by young people who had been treated by Sam as described in the petition. It was the beginning of a long battle between ALEOAC and Sam Barlow.

The complaints were mostly because of his harassment of the young people, his habit of taking them into his office and grilling them along sexual lines. At great difficulty a few affidavits were obtained from some of these juveniles, telling of his abuses. One affidavit from a fourteen-year-old girl describes how bad the problem was.

"The Affiant says that on_____, 1986, Sam Barlow picked her up as she was walking home at about 11:00 PM. He took her to his office, and after questioning her for over an hour about her sexual habits, asked her if she knew what 'giving head' was? He then asked her if she was guilty of 'giving head' to the boys he had been questioning her about."

CHIEF PROTECTOR LOSES CERTIFICATION

The ALEOAC, after reviewing the evidence and conducting interviews with the complainants, decided to hold an administrative hearing to determine if his certification should be withdrawn. Sam Barlow was notified of the hearing and given a grace period to protest it. And protest he did.

On May 4, 1987, Bill Jameson from the Arizona Attorney General's office and Hank

Shearer from ALEOAC went to Colorado City to meet with the complainants and discuss with them circumstances surrounding Sam's protest. Sam produced affidavits from the parents of the juveniles, denying their children's testimony. And one of the young men (who was now eighteen) recanted.

When the young man was questioned, he answered that Fred Jessop and Sam Barlow had told his mother, a school teacher in the public school, that if her son did not withdraw his accusations against Sam's conduct, she could lose her job. He felt he had no choice but to protect his mother.

Likewise with the other juveniles who had sworn out affidavits, their parents were told that if the charges were not withdrawn they would be evicted from their homes and forced to leave the community.

State Officials were stunned. In all their experience, never had they come up against an entire community so under the control of a religious cult. Being all the more determined to remove Sam from his position of control, they resolved to go forward. They felt their case had been weakened by the juveniles' renouncing of their complaints, but still felt they had an ace in the hole with the fact that Sam Barlow was a polygamist. He had taken an oath to uphold the Constitution of the State of Arizona when he was granted peace officer certification.

Since the Arizona Constitution states that polygamy shall forever be prohibited, he had violated his oath and for this cause only, they felt he should be decertified. If they could get him out on the polygamy issue, it would still get him out, even though the real reason was his unethical actions.

The UEP leaders contacted their Phoenix attorney Charles Ditsch and asked him to represent Sam Barlow against the State, and he referred them to Marc Cavness, a criminal law lawyer.

Sam Barlow considered Mr. Cavness a "real big gun" in the legal field, and it caused him to act in a very arrogant manner when dealing with the state officials. Standing on the premise that he had been called to his position by "one of God servants, Leroy Johnson," he proceeded to go all out to vindicate himself.

A meeting was set up between the complainants and Mr. Cavness, with Bill Jameson (the Attorney General's representative) present. The meeting took place in Colorado City, beginning on October 26, 1987. Mr. Cavness grilled these people unmercifully, with some of the interviews lasting nine hours.

At the end of these interviews, neither the State nor Mr. Cavness felt very secure in their positions. There was just enough evidence against Sam to worry Cavness, and Mr. Jameson could see that it would also be hard to prove the State's case. At this point a compromise was reached. Sam Barlow agreed to admit to being a polygamist, if the State would drop all of the other charges against him. The State agreed, supposing that since he was in violation of the State Constitution, it would be simple on this basis alone to have him decertified. Sam Barlow finally realized he could not win. To protect his reputation, he decided to step down. However, he did not do so for another year, remaining a peace officer long enough to be eligible for retirement.

THE BAPTISTS BRING CHANGES

Several Baptist preachers began talking with UEP dissidents about establishing a Bible study class at Colorado City, and said they would need a building to hold these classes. Since the Polygamists were using the school building for their religious meetings, the interested parties went to the local school board and asked for the same privilege, offering to pay rent. The school board said "no." This did not seem lawful to them, so they filled a complaint with the County School Superintendent at Kingman.

When the Superintendent learned that the Polygamists were using the school buildings for religious purposes and had been for the last twenty years, he gave the school board an ultimatum: the Polygamists could only use the school buildings for religious purposes for one more year.

This came as no little shock to Fred Jessop, the person who, since his appointment as UEP trustee, was managing the affairs for the Polygamist Group. He went to Leroy Johnson and told him they would finally have to build a church house. He was reluctant to give Fred the go-a-head on such a project, but Fred prevailed and got permission to construct a modest building for their religious meetings. A modest building indeed!

Fred got carried away, beyond the wildest imaginations ever envisioned by the Polygamists. The dimensions when completed were 200' by 270'. Work on "his masterpiece" began in early 1986. It was called the Activity Center at the beginning of construction, with hope of obtaining government money. But in a few months it was decided that to keep it under religious control, it would have to be built with private funds.

This was taking place the same time as the peace movement in the nation called Hands Across America, where people attempted to form a human chain holding hands from coast to coast. Fred Jessop copied this slogan, naming his Hands Across The Creek.

He had the people come out to a gathering and hold hands to form a human chain from Leroy Johnson's house in Hildale all the way to the new church building under construction in Colorado City, about two miles. For the privilege of standing in this line the participants had to pay Fred Jessop $2.00 each, the money to go for the new building.

For the $2.00, they were "honored" by seeing their prophet Leroy as he was driven by sitting in the rear seat of his van, attended by his nurse (one of his younger wives), and the ever present oxygen bottle and tubes to his nose.

This occasion occurred on June 12, 1986, his ninety-eighth birthday. It was a big enough event that TV news reporters covered it. Several people were interviewed by the media and asked why such loyalty was given to their Prophet. The answer: "Leroy is just like Jesus Christ to us." The one astounding news item that was heard and broadcast: "The Lord told Leroy he is not going to die, he will still be around for his 100th birthday."

The work on the new church building progressed enough by August 1986 that part of it could be closed in for meetings by the one year deadline. Prophet Leroy Johnson, who told his people he would not die until Christ returned at His Second Coming, did not see the completion of this building. He died on November 25, 1986. His funeral was a very elaborate affair, attended by more than 3,500 people. The new building would be dedicated in honor of Leroy Johnson and called the Leroy S. Johnson Meeting House.

LEROY JOHNSON PASSES AWAY

The funeral, held in the unfinished church house, was attended by TV reporters from Salt Lake City and Phoenix. The Polygamists were worried about the possibility of violence at his funeral, so armed Sheriff Deputies from both Washington and Mohave Counties were in the building, along with the Colorado City Town Marshals.

The highlight of the service was when Truman Barlow, in his eulogy of the Prophet, made this statement: "Everyone in this building will have to pass by Uncle Roy, getting his permission and OK before you can get into heaven." This statement seemed arrogant and out of place to the reporters scattered throughout the audience.

After the funeral, the casket was carried on a horse drawn wagon, driven by Leroy's oldest son Orval to the cemetery, a distance of two blocks. After the dedication of the grave, the casket was lowered into the ground and Leroy Johnson was buried. A gravestone was placed at the head of the grave stating: "Prophet, Prince Of Peace."

Leroy Johnson had told people that he was going to live until Christ's return at His Second Coming, that he would be here to turn the "Keys of Priesthood back to Him." He had set the date of this event to be in the year 1998. This is recorded in the minutes of a UEP Board Meeting held at the home of Rulon Jeffs in Salt Lake City on September 1, 1984. In this meeting Leroy was asked by Jeffs about making some amendments to the Trust Document, regarding its life limit of 100 years. Quoting from the minutes, Leroy said:

"We won't be under any trust law then. It will come under the jurisdiction of the Prophet Joseph Smith and his kingdom…. It's been tested pretty much in the courts. The lawyers are afraid of it so let's not make any changes. There is only 14 years and that won't be long. We'll be dealing with the Kingdom of God then."

Rulon then said: "It will be a very great pleasure to have you govern us in the millennium under the direction of Jesus Christ and Joseph Smith."

So Leroy had taken the position that he would need no one to take his place because he expected to be on the earth till the coming of Christ. Since this did not happen, Rulon Jeffs became the new Prophet.

Following their attorney's advice to keep all the legalities in place, the day following Leroy's death the UEP Trustees filed an amended affidavit, with the names of Trustees: Rulon T. Jeffs, Fred M. Jessop, Leroy S. Jeffs, James K. Zitting, Winston K. Blackmore, Parley J. Harker, and Truman I. Barlow.

CENTENNIAL PARK SECOND WARD LAUNCHES

Marion Hammon was recognized by Second Ward as the new leader. The work on their church house was progressing and on September 27, 1986, the first meeting was held in their new building. It was a program to honor the day Prophet Joseph Smith allegedly came to John Taylor in 1886, commanding him to keep plural marriage alive. This was the centennial of the occasion, September 27, 1886, from which the name for their town was derived: Centennial Park City.

A motivating force behind the construction of the building for Second Ward had been the Williams' boys, who were interested in activities for the young people such as ball games, dances, plays, etc. Their understanding was that those in leadership positions such as Marion Hammon and Alma Timpson would allow the building to have a gymnasium constructed inside with basketball backstops, and where plays could be put on. The boys worked hard with John Williams, the superintendent over the works.

Within a year the building was completed and religious meetings were held, and the Colorado City Academy began holding classes. The basketball court was completed, sports activities were held, and some plays and dances. A baseball diamond was constructed on the grounds of the chapel and baseball games were enjoyed by young people, boys and girls mixing together.

BASKETBALL, PLAYS, & DANCES STOPPED

An unfortunate situation developed within Second Ward not too long after the new building was completed. Alma Timpson had called a new priesthood council and placed his son, John Timpson, at the head of the council. And one of Marion Hammon's sons, Jed Hammon, was also appointed a council member, and he was placed in charge of the Colorado City Academy. Surprisingly unlike his father, it was not long until Jed would no longer allow basketball games, plays, or dances to be put on in the building that was constructed partially for that purpose. And the baseball games outside on the baseball park were stopped because the boys and girls were playing together. Jed Hammon did not like this. Many of the followers of Marion Hammon eventually broke off as a result and began meeting together in the home of their friends.

MARION HAMMON PASSES AWAY

Marion Hammon passed away on August 28, 1988, a broken hearted man. Just prior to his death he conceded that his only Priesthood power and calling was to keep Plural Marriage alive. The control he had imposed on the people had merely been because of his ego, in trying to prepare them for entering the Kingdom of Heaven. His funeral was held the next Sunday at the new chapel in Centennial Park.

Prior to the funeral, Fred Jessop told First Ward members that they "could not go onto the Devil's ground," thus many of Hammon's friends and family members could not attend the service. He was laid to rest in a family plot in the front yard of his home, where several members of his family were buried.

Several months later, Fred Jessop attempted to have him and the other buried members in this plot, dug up and moved off the United Effort Plan property. His scheme was foiled and the attempt to evict the dead, was not carried out.

CONTROVERSY SPLITS THE GROUP

The death of Marion Hammon left Alma Timpson as the leader of Second Ward. He felt very much alone under the weight of this calling, and in the spring of 1989, he called Frank Naylor as a High Priest Apostle to assist him in the Priesthood Council. Later in 1990, Timpson would call others and fill up the Council.

Frank Naylor had been called as a patriarch by Leroy Johnson a few years before and was readily accepted by Second Ward into this position. Naylor was very conscientious and performed well in his new calling, too well in fact, for his act of living by his conscience rather than by an edict of "his file leader," would soon cause problems.

When Timpson approached Apostle Naylor for his endorsement in calling John Timpson (his own son), and Claude Cawley (his stepson) into the Council, Naylor was vehemently against it. He had problems with the moral character and honesty of both, and he felt there was some nepotism involved.

In the next year Alma Timpson called four more men into his Council: Clayne Wayman, Jed Hammon, Joe Knudson, and Lorin Zitting, thus filling it up to the required number of seven.

This action on Timpson's part caused another split in the Priesthood Work. When Frank Naylor learned what he had done, his conscience would not allow him to support Timpson's actions. According to what he had been taught, Timpson had violated the most important rule that governed the calling of new members into the Priesthood Council. In his frustration, he went into the hills to pray and ponder what he should do.

One of his sons owned a mountain cabin near Duchesne, Utah. He took part of his family and moved there. He did not want to be bothered; he just wanted to be left alone to consider what he was supposed to do. Others who did not agree with the actions of Timpson sought Naylor out to convince him that because Timpson had acted contrary to Priesthood Doctrine, Naylor was duty bound to step up and lead those who were willing to follow him. Naylor, very reluctant, told these people that he had received no revelation to lead anyone, that he just wanted to be left alone and let the Lord work things out. These people persisted in trying to persuade him that it was his duty to come home and lead the people.

He was finally convinced and after a few months came back to Centennial Park to take up the duties of presiding over the flock. By the fall of 1990, he began holding regular meetings, alternating between Centennial Park and Salt Lake City, meeting every other

Sunday respectively. About one half of the Second Ward members in Salt Lake City chose to follow him while only about ten per cent of those in the Colorado City/Hildale/Centennial Park area gave him their allegiance.

Frank Naylor was an honest man. He tried to lead his followers in a righteous manner. He eventually moved to Missouri with some of his followers, but still maintained a small group in Salt Lake City and Colorado City. Because he had not ordained any successor to his priesthood authority, members of his group were putting pressure on him to ordain someone, in case he should die. He flew back to Salt Lake with the intention of ordaining his son, Frank Jr., to be his successor as the leader of the group. When he arrived in Salt Lake City, he was very tired and needed to rest a few days. He took one of his young wives and they went into the Uinta Mountains where his sons owned a cabin. He decided to spend a few days there, resting up. The first night he had a heart attack and died. His young wife was the only person with him and she had to drive several miles to find a telephone to notify someone. Since he had failed to perform any ordinations, this line of the alleged Lorin Woolley priesthood ended. Prior to his going to Missouri, he had ordained Ivan Nielson as a bishop, giving him authority to perform marriages for time only, but not authority to seal for time and eternity.

In 1998 Alma Timpson died, thus leaving his son, John Timpson, as the leader of Second Ward, and he is still the leader in 2004.

THE UEP LEADERS MOVE FORWARD AGGRESSIVELY

The instructions of Leroy Johnson before he died, of not ordaining any new members to the Priesthood Council, placed Rulon Jeffs in an awkward position. He could not call any new apostles and had only his First Counselor Parley Harker and Second Counselor Fred Jessop.

As the work on First Ward's new church house progressed, there were a few setbacks, one being several cubic yards of walls that had to be torn down because of an improper mix of concrete. This created an unexpected expense for Fred Jessop. When he asked Rulon Jeffs for money to help, Jeffs went to the people.

On October 25, 1987, Rulon Jeffs asked his followers to donate more money for the new building. He told them that for every $1,000 turned in for the new church house, that contributor would be guaranteed a ticket to Jackson County, Missouri (where the Second Coming was to occur) and title to one lot there. This promise was believed by many and they went to great sacrifice to contribute.

UEP DOUBLES ITS LAND ASSETS

Also in 1987, the UEP bought land to double its acreage. A 700 acre farm southwest of Colorado City had been homesteaded by Louis Black, one of the early settlers in the 1930s.

He had sold it to a couple of Newel Steed's sons who were promoting and selling circle sprinkler systems. They were in debt to the Farm Home Administration (FHA) for close to two million dollars on the project and were unable to meet the payments. In a couple of years the FHA foreclosed and took possession of the farm, called The Berry Knoll Farms. It was put up for auction, requiring a minimum bid of $1,800,000. There were no bidders. In another year or so it was put up for auction again, with a lower minimum. There were still no bids. The desperate FHA asked for any offers it could get to try and negotiate a deal. Fred Jessop and Rulon Jeffs sent Parley Harker to contact the FHA.

First Counselor Parley Harker was a successful farmer living in the Beryl, Utah, area. Because he had previous dealings with the FHA, he had credibility with their agents. He was able to arrange a deal to purchase the Berry Knoll Farms for $330,000, a fraction of its worth, and the purchase included the sprinkler systems, wells and pumps.

The money to buy the farm was raised by asking the people to donate to the United Effort Plan. Rulon Jeffs told the men of his Group in a Priesthood Meeting at the new church house one Sunday morning, "If you want to be a member of the United Effort Plan, just donate a thousand dollars toward the purchasing of the Berry Knoll Farms." His plea was honored and over $330,000 dollars was raised. Parley Harker paid the FHA and the farm was acquired.

One little problem developed. Ron Bradshaw, the man who had drilled the wells and furnished the pumps, had not been paid for some of them. When he could not collect his money he went to the farm and proceeded to pull some of the pumps to try and recoup part of his losses. Sam Barlow showed up with some of his Goons and threatened Mr. Bradshaw with physical force if he did not leave the premises. Mr. Bradshaw then filed a claim in the District Court at St. George to either collect the money owed him or repossess his pumps. The day before the scheduled hearing was to take place, his pickup truck was burglarized while parked on the street in St. George and his briefcase, with all the documents and papers, etc. necessary to prove his case in court, was stolen, thus he was unable to prove his claim.

With the acquiring of the Berry Knoll Farms and Sam Barlow's orchestrated evictions, the new leaders of the UEP became quite arrogant and bold. They decided to legally secure their position that its members/beneficiaries could hold no equity claims on the homes they had built on UEP property. In other words, they could be evicted from the homes they had built and paid for, based on any reason thought valid by the leaders.

"TENANT AT WILL" PUTS HOMES AT RISK

Now under the counsel of an attorney, the Trustees were learning how to legally bring to pass what they wanted. In a UEP board meeting held in April of 1987, a letter was drafted and adopted by the board and was signed by Rulon T. Jeffs, President of the United Effort Plan. About 600 letters were sent by regular mail and sixty-five were sent by certified mail. The ones who received the certified letters were those whose names had been removed as beneficiaries in the 1976 affidavit of disclosure:

TO ALL OF THE PEOPLE RESIDING UPON UNITED EFFORT PROPERTY

As you know and as was explained to you in great detail when you became residents on the property, you are tenants at will and reside on the property at the pleasure of the trustees.

Some or all of you have made improvements (homes built) to the property with the consent of the administration of the trust. Any such voluntary improvements become part of the land and are not to be moved, transferred, demolished or assigned to other occupants without the consent of the United Effort Plan.

The above policies have been in effect since the creation of the United Effort Plan and this letter is not intended to represent any change but merely the written clarification of pre-existing policy.

Since the incorporation of both Hildale and Colorado City certain additional formalities are required before any improvements can be constructed on the property located in either of those towns. The United Effort Plan is most supportive of the governments of those towns and desires that all of the ordinances with regard to building permits and inspections be complied with.

The United Effort Plan will require that building permits be issued by the proper authority before any improvements are made on the property. As the residents have no authority to improve the land without the consent of the United Effort Plan, the application for each building permit must be approved by one of the agents for the Plan and we are notifying the towns of Hildale and Colorado City of this fact and request that they not grant any building permit unless approved by an agent.

The agents of the trust authorized to approve applications for building permits are the trustees of the Plan: Rulon T. Jeffs, Fred M. Jessop, LeRoy S. Jeffs, Parley J. Harker, Truman I. Barlow, James K. Zitting and Winston K. Blackmore.

The willful violation of any of the policies set forth above shall constitute grounds to terminate the violator's *tenancy at will* on the property.

> Very truly yours,
> (signed) Rulon T. Jeffs

The term Tenant At Will was an unknown phrase to the people receiving the letter. Mike Pipkin looked it up in *Blacks Law Dictionary* to try and understand what had been "explained to you in great detail" before they had built their homes on Trust property.

TENANT AT WILL – One who holds possession of premises by permission of owner or landlord, but without fixed term. Where lands or tenements are let by one man to another; to have and to hold to him at the will of the lessor; by force of which lease the lessee is in possession. In this case the lessee is called "Tenant At Will," because he has no certain nor sure estate, for the lessor may put him out at what time it pleases him.

The interpretation of "tenant at will" sent a chill through the people who had been removed from the beneficiary list. They knew they needed legal advice, so a committee was sent to Washington County Attorney Paul Graf. He told the men it was evident what the Barlows intentions were. He also told them that if the letter was not protested in court, that in a very short time the statute of limitations would run out and those living on trust property would in indeed become Tenants At Will. He told them they had two choices, 1) start looking for somewhere else to live, or 2) file a court action against the UEP Trustees contesting their actions.

Several approached Judge Burns of the 5th District Court for advice. His answer was about the same as Paul Graf's. The choices for the disenfranchised beneficiaries looked bleak. At any moment these families could receive an eviction notice. Not knowing what else to do, they filed a protest with the respective county recorders in St. George and Kingman:

"We the undersigned beneficiaries do hereby register our protest and objection to being summarily disfranchised as Beneficiaries of the United Effort Plan Trust without any official notification. As evidence we submit Exhibit A; Affidavit of Disclosure dated Oct. 16, 1976 listing the undersigned as Beneficiaries, Exhibit B; First Amended Affidavit of Disclosure Dated Nov. 12, 1983, disfranchising undersigned without official written or oral notification, in violation of Arizona Revised Statutes #14-77303."

DEFENDING THEIR HOMES

If they wanted to stay in their homes, it looked like the only safeguard would be to file a lawsuit.

Several of the people who received the Tenant At Will letter contacted an attorney in Victorville, California, who professed to have some knowledge concerning Cults and their questionable use of Trusts to defraud innocent and gullible people. A meeting was set up with Mr. Ruskjer and on July 28, 1987, four men traveled to meet with him.

He offered to call Rulon Jeffs, acting as a mediator, in an attempt to negotiate some kind of settlement for the disenfranchised UEP members. And in this telephone conversation, Jeffs seemed to be willing to work out some kind of resolution in order to avoid going to court. This was good news to those who had driven to California for the meeting. Their euphoria was short lived. In about thirty minutes time Mr. Ruskjer received two telephone calls. One from Dan Barlow and, soon after, another one from Truman Barlow.

After talking to these two men, two things were clear to him: 1) Rulon Jeffs was not the one making decisions for the United Effort Plan; it was the Barlows, and 2) There would never be any settlement made with the "apostates." The visitors returned home, determined to look for an attorney to take the case.

Finding an attorney became a real challenge because several asked for a $40,000 retainer before they would even look at the case, and they would need a guarantee of at least $100,000 a year for what could last for as long as eight to ten years.

160

When the Barlow Cabal initiated the Tenant At Will document, they knew what it would cost for anyone to challenge them in court. None of these people legally owned their homes, they had donated any extra money they earned to the UEP, who was regularly asking for donations, and they paid tithing money each month. These people had few assets and the Barlows knew it.

But as sometimes happens, unexplained events transpire. A son of one of these disenfranchised members was working for a legal firm in Salt Lake City, Woodburys & Associates. They dealt mostly in real estate matters. At this particular time the owners of Woodburys & Associates were considering launching out into ligating real estate disputes. When the young man from Colorado City told them about the dilemma of his parents and others in the community, the owners of the firm became interested.

On August 9, 1987, the young man took the information to his employers and, after going over the details, they seemed confident about taking the case. A meeting was set up to meet with twenty-five of the disenfranchised members. This meeting was held on August 23, 1987, in a private home in Colorado City.

John Kesler was the representative for the firm. He proposed that it would be easier and cheaper to break the disenfranchised members out of the UEP than try to break up the Trust. He thought that if they could raise $100,000, they would be able to force the UEP Trustees to make an out of court settlement. He recommended that thirty people raise one thousand dollars each up front money and then guarantee a monthly payment of a hundred dollars a month until the case was terminated, which he estimated would take one year.

Mr. Kesler went back to Salt Lake City and began the work of preparing a questionnaire for each of the would-be plaintiffs to fill out, detailing their individual circumstances.

The lawsuit was filed in The Utah District of the Federal Court in Salt Lake City on November 25, 1987. UEP attorneys would use many legal delaying tactics to make the effort more expensive.

FIRST WARD HIDING ITS ASSETS

Just prior to Leroy Johnson's death in 1986, Joe Barlow convinced him that many of the assets of the UEP should be hidden in a new Trust to hide them from any who might apostatize and attempt to claim equity on their homes. With Uncle Roy's permission, he formed a new trust called The Majestic Security Trust. Only three people were named in this trust, Leroy Johnson, Joseph I. Barlow, and Fred Jessop.

When Leroy Johnson died, he was replaced by Rulon T. Jeffs on this new trust. When the lawsuit was filed in 1987, Joe Barlow and Fred Jessop were already in the process of transferring assets of the United Effort Plan into the Majestic Security Trust. In a deposition of Rulon Jeffs taken on May 4, 1989, he testified that he had known nothing of this new trust until a few days before this deposition when Jethro Barlow, son of Joe Barlow, had handed him a paper showing the names of several companies that at one time were owned by the United Effort Plan, but had been changed over to other ownership.

These included the Majestic Security Trust, General Cooperative Association, Twin City Improvement Association, Colorado City Improvement Association, Cooperative Mercantile Corporation, General Rock and Sand, General Concrete Products, Danco Manufacturing Co., Color Country Care Center, J&B Service, and Cooperative Financial Service.

When the lawsuit was filed, it stopped the transfers, thus thwarting the plans of Joe and Fred from gaining complete control of the United Effort Plan assets. If this lawsuit had not been brought against the UEP at this time, the Barlows would have completely owned and controlled all the property of the United Effort Plan.

13

Case Against The United Effort Plan

In a memorandum, filed on August 30, 1989, by the attorneys for the plaintiffs, in support of a motion before the court for partial summary judgment, one of the attorneys summarized the situation of the Polygamists at Colorado City. He compiled the following from the depositions and interrogatories of the UEP Defendants.

Defendants would have this Court believe that Plaintiffs' causes of action against the Municipal Defendants are mere 'window dressing, meritless, specious and brought in bad faith.' Such statements could not be further from the truth and only tend to show the cavalier attitude of Defendants and reaffirm that the communities of Hildale and Colorado City were established for and are totally controlled by one religion.

Hiding from its own past following the 1953 raid, the community of Short Creek ultimately changed its name to Colorado City. The town of Hildale, Utah, was created in 1962 and the Arizona side of the community continued to be called Colorado City. Finally, in 1985, Colorado City was finally formally organized.

There is little question but that Fred Jessop, with the support of church leaders in the past and sustained by the individual Defendants in the present court action, controls virtually every aspect of the communities of Hildale and Colorado City. Wearing almost every conceivable hat while at the same time professing that all he does is church work, Fred Jessop sits as a chameleon as the Hildale town clerk, and effectively pulls strings to control and manipulate all that goes on in the communities. Although their motives may have been pure in the beginning, those in control have become rapacious as they have sought to protect what has transpired in the past from those who have trusted them and preserve their power base in the future. Those motives have led to involvement in the municipalities through rubber stamp town councils and the law enforcement threat of Sam Barlow who was hand picked by church leaders to carry the fear of color of law in enforcement of all of their actions.

Sam Barlow was hand-picked to be 'the man that the priesthood has set as a police officer in this place' in the very words of the former prophet, Leroy S. Johnson. Sam has fulfilled that role by doing the bidding of both President Johnson and now of President Rulon T. Jeffs. Operating in uniform as an employee of Mohave County working in the Colorado City area prior to its formal incorporation and as a Deputy Marshall within Colorado City; and through cross-deputization, acting as a law enforcement officer in the town of Hildale, Sam has brought law enforcement authority to the whims and dictates of the prophets.

Sam was raised in his formative years from ages 12-19 by Leroy S. Johnson and in the waning months of President Johnson's life, he accompanied Leroy Johnson when he traveled until Leroy Johnson's death.

If righteous conduct needed to be enforced, Sam was there. If 'Uncle Roy' needed to see you about your behavior or the behavior of your children, Sam was there in uniform to deliver the message. If you were being evicted from trust property, Sam was involved in serving Notice upon you. His mere presence created an aura of fear in those who felt they may not be entirely in harmony with the teachings or practices of the dominant religious group.

The actions of Defendants and their subordinates have gone well beyond constitutional limits and have severely impacted the lives of Plaintiffs.

Plaintiffs specifically deny that the evidence available in this case involves either non-specific conclusory allegations or claims against a non-party. Plaintiffs do not deny the facts set forth in the memorandum of Defendants in this action, (they) do however specifically deny that Defendants' list of facts is complete. The municipal Defendants appear to have overlooked the significant additional facts brought forth in the form of testimony over the past four months to which this Memorandum shall draw the Court's attention as follows:

TESTIMONY OF FRED M. JESSOP

Facts gleaned from the Testimony of Fred M. Jessop, Hildale Town Clerk:

1. Fred M. Jessop is the Vice President and a Trustee of the United Effort Plan, Bishop and a counselor to Rulon T. Jeffs in the presidency of the Fundamentalist Church of Jesus Christ of Latter Day Saints, the Town Clerk of Hildale, the President of Twin City Waterworks, the editor of the Twin City Courier, the only locally printed newspaper of general circulation in the area, as contemplated trustee of the Majestic Security Trust, which was created to hold the businesses of the United Effort Plan at a distance from those who may apostatize from the Work, the President and a member of the board of the Colorado City Improvement Association, the owner of the town's only health center, the owner of Standard Supply, the owner of the only restaurant in town, the Early Bird Café, the general election Judge for the Town of Hildale, and the municipal election Judge for off year elections. Further, during the last 50 years, Mr. Jessop testified that he has labored full time in church work.

2. In response to a question as to how he has time to do all the things that he does Fred Jessop said 'My whole interest is to carry out the expectations and hopes and aspirations of Brother Barlow (John Y.) and Brother (Leroy) Johnson and Brother Jeffs and all Presidents of the Fundamentalist Church of Jesus Christ of Latter Day Saints. And all these other incidental so-called hats are just in a day's work. That's the way I view it.'

3. During all the time that Hildale has been in existence there has never been more than

one name listed on the ballot for the election of mayor or the election of each position as a member of the town council.

4. Fred Jessop was recommended to become town clerk in 1962 by Marion Hammon, 'since I (he) had been doing some clerical work for the prophet it was recommended that I continue in that capacity when this was done.'

5. Fred Jessop admitted that he was the principal person involved in preparing the list of beneficiaries to attach to the 1983 Amended Affidavit of Disclosure which list deleted 117 names which appeared in 1976 as beneficiaries, This was done while Fred Jessop was serving as town clerk of Hildale but before he was appointed as a trustee of the United Effort Plan.

6. Fred Jessop admitted that he composed the list of beneficiaries which appeared on the original Affidavit of Disclosure filed in 1976, again, years before he was appointed as a trustee of the United Effort Plan but while he was serving as Hildale Town Clerk.

7. Fred Jessop, in talking about his close relationship with the prophet, Leroy Johnson said, 'I felt like I was his right hand man.'

8. Fred Jessop admitted to having the seal of the United Effort Plan for 'quite a long time;' doesn't recall if he used it, but said it was 'just my nature to take care of things.' That was long before he became a trustee of the United Effort Plan and while he was serving as the clerk of Hildale.

9. Fred Jessop holds a private Sunday School in the Hildale town office building 3 times a month for between 150 and 200 people.

10. Sam Barlow, Deputy Town Marshal of Colorado City, was sent by Fred Jessop as the representative of the Fundamentalist Church of Jesus Christ of Latter Day Saints to negotiate with Mohave County officials for the tax exempt status on the Church's meeting house in February of 1988. His negotiations led ultimately to the recording of Notification of Dedication to Religious Use.

11. Fred Jessop has personally leased a building and land owned by the United Effort Plan to the United States Postal Service for a post office in Colorado City and has personally taken the lease money over the years for his own subsistence in amounts in excess of $5,000.00 per year.

12. In his own personal financial statements filed with 3 different banks in 1983, Fred Jessop claimed (and) showed ownership in his own name of his home located on United Effort Plan property with a value of $185,000.00.

13. Fred Jessop prepared a financial statement for the Stockman's Bank in 1983 identifying as his occupation 'City Manager.'

TESTIMONY OF RULON T. JEFFS

Facts gleaned from the testimony of Rulon T. Jeffs the President of the United Effort Plan and the President of the Fundamentalist Church of Jesus Christ of Latter Day Saints:

1. Fred Jessop, while serving as town clerk and also as a trustee of the United Effort Plan signed as many as 7 different lease agreements between the United Effort Plan and individuals living in the town of Hildale wherein the United Effort Plan leased property to those individuals for a period of 5 years for the purpose of obtaining funding from the Community Development Division of the Utah Department of Community and Economic Development. Each of the leases was signed by Fred Jessop, the Town Clerk, as 'Authorized Representative' of the United Effort Plan, without the knowledge of its president, Rulon T. Jeffs, and without a resolution of its Board of Directors.

2. Rulon T. Jeffs, when he was secretary of the United Effort Plan, gave the seal of the United Effort Plan to Fred Jessop, at Fred's request long before Fred Jessop became a trustee of the United Effort Plan but while Fred was serving as a clerk of the town of Hildale. The seal was to be used on legal documents signed by the United Effort Plan requiring a seal.

3. The beneficiary list attached to the 1983 Amended Affidavit of Disclosure which list deleted 117 names from the 1976 beneficiary list, was prepared by Fred Jessop while he was serving as town clerk and before he was appointed a trustee of the United Effort Plan.

4. The United Effort Plan leased real property to Hildale for the city offices on the 16th of April, 1979 for a 49 year term at $100.00 total rent. There was no meeting of the trustees or a resolution of the trustees to authorize the lease.

5. The Colorado City town hall sits on United Effort Plan land without a lease agreement and is a 'Tenant at Will' on United Effort Plan property.

6. All those who chose to follow J. Marian Hammon and Alma Timpson into what has now been termed as the 'Second Ward' stand in jeopardy of being asked by Rulon T. Jeffs to leave the homes they now occupy.

7. Sam Barlow, while drawing a salary from Colorado City, has served as an agent for the Fundamentalist Church of Jesus Christ of Latter Day Saints in helping it throughout this lawsuit.

8. Rulon T. Jeffs as president of the Fundamentalist Church of Jesus Christ of Latter Day Saints and the United Effort Plan has relied on Sam Barlow to answer interrogatories and requests for production of documents in his own behalf and on behalf of those entities.

9. Rulon Jeffs turned over all of the original files of the United Effort Plan to Sam Barlow at the beginning of the lawsuit 'because he was actively working with our attorneys in preparing the case.'

TESTIMONY OF LYNN COOKE

Facts gleaned from the testimony of Lynn Cooke, Mayor of the City of Hildale from its inception in 1962 until 1985, a period of 23 years:

1. The appointment of Lynn Cooke as Mayor was initially suggested by a member of the Priesthood Council, J. Marion Hammon.

2. During the 23 years Mr. Cooke was Mayor of the town of Hildale he was never opposed in an election due to influence of the United Effort Plan and the Priesthood Council.

3. 'Marked, stray ballots' already filled out were left 'promiscuously around the polling place' in Hildale elections and if citizens asked to see them that request would be made to the election judge.

4. Fred Jessop 'was in fact the real mayor.'

5. Once 'Uncle Fred' stated his opinion, no one on the town board would vote against him.

6. 'Uncle Fred' would often tell the town council what Leroy Johnson (the then President of the Priesthood Council) wanted them to do.

7. Fred Jessop was a mediator between the Priesthood Council and the town Council.

8. Fred Jessop was the mediator between the President of the United Effort Plan and the town Council.

9. As Mayor, Lynn Cooke was asked to pre-sign checks and give them to Fred Jessop 'in blank' to be used by Fred Jessop to pay town expenses.

10. Lynn Cooke, as Mayor, had agreed with Lorin Webb of the Spectrum (local newspaper), in St. George, to send the Spectrum the agenda of the town meetings and minutes of town meetings. He was overruled by Fred Jessop who said that the Spectrum would 'have to go to Court to get them.'

11. In a meeting Cooke had in the home of Fred Jessop, Fred required that they get Sam Barlow on the telephone to have him participate in their conversation regarding Lynn's discussion with Lorin Webb.

12. Fred Jessop holds his weekly Sunday School meeting for friends and family in the Hildale City offices without payment of rent therefore.

13. J. R. Williams was removed as a Justice of the Peace because he had a difference of opinion with Fred Jessop regarding Priesthood Order.

14. Cooke was recently selected by Hildale as a recipient of the largest single grant in Hildale from the Community Development Division of the Utah Department of Community and Economic Development for work on his home in May of 1989. The amount of the grant was $10,000.00. In order to qualify, Mr. Cooke had to demonstrate to the Department of Community and Economic Development that he had at least a 5 year lease from the United Effort Plan on the property on which his home was located. The lease between Mr. Cooke and the United Effort Plan was delivered to Mr. Cooke by David Zitting, the Mayor of Hildale, in May of 1989. The lease had been pre-signed by Fred Jessop on behalf of the United Effort Plan. Mr. Cooke refused to signed the lease as it was drafted because in two portions thereof it required him to acknowledge that he occupied his property as a tenant at will. Mr. Zitting, the mayor of Hildale, then offered to strike out those portions of the lease if Mr. Cooke would sign it. Those portions were whited-out by Mr. Zitting. At no time did Mr. Cooke have any negotiations with any of the Trustees of the United Effort Plan regarding the lease but only with the Mayor of Hildale and another

member of the town council who were in Mr. Cooke's home acting as agents for the United Effort Plan.

15. Sam Barlow, who was not a citizen of the town of Hildale, would occasionally attend town council meetings and express his views. In at least one instance where a decision had already been made by the council, Fred Jessop responded to a late comment by Sam Barlow and recommended that the matter be opened up for further discussion. The decision of the council was changed.

16. Until last year, the audits of the Town of Hildale were always performed by Rulon T. Jeffs, a trustee of the United Effort Plan, and now its president and president of the Priesthood Council, or in later years, by Mr. Jeffs' son, LeRoy Jeffs, who is now a trustee of the United Effort Plan.

17. Lynn Cooke often cast his vote against his will, 'to make voting on the council unanimous because of the psychology of being united, of being one heart, of one mind…it was ecclesiastical psychology that has come down to us through the years, and now I realize that some of the things I permitted and tolerated and participated in wasn't quite right. When they refused to cooperate with me, according to their promise, and send Lorin Webb a report, why I just backed clear out. I didn't say anything to them. I just never did show again.'

Note: In the preceding testimony by Lynn Cooke, there is an underlying story to be told. Fred Jessop needed favorable testimony from Lynn Cooke's deposition about his experience as the Mayor of Hildale. It appears Fred attempted to buy him off by "giving" him the grant money of $10,000 from the Utah Community and Economic Development Agency that Hildale was eligible for in 1989. Each year a cash grant was given to Hildale for improvements on homes owned by poor people. Since the United Effort Plan "owned" all the homes in Hildale, the only way the money could be obtained was for a five year lease to be given to the person Fred chose to receive the grant. The new mayor of Hildale, David Zitting, presented the lease to Mr. Cooke to sign. Mr. Cooke was not happy with the clause making him a Tenant at Will, so the clause was eliminated. But Lynn's testimony about Fred's "running of the town board" was a help to the Dissidents. When Lynn's five year lease was up in 1994, Fred attempted to have him evicted. He would have succeeded had not Rulon Jeffs interceded.

TESTIMONY OF SAMUEL S. BARLOW

Facts gleaned from the testimony of Samuel S. Barlow, law enforcement officer from 1968 to the present:

1. Sam Barlow lived in the home of Leroy Johnson from the age of 12 until he got married at age 19.

2. Sam Barlow finished only the 8th grade; he was able to be certified as a law enforcement officer in the State of Arizona without ever attending high school only by

providing an honorary diploma given him by the Colorado City Academy; he was a range Deputy in the State of Arizona in the Colorado City area from approximately 1968 to 1974 and was cross-deputized in the State of Utah during that same period of time as a Deputy Sheriff serving in the Hildale area; he became a Deputy Sheriff in the State of Arizona in approximately 1974; he traveled with President Leroy S. Johnson in the last months of Leroy S. Johnson's life, however he refused to testify from whom he received compensation at that time; and began serving as a Deputy Marshall for Colorado City in December of 1986.

3. In the summer of 1985 Rulon T. Jeffs set up a meeting with Leroy Johnson, J. Marion Hammon, Alma Timpson, Truman Barlow and Fred Jessop at Rulon's office in Salt Lake City. The meeting was an effort to settle a controversy over the Colorado City Academy and the property on which it was located. Sam Barlow testified that 'I was there at the request of the South Salt Lake police department,' indicating that he had told the police department that, 'there had been some threats – not from the persons involved in this contention – but some threats against Mr. Johnson.' He further said, 'and my communications to the police was that I didn't anticipate any violence but I didn't want to be negligent in my responsibilities. And I was not a rookie.'

4. While traveling with Leroy Johnson, he kept his 'duty revolver' in the car with him and carried a radio.

PLAINTIFF'S ATTORNEY SUMMARIZES THE CASE

The admissions of Defendants and testimony set forth herein as well as the affidavits demonstrate a simple, yet terrifying, reality. There is one dominant religious group with strict hierarchical lines of authority which completely controls the municipal government authority in both Hildale and Colorado City that, with threat of force and under color of law, systematically deprives Plaintiffs of their constitutional rights.

Plaintiffs, who live in those cities and surrounding areas, exist in fear of speaking or acting freely and have no effective redress for grievances which would challenge the civilly imposed opinions and acts of discrimination on Plaintiffs of the leaders of Defendant Fundamentalist Church of Jesus Christ of Latter Day Saints and Trustees of the Defendant, United Effort Plan who are effectively the same individuals. Plaintiffs, who have different religious and trust beliefs, could solve the problem simply by leaving, as these religious leaders want them to do. Yet (under the protection of law), there should be no place in these United States where an individual or a family cannot live peacefully and enjoy the religious and civil diversity and freedom guaranteed by the Constitution.

As adherents of particular religious beliefs, individual Defendants had the right to isolate themselves in a sparsely populated part of the country to practice their religion as they saw fit, but they now have no right to ostracize, persecute and expel people with different beliefs who arise within their midst, particularly by force or through color of law.

The incredible reality is that particularly Defendants Fred M. Jessop and Samuel S. Barlow do not even try to conceal their scorn for the principals of separation of church and state while being employed by the municipalities. They flaunt the subservice of their public duties to their religious allegiance through their current testimony and actions.

Fred M. Jessop is acknowledged generally as running the affairs and being the power behind the scenes in Hildale. For instance, Lynn Cooke, Mayor of Hildale from its inception in 1962 until 1985 stated in his deposition that Mr. Jessop's power and influence in Hildale were such that during all the years Mr. Cooke was legally the Mayor, Mr. Jessop 'was in fact the real mayor.' In other words, he controlled the policy decisions and affairs of the City.

It is clear that Mr. Jessop plays a major and possibly a dominant role in the temporal affairs of the Trust and Church Defendants and the City of Hildale. Fred M. Jessop is the Vice President and a Trustee of the United Effort Plan, a Bishop and a counselor to Rulon T. Jeffs in the presidency of the Fundamentalist Church of Jesus Christ of Latter Day Saints and the Town Clerk of Hildale. He is the President of Twin City Waterworks, the editor of the Twin City Courier, the only locally printed newspaper of general circulation in the area. He is a contemplated trustee of the Majestic Security Trust, which was created to hold the businesses of the United Effort Plan at a distance from those who may apostatize from the Church. He is the President and a member of the Board of the Colorado City Improvement Association, the owner of the town's only health center, the owner of Standard Supply and the owner of the only restaurant in town, the Early Bird Café. Mr. Jessop serves as the general election Judge for the Town of Hildale, and the municipal election Judge for off year elections. It is extremely revealing that Mr. Jessop testified that in spite of these public and business designations, he represents that, in fact, he considers himself to be laboring full time in church work.

Mr. Jessop is frank about his true purposes and intentions as the de facto mayor of Hildale, 'town clerk, town auditor,' election judge and man in charge of other corporations and enterprises. He testifies without equivocation that his 'whole interest is to carry out the expectations and hopes and aspiration of Brother Barlow and Brother Johnson and Brother Jeffs (all presidents of the Fundamentalist Church of Jesus Christ of Latter day Saints). And all these other incidental so-called hats are just in a days work. That's the way I view it.' In other words, his publicly acknowledged loyalties and priorities at all times are to promote and protect the best interests and the objectives of the church leaders. His duties and responsibilities as a public official of Hildale are at all times sacrificed at the altar of his primary loyalty to these religious leaders and Defendant Church.

This loyalty to his religious leaders creates a constant state of fear among Plaintiffs and a dramatic chilling effect on Plaintiffs and other residents of Hildale and Colorado City, who hesitate, for fear of reprisal, to insist on their constitutional rights that the Defendants regularly trample upon.

One of the most blatant and arrogant shows of inappropriate allegiances to the leaders of the Defendant Fundamentalist Church of Jesus Christ of Latter Day Saints and the

Defendant United Effort Plan and against Plaintiffs can be found in Mr. (Sam) Barlow's behavior during this lawsuit. This full time Deputy Town Marshal of Colorado City, sworn to impartially uphold the law of the land and the rights of citizens, is spending virtually all of his time at the tax payers' expense leading the defense of the lawsuit for all the Defendants and functioning as an agent of the Church and Trust Defendants. Defendant Rulon Jeffs, the president of Defendant Church, admits that Sam Barlow is functioning as an agent of the Church in this lawsuit and that Mr. Jeffs as the current leader of the Church has relied on Sam Barlow to prepare answers to interrogatories and requests for production of documents for the Defendant Church and Trust. Rather than being an even handed enforcer of the law and impartial protector of the rights of the citizens in the municipalities where he is employed, he has been taking notes and functioning as a paralegal to attorneys for all Defendants. He is publicly acknowledged by most of the parties to the lawsuit as the wholly committed armed enforcer, defender and lieutenant companion of the Defendant Church and Trust and their leaders.

Just as much as Defendant Barlow is the official enforcer of the dictates of the Defendant Church and Trust leaders under color of law, the Defendant Church insists on strict recognition and sustaining support of Defendant Barlow as the Church's armed enforcer.

Defendants make no attempt to conceal their insidious disregard of the principal of the separation of church and state. The actions of Defendants Jessop and Barlow are merely pertinent examples of how the Defendant municipalities of Hildale and Colorado City are permeated by the influence and control of the Defendant Church and Trust and its Defendant leaders.

The governmental practices of the Defendant municipalities, Hildale and Colorado City, are permeated with a strong underlying endorsement of the majoritarian religion. Dissenters are ostracized, discouraged from political office as well as deprived of material benefits such as continued patronage in their livelihood or the peaceable enjoyment of their homes.

Hildale and Colorado City are small and the customs and practices of these municipalities are manifested by a close group of people related by both blood and position in the hierarchy of the Defendant Church and Trust. The Plaintiffs and even Plaintiffs' legal counsel are taking their lives in their hands to oppose these religious and trust leaders who preach a doctrine of blood revenge against those who oppose them and who have armed lieutenants functioning under the banner of civic authority.

UEP ATTORNEYS RESPOND

This characterization of the status of the community and the United Effort Plan was answered by the attorneys for the UEP Defendants in a lengthy memorandum that ended with the following paragraph, the only intelligent claim made in the whole memorandum:

Plaintiffs' effort to portray the United Effort Plan as some sort of selfish 'CABAL' does a base injustice to the selfless struggle of the Trust Defendants and the majority of the community for more than 50 years to create a just, prosperous, and religious community surrounded by the harsh beauty of the Arizona Strip. Quite simply, Plaintiffs' goal in this action is to destroy the 'community chest' and to distribute the 'loot' among themselves, so as to satisfy (in part) their own greed.

The attorney for the UEP relied solely on strategy to prove that the United Effort Plan was created by a "Church" for religious purposes and that all activities of the United Effort Plan were really activities of this "Church," thereby *claiming they did not have to furnish any of the information the Plaintiffs were asking for in the discovery process.* They cited the Religious Freedom Restoration Act of 1993. The only evidence they could produce proving they were a "church" was the document Sam Barlow had filed in the Mohave County Court House, claiming tax free status on the new church "building" that was under construction.

Depositions on the lawsuit began with the lawyers for the defendants taking Marion Hammon's on June 27, 1988. Throughout the lawsuit, Scott Berry, attorney for the United Effort Plan, would accuse the plaintiffs of all belonging to a "religious schism" that had broken away from the "true Church," and were just trying to "steal the UEP assets."

With the beginning of these depositions, the lawsuit got under way. It would be longer than seven years before it would be resolved, costing both sides an enormous amount of money, totaling over $3,000,000 counting the expense on both sides, with the UEP defendants' portion amounting to about five times what the plaintiffs would pay. There would be suits and countersuits.

DISSIDENTS RUNNING OUT OF MONEY

With the arrival of 1989 the dissidents had to face a financial decision. Their attorneys had speculated that the lawsuit could be over within a year, believing that the UEP defendants would use reason, come to the bargaining table and negotiate a settlement. This did not happen and at the end of the year and the $100,000 dollars paid to attorneys, the lawyers wanted to negotiate a new contract for more money.

By now the Plaintiffs could see the position they were in, that of paying their attorneys much more money than any of them had ever dreamed, or trying to settle with the defendants on their own. A few of them did just that. The response they received was shattering.

They were told by the Cabal that they would be evicted, and a counter suit would be filed against anyone who would drop out of the lawsuit, taking any and every asset they might have. When they were reminded that none of the plaintiffs had any assets, the response was that a judgement would be levied against them, just for the purpose to embarrass and punish them for "fighting against the Priesthood."

These plaintiffs were in a position of riding on a tiger; they could not get off for fear of being destroyed.

The Defendants (UEP) had asked the judge to delay the court proceedings to allow the attorneys of both sides to attempt a settlement agreement. As it turned out, their request was only another attempt to drag the proceedings out a little longer, *hoping to run the plaintiffs out of money.*

During these negotiations the Defendants refused to consider any offers from the Plaintiffs. The only "compromise" they offered in return was that they would allow the Plaintiffs to move out of their houses in peace, not filing a countersuit, if they would withdraw the present lawsuit and reimburse the United Effort Plan their attorney's fees.

Finally the Judge ruled that the UEP was a religious entity and the Plaintiffs appealed the ruling to the Federal Court in Denver. It would take almost six years for that court to rule.

APOSTATES TO BE EVICTED

On June 16, 1993, Federal Judge Bruce Jenkins dismissed an appeal by the Plaintiffs, ruling that the disputes did not come under the jurisdiction of the Federal Court. This was quite a shock to the plaintiffs because the case had been in the Federal Court for *almost six years.* The Defendants were ecstatic, and claimed to their people that this ruling was a great victory, that the lawsuit was over and they had won.

The Barlows expected the plaintiffs to just lie down and give up, but that did not happen. Their attorneys drew up a new complaint to be filed in the District Court at St. George in Washington County, narrowing the issues down to simple equity claims rather than claims of fraud. It was filed in Washington County, Fifth District Court on July 26, 1993.

But because the UEP Defendants were not served until a couple of months later, they had concluded in error that the Plaintiffs could not afford to continue. Their confidence running high, they moved forward aggressively to get rid of the apostates.

Chief Protector Sam Barlow announced in a meeting of First Ward that the *apostates must be removed from the homes* belonging to the Priesthood and he proceeded to read off a list of forty-five names. Certified letters were sent August 13, 1993, to those no longer worthy to stay in the community. It stated in part:

". . . . The Fundamentalist Church recognizes a solemn obligation to preserve and advance the religious purposes of the United Effort Plan. To meet that obligation, those individuals who voluntarily and publicly reject the Priesthood must be disassociated from the United Effort Plan, and from its parent, the Fundamentalist Church (see Section 84, verses 35 through 44; Also see the *Teachings of the Prophet* Joseph Smith, pages 155 and 156). To allow otherwise would result in compromise of the effort to implement the eternal principles of the United Order, as restored by revelation through the Prophet Joseph Smith.

"The United Order effort, to be acceptable to God, must be directed by the President of the Church and the holder of the keys of the Holy Priesthood. President Rulon T. Jeffs holds those keys and that responsibility at the present time. Those who have altogether turned away from the President and his teachings are apostates, and must be excluded from the congregation of saints whose labor and devotion give visible expression and vitality to the principles of the United Order.

"Your words and actions over a period of many years show that you have forsaken the Fundamentalist Church and the teachings of President Johnson and President Jeffs. The Fundamentalist Church hereby recognizes your withdrawal from the congregation of saints, and declares you disassociated from the Fundamentalist Church, including the United Effort Plan.

"For this reason, the Fundamentalist Church declines to accept any further donations or offerings from you."

On September 3, 1993, these same people were sent a second letter:

"The Fundamentalist Church of Jesus Christ of Latter Day Saints, including the United Effort Plan, has always deemed all improvements (building a home or improving it) to land owned by the United Effort Plan to be religious consecrations to the Fundamentalist Church, freely donated to support the work of the Church. . . .

"As I stated in my letter to you dated August 13, 1993, the Church has recognized your withdrawal from the congregation of the saints, and declared you disassociated from the Fundamentalist Church, including the United Effort Plan. The Fundamentalist Church declines to accept offerings or contributions from you, or any improvements which you may desire to make to United Effort Plan property.

"Because donations or offerings from you are not acceptable, you are hereby directed to not make any substantial improvement to the property at the above mentioned address. A substantial improvement is any improvement in which the cost of materials and/or labor exceeds five hundred dollars.

"*Until arrangements are made for your relocation*, you are directed to maintain the property in its present condition, and to take reasonable care to protect the safety of the persons residing on or using the property." (Italics added)

Threats made in a 1985 sermon by Leroy Johnson were included in this "eviction notice" by Sam Barlow to intimidate his victims. The UEP leaders were stunned when they learned that the Plaintiffs attorney had filed a new lawsuit in the State Court at St. George.

14

The Trial Begins

Utah state statutes only allow about one year for cases like these to be resolved. Thus it would not allow the UEP to drag the case out with ridiculous motions.

Judge J. Philip Eves divided the issues of the lawsuit into two different phases, seeking to determine two facts:

1) whether the plaintiffs had any equity in the homes they had built and,
2) whether or not they were beneficiaries of the United Effort Plan Trust.

Depositions began on December 6, 1993, at St. George, Utah. These depositions began with the lawyers for the defendants taking Plaintiffs' testimony first, then took testimony from the Defendants. The most significant factor surrounding these depositions is the involvement of Sam Barlow and his role in the case.

Sam Barlow was not a defendant, but he was appointed by Rulon Jeffs to be the official representative for the United Effort Plan. A person who was a non-party to the lawsuit read Sam's deposition and commented: "The only truthful statement Sam made in the whole deposition was at the first part where he stated his name."

One of the first questions asked of Sam: "Do you receive any income from the Trust (UEP)?"

Sam: "I don't receive any income from the Trust. The Trust has no income. I don't receive any income from the church either, but the church does allow me to continue on my mission that sustains me on my mission."

The next set of questions dealt with whether the UEP was indeed a Church or was simply a Business trust. The UEP was still claiming they were and always had been a Church, and that anything donated to it was given freely. Sam's answers were such that Scott Berry, attorney for the defendants, jumped in and answered for him.

Mr. Berry: "Obviously Sam, you haven't gone to the Trust or the president of the Trust or the president of the church and asked him to give you guidance on the questions that Reed is asking you. So, the fair answer in the case would be that you don't know what the Trust claims."

This statement by Scott Berry is so inconsistent that it causes one to ask why Mr. Lambert, attorney for the Plaintiffs, did not stop the depositions and insist that if Sam Barlow were going to answer questions for the trust that he indeed go to the president of the trust and the "church" and learn what "his guidance on the questions" were. This little stalling act on the part of Sam and Scott is a prime example of how the deposition of Sam Barlow went.

A few more examples:

Question: "My question is, does the Trust agree that the trustees are liable to the members for acts that they might commit in bad faith?"

Answer: "They (fundamentalists) do not believe the priesthood leadership over them are accountable to the members of the church."

Question: "Okay. If a trustee were to do something in bad faith…would the Trust agree that they could be subject to the civil laws?"

Answer: "Absolutely."

Going to the trust document, Mr Lambert then asked:

Question: "Let's look on page 6…Short sentence. 'Evidence of membership shall be shown in the books of the association.' Have such books been maintained by the Trust?"

Answer: "Maintained by the church."

Question: "And there is a book that records membership?"

Answer: "No, records of baptisms into the church."

Question: "Does the Trust admit that at some point the plaintiffs were members of the Trust?"

Answer: "They were at one time regarded as members of the church."

Question: "Were their names ever noted in the book of the Trust or shown in the books of the association?"

Answer: "I think you'll find that they were baptized and recorded as being members of the church, designated the Fundamentalist Church."

The reader is reminded that there was no Fundamentalist Church organized until several years after the Plaintiffs initiated the lawsuit, so Sam's answer is a falsehood. None of the Plaintiffs ever belonged to any so-called "Fundamentalist Church."

Question: "Are you aware of anything that you have seen that is a separate record, not a baptism record, but a separate trust record of membership in the Trust?"

Answer: "No."

Question: "(From the trust document) A membership certificate may, in the discretion of the trustees, be issued to each member. My question is, were such certificates ever issued?

Answer: "I don't think they were, I have never seen them."

Question: "Rulon Jeffs testified in deposition that there were some – there was some kind of agreement and he testified that it was possibly a dozen pages long."

Answer: "I've never seen that."

Then Sam was asked why Leroy Johnson and Rulon Jeffs gave Marion Hammon the deeds to certain large parcels of land.

Question: "The Trust at one time conveyed real property to Marion Hammon and I realize Marion Hammon lost that property."

Answer: "I don't know entirely what arrangements was made, but I know quite a degree what arrangements were made. And it was not giving the property, it was allowing him to use it to establish a contingent in Idaho which he wanted to do…when it didn't work out, they called him into an accounting for that and asked him to step down as a trustee."

A major falsehood told by Sam Barlow in this deposition dealt with whether members who donated property to the trust were told at the time where they could read a copy of the trust document. He claimed they were told that the document was filed in the courthouses of two counties and they could find it there if they wanted to read it. But, of course, they were *not* told the documents were recorded in the courthouses. In fact, spiritual coercion was used. They intimated that the document was sacred and anyone asking to see it was demonstrating a lack of faith.

He was asked: "How would the trust define support of the priesthood?"

His answer was, "Speak well of the leading brethren and to not do things that damage the faith of others and cause dissension or division." Another prerequisite was that you give generously of "your treasure."

He was asked about the accusation of the defendants that the plaintiffs had violated the standards of moral conduct of the trust.

Question: "Does the Trust contend that any plaintiff has violated one of the standards of moral conduct that it referred to in the excerpt we have read?"

Answer: "That's set forth for the reason that moral standards are important and not for the reason we want to go and ferret out somebody's misbehavior, but certainly gambling and lying and misrepresenting and filing non meritorious, fictitious lawsuits is outside of the purview of the gospel plan."

Besides these misdemeanors, Sam included the act of apostasy and adultery as being paramount sins, giving the trust cause to disassociate members.

He was asked to be specific as to which individual plaintiffs were guilty of these moral faults.

Answer: " I don't wish to accuse these folks. I wish to defend the church and the United Effort Plan and in the process of that defense, it's really gauged on how you make your attack on the church. I can't answer that question you just asked about without some time to work on it."

Question: "So at this point, you haven't – you don't know of any specific instance of the type I'm talking about that the Trust would contend is, other than what you've told me about, the lying and apostasy, being disassociated with the church, other than those things, you can't point to any specific instance of conduct by any plaintiff that you would say is conduct inconsistent with these moral standards we're talking about?"

Answer: "I think bringing publicity upon our people that is designed to create a collision between this small religious community and the world in general, is a breach of moral conduct."

Question: "That's a good example. Can you tell me which plaintiffs you believe have done that?"

Answer: "Yes. Some of them have said it in deposition that they had participated in alleging that we were a gun-toten people, that we're using the Bishop's storehouse to store firearms. And some of them worried in front of the television about bloodshed and that sort of thing, which has never ever been proved at all."

Question: "Do you know who those individuals were?"

Answer: "Yes, Ben Bistline, Harold Blackmore, Cyril Bradshaw, Don Cox, and some of them."

Question: "Is there any other conduct, the type we're discussing, that you can identify at this time?"

Answer: "Claiming a women is your wife while she's married to someone else."

Question: "Tell me who's engaged in that kind of conduct?"

Answer: "David Stubbs was reportedly engaged in that."

Question: "At the present time?"

Answer: "I don't know about the present time."

Question: "And the position of the Trust is that at that (same) time she was someone else's wife, not his?"

Answer: "Someone else claims she was."

It is interesting to note that Sam's Uncle Fred Jessop was living in adultery with wives of two of the plaintiffs. Fred had convinced the women they should be "married" to him instead of the men to whom they had been "sealed to by the Priesthood."

When Sam was asked about businesses once owned by the UEP, his answer: "United Effort Plan only holds property. It's a receptacle for real property."

Question: "When property is sold, the United Effort Plan maintains no records of the sale, or doesn't have any books that it keeps track of it?"

Answer: "United Effort Plan is a child of the church and the church designated what happens."

He was denying that the UEP ever handles any money, claiming it is all church money.

When Sam was asked if people could be evicted for no reason at all, he said they would only be asked to leave if they had done something prejudicial to the trust.

Sam stated that no leases are given. This is untrue because Fred Jessop had been given many leases on which he has built income-producing businesses, making sure that any income produced on the property would be income to him, not to the trust.

Several months later in the spring of 1994 the Barlow Cabal decided to make one last Amended Affidavit of Disclosure to try and set the record straight as to just what they claimed was the policy of the United Effort Plan in regard to its people, the Beneficiaries.

In this sixth amended affidavit of disclosure they claimed that "the only beneficiary of the United Effort Plan is the 'Fundamentalist Church of Jesus Christ of Latter Day Saints' and has always been so. All other affidavits of disclosures filed, under oath, prior to this time were made in error."

Following this, at the suggestion of their attorneys, the Cabal began requiring those who were "given" a lot to put up a sign before they began any improvements. The sign must state that the lot belonged to the UEP and acknowledge that they were a Tenant at Will on the property.

At the end of May 1994, there was a hearing in St. George before Judge Eves on the lawsuit. Both sides had filed motions for him to consider. The Defendants were asking that the lawsuit be dismissed on the basis of religion. The Plaintiffs asked the judge to compel the Defendants to turn over their bank records and give an accounting to the plaintiffs.

On December 19, 1994, the Plaintiffs finished their presentation to the court. Afterwards the Judge called the attorneys into his chambers and told them to try and come to a settlement, but they could not. The trial lasted a few more days with only a few of the witnesses for the defense testifying, before the time allotted by the Judge ran out. So the hearings were postponed, with UEP attorney Scott Berry telling the Judge that he was prepared to put 125 witnesses on the stand when the trial resumed. The Judge asked him to proffer what they would say but Scott Berry refused. The trial was scheduled to continue in May and to take place in Parowan at the Iron County Court House.

The hearings resumed on May 17, 1995, in Parowan, Utah. The defendants began putting their 125 witnesses on the stand, their testimonies pretty much identical. After the first half dozen witnesses, the Judge proposed they began proffering the testimony of the remaining witnesses and Scott Berry finally agreed.

The trial was then postponed with the Judge setting a date of November 14, 1995, for the lawyers to give their closing statements.

This marked the end of an era. Because most everyone in the community was related, the eight year legal conflict had literally torn the community and families asunder. Anxiety ran high as the community moved into the new year, nervously awaiting the Judge's decision.

Judge Eves handed down his ruling in January of 1996. The important issue was whether the UEP was religious or business in nature, and whether by evicting people, the UEP received "unjust enrichment." The Judge ruled that the UEP *was* a religious trust, charitable in nature. Also, according to his interpretation of the trust document, the Plaintiffs were not members of the United Effort Plan, but if the trust were to evict them from the homes they had built, it would be *unjust enrichment*. Therefore he ruled that the Plaintiffs would have equity interest in the property on which their homes were situated and could remain in them for the remainder of their lives. If the UEP desired to evict them, they would be required to pay the current assessed valuation of the homes to the occupants. If any Plaintiffs chose to leave their homes on their own volition, they would forfeit any equity claims.

COURT'S FINAL DECISION

The Judge's Summary

This case presents complex issues of fact and law. The Court has heard dozens of witnesses and has received over 100 exhibits. After a thorough review of the evidence the Court finds the following facts have been established.

Plaintiffs and defendants herein generally all contend that in approximately 1886, John Taylor, then President of The Church of Jesus Christ of Latter-day Saints, directed several of his followers to continue the practice of polygamy outside that Church. The movement that resulted has been called The Priesthood Work (hereinafter The Work), and the adherents to that movement have continued the practice of plural marriage within their own religious organization to the present day. . . .

A common way for The Work to obtain land to occupy was to have its followers and sympathizers buy land and then deed it to The Work. To hold title to the land as it began to accumulate, the leadership of The Work formed a trust which was the predecessor to the current United Effort Plan Trust. The predecessor trust eventually failed and the land was deeded back to those who had contributed it, for the most part. Finally, in 1942, the 5 members of the then existing Priesthood Council signed, and later caused to be recorded in Mohave County, Arizona, a Declaration of Trust of the United Effort Plan, the trust in question in this law suit (hereinafter UEP).

After the UEP was formed, most of the land held by the predecessor trust was deeded to the UEP. As other land was made available by the adherents to The Work, it was also deeded to the UEP. The UEP currently holds legal title to much of the land around the Short Creek area, including the lands occupied by the claimants in these cases. Taxes on the UEP held land are paid by assessment of the persons occupying the land and other faithful members of The Work, if necessary. Tax money would be solicited as a donation and collected by religious leaders. No penalty was imposed on the land users who could not pay the taxes assessed to them. The shortfall would be made up by The Work, even using other donation money if necessary. The plaintiffs herein participated in this tax arrangement to one degree or another.

In the early days of the UEP, it also owned various cooperative enterprises in the community and engaged in business activities which were formed to serve the adherents of The Work living in the remote area, such as stores, a gas station, dairy, and other operations. In the 1940s many of these enterprises failed and the trust closed its accounts and determined that it would limit its functions to holding title to the land in the area. Such has been the case since the 1940s. . . .

From the beginning of the operation of the UEP, it was apparently the practice of the trustees, who were also the religious leaders of The Work, to invite certain of the adherents to build their homes on the land owned by the UEP. The adherents were aware that they were building on land to which they did not hold title. No deeds were issued and no written agreements were formalized spelling out the terms for the use of the land. The use of the land was conditioned upon religious teachings and beliefs commonly held and widely known in the community. . . .

Accordingly, it was not unusual for those occupying UEP lands or houses to be asked to move so those more needy or more deserving in the eyes of the trustees, or their agents, could take over the premises. Generally such requests were complied with willingly by the adherents to The Work. Some adherents of The Work built homes only to see the UEP move another family into the partially or fully completed structure. These occurrences were common knowledge in the community.

. . .The adherents were told that having a home on UEP land was better than having a deed because it couldn't be foreclosed for the adherent's debt. For the same reason, the adherents were frequently told that they were not free to mortgage or sell the land they occupied and that if they ever determined to leave the land, for any reason, the land and all improvements would belong to the UEP.

. . . many of the adherents, as part of their religious practice, spent countless hours on volunteer projects for the community, such as setting up water and sewer systems. They often went on work missions in which they would work without compensation for the community, or they would take jobs outside the community and contribute their pay to their religious leaders. It was also common among the adherents of The Work to serve as volunteers doing construction work on the homes of the other adherents. Some were compensated for those efforts, either with money or by trade, but many were not compensated.

Some residents did become discouraged and leave the community, as life there could be hard and lonely, and their improvements became the property of the UEP. Some were invited to leave by the leaders and some of these left voluntarily while others were bought out, "prayed out" or allowed to remain. Until recent times, the trust had not resorted to legal action or force to require occupants of the land to vacate.

Most of the communications to the residents from the UEP, or the Priesthood Council about the UEP, came from the pulpit during the frequent religious services that the adherents attended. In addition, some of the claimants in this suit claim that they had private conversations with representatives of the UEP in which they received additional representations about their right to use the UEP land. These communications will be discussed later in this opinion. All of the claimants have built improvements upon land to which title is held by the UEP.

Although the verbal arrangements for the use of UEP land were usually made with members of the religious leadership, who were also UEP trustees, or their agents such as J. Marion Hammon or Edson Jessop, the evidence clearly indicates that the provisions of the UEP Declaration and the amendments thereto were roundly ignored by everyone in the process.

In 1987 the claimants herein brought suit in the Federal Court to determine the rights, if any, that they may have in the UEP land which they have occupied. This action was commenced after the claimants received notification that they were considered to be tenants at will by the UEP. In 1989 a suit was also filed in Washington County, Utah raising many of the same issues. The State case was stayed pending the resolution of the Federal case. Eventually the Federal case was dismissed for lack of subject matter jurisdiction. The stay on the State action was then lifted and this matter has proceeded in this forum.

The Judge told the attorneys for the Plaintiffs to write the Order and he and the attorneys for the Defendants (the UEP) would sign it. After the Order was written, however, the attorneys for the Defendants refused to sign. There would be two more hearings to clear up the questions of the attorneys, held on June 10, 1996, and on August 13, 1996. The following is a partial list of the Order.

    3. The Court further orders that upon each Plaintiff's death, the land and improvements shall then belong to the UEP without the necessity of payment therefore.

    4. Each Plaintiff's right of occupancy shall terminate without reimbursement for improvements if he tries to sell or mortgage the property or the improvements, or if he abandons the use of the lot. Each Plaintiff shall be liable to the UEP for waste committed on the property by him or his co-occupants, beyond normal wear and tear, during his occupancy.

    5. Plaintiffs shall not construct any further improvements on UEP land if under applicable law the project requires a building permit, without the express written permission of the UEP, and any such project shall be submitted to the UEP for approval before it is submitted to any governmental authority or agency.

    6. Each Plaintiff is hereby ordered to pay all real property taxes accruing on the property he occupies from the date of this Judgment forward.

    7. For the reasons set forth in Memorandum Decision dated January 11, 1996, all other claims of the Plaintiffs set forth in the first through sixth claims for relief of the Amended Complaint in Case No. 930501020 CV are hereby dismissed with prejudice.

The UEP appealed, of course. They did not want the Dissidents to remain on UEP property, in the midst of faithful members of the community. In October 1997 the Utah Supreme Court heard the appeal on the judgment of the lower court wherein it ruled that the Plaintiffs could live in their homes until they died.

Before the Utah Supreme Court handed down their decision in the matter in September of 1998, Sam Barlow once again began evicting people from their homes. And he could evict any who were not parties to the lawsuit, because every other person living on UEP property was now a Tenant At Will and could legally be evicted. Sam started by picking on widows he thought would not have the courage to oppose him. And he was successful in running out a couple of old defenseless widows, and was going through court proceedings to evict more.

15

Colorado City Back In Business

The lawsuit was often the main topic of discussion among the people of Colorado City, Hildale, and Centennial Park. Families still lived their lives, women cared for children, and men worked. And the sermons of each Sunday's church meetings were to be accepted as if from God himself. Because almost everyone was related in one way or another, those in opposing Wards or involved in the lawsuit avoided one another.

An upsetting change in the doctrine of the Polygamists had been made by Rulon Jeffs in 1991. It was a complete turn around on one of the Fundamentalist stands since the 1930s, regarding the "Adam God Doctrine," wherein it was taught that "Adam is the creator of the earth and is our God." On June 2, 1991, Rulon Jeffs gave a discourse on "The Godhead" at Colorado City, explaining a new doctrine, that Adam was not the creator. He stated that Christ was.

Not too long after Rulon Jeffs delivered this sermon, Fred Jessop and the Barlows thought it "might be best for the Work" if President Jeffs would *actively resign from managing its affairs*. When this rumor spread throughout the community, Fred was forced to deny it. In December of 1991, he stood before the people in their church house and said that he had "not asked President Jeffs to step down." What is clear is that the Barlows and their Uncle Fred controlled everything in Colorado City, while Rulon Jeffs lived in Little Cottonwood Canyon in Salt Lake City. What was going on behind the scene is anyone's guess.

Later in 1996 Rulon Jeffs announced in church that he had made a mistake when he had denounced the "Adam God Theory."

THE LDS CHURCH SEES A MISSIONARY OPPORTUNITY

On June 21, 1992, the President of the Kanab, Utah, Kaibab Stake of The Church of Jesus Christ of Latter-Day Saints held a missionary meeting in the Second Ward Chapel at Centennial Park. There were about fifty Stake Leaders (men responsible for a number of congregations) who came with him. About fifty local people attended the meeting.

This was the first time in over fifty years that a meeting was held by the LDS Church among the Colorado City Polygamists. It was surprising that Second Ward Leaders allowed them the use of the building, but it does show their open-mindedness in comparison with First Ward. The message presented was the thirteen Articles of Faith (statement of beliefs) and an invitation to participate in future missionary meetings to be held in the area.

The LDS Stake Officials, however, were unable to obtain a building where these meetings could be held on a regular basis. Their only option was to hold them out-of-doors in one of the parks until the weather turned too cold in late November. They were then invited into a home of a non-member who, although she did not intend to join the Church, still had enough Christian compassion to offer her home.

The LDS Stake Mission President went to the local school board and requested permission to use the County school house, but he was told that a religious organization could not use the public school house.

President of the Colorado City School Board, Lee Bistline, called Rulon Jeffs in Salt Lake City and asked whether or not he should allow the LDS Church the use of the building. Jeffs told him that he was not going to make that decision, that the school board would have to do so. Lee then asked Fred Jessop and Fred made no hesitation, "Don't give it to them." Fred then announced in his church house that the people should not allow their children to attend any of the LDS meetings or any of their activities (The LDS Church was also sponsoring weekly activities for the young people and attendance would reach a hundred people).

This un-Christian behavior of Fred Jessop is in marked contrast to the attitude of the Second Ward Leaders, for although they did not offer their building to be used for these regular meetings (they were never asked), they did allow the first meeting to be held there.

Unfortunately, these missionary meetings were stopped in January of 1993. The General Authorities of the LDS Church were suspicious that people living in Colorado City would only join the Church to gain access to the Temples and after getting their endowments return to the Fundamentalist Cult where they could continue living polygamy.

They were somewhat justified in this concern because other Polygamist Groups in the Salt Lake City area were guilty of this charade, but none of the Colorado City Polygamists had ever attempted it. The teachings and beliefs of the polygamists are that the Temples are *out of order*, that the LDS Church does not have the Keys to Priesthood, so all temple work being done is not efficacious and will all have to be redone when they, the Polygamists, are established as the true Priesthood Leaders.

This action by the General Authorities was a disappointing blow to the local LDS Church leaders. But, they complied with the instruction given and suspended all missionary activities on the Stake level. By the end of 1993 there were over twenty active members living in Colorado City and Hildale, who attended the Kaibab/Moccasin Ward. These active members and the influence of The Church of Jesus Christ of Latter-day Saints was felt in the community, thus opening the way for people to some day find the truth of their religious history.

Five years later the LDS Church did give their approval for a Branch to be organized in Colorado City. The plan was to establish a Church Institute in connection with the Mohave County Community College, using the building not only for a chapel and activities building, but for Institute classes as well. This would have been a big milestone in the history of the community, it being over 60 years since there was an LDS Branch in the community.

But in January of 1999, representatives of the LDS Church met with Dan Barlow, mayor of Colorado City and David Zitting, mayor of Hildale, to discuss the legal aspects of building permits. Dan Barlow's answer: "We want you to build your church house in Cane Beds; we don't want it here. If you attempt to build here, we will condemn the property and build a road through it."

PRIESTHOOD TAKES CARE OF ITS OWN

On July 2, 1995, Truman Barlow's mansion, built and paid for by the UEP, caught fire and was a complete loss. He had to move into Uncle Roy's house while the UEP rebuilt his house. It took several months before it was finished, but was far more imposing and grand than had been the old one. And this all was done and paid for by the UEP Priesthood at no cost to Truman. The Priesthood takes care of its own.

GUNS OUTLAWED

In October of 1995, Fred Jessop "sent down a decree" that no one in the community could own guns. All guns were to be disposed of. Only those who had been commissioned by proper authority could have guns in their possession, and this edict was followed by First Ward followers. This was the third time in the Colorado City Polygamists' history that the people have had their guns taken away, perhaps as one more control issue. The leadership, however, had a cache of guns ready and waiting.

BLOOD ATONEMENT

During the 1990s Rulon Jeffs began publishing several volumes of his sermons and doctrine, and in 1997, he talked of Blood Atonement. This was not a new doctrine. Brigham Young had delivered a speech at the Salt Lake Tabernacle in 1857, "*Journal of Discourses*. Vol 4, p 219, stating : "... he [that] has committed a sin that he knows will deprive him of that exaltation which he desires, and that he cannot attain to it without the shedding of his blood, and also knows that by having his blood shed he will atone for that sin, and be saved and exalted with the Gods, is there a man or woman in this house but what would say, 'shed my blood that I may be saved and exalted with the Gods?' All mankind love themselves, and let these principles be known by an individual, and he would be glad to have his blood shed. That would be loving themselves, even unto an eternal exaltation. Will you love your brothers or sisters likewise, when they have committed a sin that cannot be atoned for without the shedding of their blood? Will you love that man or woman well enough to shed their blood? That is what Jesus Christ meant. He never told a man or woman to love their enemies in their wickedness, never."

Not only did Rulon Jeffs quote from the Brigham Young "Blood Atonement" sermon in his book entitled *Purity in the New and Everlasting Covenant of Marriage*, he also put it in a 1997 volume of his own sermons.

"I could refer you to plenty of instances where men have been righteously slain, in order to atone for their sins. I have seen scores and hundreds of people for whom there would have been a chance (in the last resurrection there will be) if their lives had been taken and their blood spilled on the ground as a smoking incense to the Almighty, but who are now angels to the devil, until our elder brother Jesus Christ raises them up – conquers death, hell, and the grave. I have known a great many men who have left this Church for whom there is no chance whatever for exaltation, but if their blood had been spilled, it would have been better for them. The wickedness and ignorance of the nations forbid this principle being in full force, but the time will come when the law of God will be in full force.

"This is loving our neighbor as ourselves; if he needs help, help him; and if he wants salvation and it is necessary to spill his blood on the earth in order that he may be saved, spill it."

Soon after presenting these, he told people in a public meeting that they should come forth and confess their sins to him, that he could let them be rebaptised and their sins forgiven. A number of trusting people did go to him and confess to sins of immorality. But he did not forgive their sins, he excommunicated them. In the case of men, he took the wife or wives from them and gave them to someone else. They were then expelled from the society and forced to leave the community.

WARREN JEFFS BECOMES FIRST COUNSELOR

In January of 1998, Parley Harker, first counselor to Rulon Jeffs, died. Rulon then appointed his son Warren Jeffs as first counselor, leaving Fred Jessop as second counselor. A few weeks later, there was a notice filed in the Salt Lake County Recorder's office declaring that a document had been filed declaring that brothers Warren and LeRoy Jeffs had been appointed UEP agents. Then a Certificate of Authority was filed April 7, 1998, with the Corporation Commission naming Warren and LeRoy Jeffs as agents for Rulon Jeffs.

It looked to the Barlows as if something was up. Soon after this, Warren Jeffs, acting in the name of his father who had just had a mild stroke, got up in Church and told all the Barlows they could no longer sit on the stand. The Barlows weren't on the Priesthood Council, but they had been accustomed to sitting on the stand as was befitting their positions in the community.

John Y. Barlow had taught and prepared his sons to one day rule the Group. They never lost sight of that goal, even as there were other people in power in the interim. Rulon Jeffs was a distant leader living in Salt Lake, with Fred Jessop and his Barlow nephews actually running the town and the Trust. It is reasonable to consider that Rulon's sons felt deep resentment toward the Barlows. But Warren was now in a position of power as First Counselor. And he had been designated by his father, the prophet, to be his spokesperson.

Everyone was asking themselves why Warren had been chosen as First Counselor and not one of the Barlows.

Many had heard of Warren's control of the Salt Lake City Alta Academy. As the administrator he quickly developed a reputation. It was rumored that he was forcing young children to be righteous through fear of being physically whipped, or of being expelled from school for minor infractions. His goal was to force the children into submission. And if Warren overhead something, he would bring in the parents to question them about intimate things in their personal lives, or beliefs not consistent with correct teachings.

As Warren's control and influence among the children grew, he taught them to spy on their friends and family, then informing him about any doctrinal differences of opinion they overheard.

Warren taught them that after informing on someone, they should feel good about building the Kingdom of God. Soon informants were everywhere. Children against parents, wives against husbands, and brethren against brethren.

Rumors had also made their way to Colorado City that are described in a report by John Dougherty of the *Phoenix New Times* on January 29, 2004, "Warren Jeffs…may have been secretly making audio and video recordings of confessions by church members…in the decade before assuming control of the church…according to allegations made by a longtime member of the church who was recently excommunicated. Reportedly he has accumulated thousands of audio and video tapes that detail church members'…confessions…."

It is clear that Warren had an established agenda that worked for him. The Barlows would soon discover a force of will even greater than their own.

On December 8, 1998, Warren Jeffs sent a new letter and a copy of a revised United Effort Trust Document to the members living on UEP property, but not to any of the plaintiffs. It reiterated again the "tenant at will" language, one more control to keep the people faithful to their leaders, who held their very lives in their hands.

END OF WORLD WARNINGS & PREPARATIONS

In the fall of 1998 and in the early part of 1999, there was a lot of hype and rumor among the polygamists of the First Ward, that the righteous people among them were going to be lifted up into the heavens while the wicked people would be destroyed. The righteous people would then return to the earth and continue to live their religion in peace.

Leroy Johnson in 1984 had said: "We will have to have the spirit of God upon us enough to be caught up when the judgments of God go over the earth, then we will be let down again. That is the only way the Lord will protect his people. He says he will protect his Saints if He has to send fire from Heaven to do so; and this he will do."

In 1992 Rulon Jeffs had also taught: "We must be lifted up to be protected. Keep sweet, Keep the Holy Spirit of God, it is the only way we are going to get through the narrows and overcome this complacency, lack of faith. Keep sweet means keep the Holy Spirit of the Lord, until you are full of it. Only those who have it will survive the judgments of God, which are about to be poured out without let or hindrance upon the earth, beginning at the house of God, where the Mormons are. I mean the Mormon Church which is now apostate, completely, and will never be set in order. We have the true and living Church of Jesus Christ of Latter Day Saints, under our administration. We add the word 'Fundamentalist' in order to distinguish the true Church of Jesus Christ of Latter Day Saints from the name of the one that now is a complete Gentile sectarian church, The Lord has rejected it."

On three occasions a date had been set by Rulon Jeffs for the lifting up, and everyone faithfully came out for the sacred event. But thus far, no one had been lifted up. Now Rulon Jeffs set the date for June 12, 1999, the 111th anniversary of Leroy Johnson's birthday. Much anticipation and excitement traveled through the First Ward members. When the day came, the people gathered in the parking lot of the LSJ Meeting house at 6:00 a.m.

Fred Jessop welcomed them and they sang "We Thank Thee O God For A Prophet." After the opening prayer and another song, the people were addressed by Louis Barlow. Then "Uncle Rulon's Sons of Helaman" were marched past the Brethren, presenting an honor guard. Everyone formed a prayer circle and held hands as a prayer was said. Forming a procession, they then made their way to Cottonwood Park, a distance of about two blocks, and engaged in a day long celebration. During the day, people went to the store to buy a supply of groceries to take with them. However, before the day ended, word came down from the prophet that the people lacked the faith for this event to take place. They were told that another date would be set for it to happen, thus giving them a little more time to repent.

Six months later, Rulon issued a warning to all the polygamists living in Salt Lake City. He said that terrorists would strike during the 2002 Salt Lake City Winter Olympics, and great devastation would occur. He said they needed to begin to move to Colorado City, and they did. Many abandoned homes they were buying, allowing them to be foreclosed on. They weren't concerned about losing their equity, because if the end of the world was coming, money would no longer be needed. Rulon left his large home in Salt Lake City and moved his family to Colorado City.

16

Warren Jeffs Takes Over

When Rulon moved to Colorado City in the year 2000, he designated his son Warren to be his mouthpiece. Rulon had already made Warren his first counselor, and the Barlows were getting more nervous by the day.

The Barlow boys immediately began pressuring Rulon to ordain one of them to the High Priesthood, while there was still time. He was getting old and was not expected to live much longer. But he rejected their badgering, telling them he would live long enough to witness the Second Coming of Jesus Christ and would return the keys of the priesthood to him.

What he did do was begin to take away local operations from the Barlows and turn them over to his son Warren. For years the Barlows had easily controlled who and what they wanted because aging Leroy Johnson was easily manipulated and Rulon lived in Salt Lake City. But now Rulon lived among them and so did Warren. Not a reticent man like his father, Warren became a tyrant when the Barlows tried to deal with him as they had with his father.

Warren knew he had to replace the Barlow's power with his own, but he had more than sixty years of their influence to overcome, so he began making demands on the people of the community, forcing them to acknowledge his position as leader. He said anyone who would not accept and believe everything he stated would be excommunicated and forced to leave. Organizing a group of young men thirteen, fourteen, and fifteen years old, and calling them "Uncle Warren's Sons of Helaman" (young warriors in the Book of Mormon), he sent them into people's homes, forcing them to make a statement that they would acknowledge him as their leader and would accept whatever doctrine he preached to them.

NO MORE PUBLIC SCHOOL

Next he decreed that all members of First Ward withdraw their children from public school. He organized several private schools in the community so he could have complete control. The Phelps School in Hildale, a public school owned by Washington County, Utah, operated one more year before it closed due to lack of students. These few Hildale students then attended the Colorado City public school. After the Phelps School building remained vacant for a year, the Washington County School Board sold the building to Warren Jeffs for one million dollars, to be paid at $100,000 a year for ten years.

Mohave County had just completed a new school building for Colorado City based on an attendance of about 1,200 students. But due to Warren's edict, less than 400 students use this new building. All First Ward teachers at the public school were ordered by Jeffs to resign, which left only teachers from the Second Ward teaching at the school. However, First Ward member Alvin Barlow remained as school superintendent, and the principals and all maintenance people, including bus drivers, were First Warders. So this public school was still controlled by Warren Jeffs. One staff member per three students worked at the school.

WINSTON BLACKMORE vs WARREN JEFFS

A serious dispute arose between Warren Jeffs and Winston Blackmore over a girl who rebelled against Warren Jeffs' dictates. It is rumored that he asked her to marry one of his brothers when she was sixteen, but three weeks later she left the community with a different brother. The two began living together but after a short time their consciences began to bother them, and perhaps they were afraid, so they decided to seek forgiveness from someone other than Warren.

Rulon Jeffs had commissioned Winston Blackmore to be the leader of a branch of the polygamists at Bountiful, British Columbia. This commission entitled him to forgive sins and to perform ordinances such as marriages. The young couple decided to go to Canada to seek forgiveness from Winston Blackmore. Blackmore contacted Rulon Jeffs by telephone, seeking his permission to perform the forgiveness and Rulon agreed.

Warren was infuriated that Blackmore had bypassed him in the chain of authority. In defending himself, Winston claimed that the commission given him by Rulon entitled him to authority equal to Warren. Warren immediately excommunicated him and ordered him off the United Effort Plan property at Bountiful.

When Warren discovered that the property was in Winston's name and not in the United Effort Plan Trust, he filed a lawsuit. Before it went to court, Winston offered to split the assets and the debts equally with Warren. But Warren refused the offer, telling Winston he must take all the debts and that all the assets and the property would go to the UEP. Meanwhile Winston had purchased other property in his own name without any United Effort Plan strings attached to it, both in Canada and also in northern Idaho.

Back in Colorado City, zealous Warren ordered all business owners to turn ownership of their businesses over to him. He also demanded that they draw out all their money held in 401(k) programs and give it to him. A number of the people rebelled and several families began leaving Colorado City, moving to northern Idaho to settle on property that belonged to Winston Blackmore. Winston therefore acquired a following that is now a rival group to Warren Jeffs.

WARREN EVICTS DISOBEDIENT MOTHER

A sixteen-year-old daughter of Lenore Holm was told to marry a man twenty-three years her senior, as a second wife. The girl's mother did not object to her daughter's marriage, only stating she did not want her to marry the man until she was eighteen. Warren Jeffs agreed but wanted the girl to live in his home until she became eighteen so she would receive proper training, Warren's kind of training. Lenore objected to this arrangement, demanding that her daughter remain in her own home until she became of age. But the girl wanted to go, and ran away. Her mother went to the Colorado City police department seeking help. Although the police knew where her daughter was (either in Warren Jeffs' home or in the home of the man she was to marry), they wouldn't assist Lenore in returning her daughter.

Because of Lenore's rebellious attitude, her husband was told to divorce her and expel her from his home and the community. This he refused to do, and was served an eviction notice from the United Effort Plan. He and Lenore refused to move and the case was taken to trial at Kingman, Arizona. The judge in the case ruled in favor of Lenore and her husband and ordered that the United Effort Plan would have to pay for the equity in their home if they wanted them to move. This was a big loss for the UEP because it set a precedent that people could not be evicted from their homes in Colorado City unless they were paid for their equity.

MOLDING GIRLS TO BECOME OBEDIENT WIVES

All the little girls growing up in First Ward are being indoctrinated with one hundred years of Mormon Fundamentalism. Polygamy, public welfare lines, and secretive religion is their way of life, and their world is as strange to mainstream Americans as would be life in Iraq.

Many of the girls feel personal value only when they are finally married to a man holding the priesthood, whether a young man or a man old enough to be a grandfather. A girl is there to bear children, as many as she can produce, for as long as her body will hold out. The religious programming begins at birth and it is the "only truth" about themselves they will ever know. And if the girl wants the love and approval of her parents, she has no choice but to comply and appear happy about it. But occasionally a girl will rebel and run away. But what does she run to? Another man who will enslave her? How does she undo years of programming and learn anew what life really can be?

Five of independent polygamist Tom Green's wives came from Colorado City. One of his first wives was Beth Cook. When Beth was twelve years old, Leroy Johnson gave her as a plural wife to a man old enough to be her grandfather. And he gave Beth's nine-year-old sister to the same man. In time, they escaped. Tom liked his new wives young, which is evident by their ages: twelve, thirteen, fourteen, and fifteen. Tom told a friend he should marry his wives young so he could train them the way he wanted.

POLICE OFFICER RODNEY HOLM CHARGED, SEX WITH A MINOR

Another story that made headlines is about Rodney Holm, a Colorado City police officer, who married Ruth Stubbs as his third wife when she was sixteen and he was thirty. After having two children and pregnant with a third, Ruth decided to leave the community. She was unable to take her children with her, because she had to sneak out in the night and flee. She sought help from the local law enforcement in St. George, Utah, to try and gain custody of her children.

In all the news stories about child brides, many complaints had been made about law enforcement and government agencies not wanting to become involved in polygamist disputes. But by now, media exposure had brought such a spotlight on the situation that she was granted custody of her children. She also agreed to press charges against Rodney. He was arrested and charged with one count of unlawful sex with a sixteen-year-old girl and one count of unlawful sex with a seventeen-year-old girl and also one count of bigamy. At his trial in August of 2003, he was convicted of all three counts. He was sentenced in October of 2003 by Judge Beacham, Fifth District Court of Utah at St. George.

Sentenced to three years probation and one year in prison on work release for each offense, all three sentences were to run concurrently. On the 10th of June 2004, Rodney Holm was released from this mild sentence by the Fifth District Court, dismissed with time served. Prior to the trial of Rodney Holm, the Utah State Attorney General's office had solicited the help of the Colorado City police department in serving a subpoena on Warren Jeffs to be called as a witness. Police Chief Sam Roundy not only refused to help, but actually dispatched a policeman to barricade the way to Warren Jeffs' home when investigators tried to serve the subpoena.

Due to the trial and conviction of Rodney Holm, Warren Jeffs (who was guilty of the same offenses) became very paranoid. He ordered an eight-foot concrete wall be erected around the city block where his homes were located. He also spent several hundred thousand dollars installing a security system to protect him from being subpoenaed or arrested by officials, thus sealing himself in seclusion from any outside access.

RULON JEFFS PASSES AWAY

In September of 2002 Rulon Jeffs died, contrary to his prediction that he would live to hand the keys of the priesthood over to Jesus Christ at His Second Coming. At the time of his death Fred Jessop and Warren Jeffs were standing at his bedside. Tearful Warren turned to Fred Jessop and said, "I guess you're the one who takes over now." Fred responded, "No, you're the one to be the leader." This exchange between these two men was the only ceremony that took place allowing Warren Jeffs to become the leader of the Group.

Fred Jessop would regret the moment he surrendered power to Warren Jeffs. But he had been taught for decades to yield his personal opinion and desire to the "leader." And Warren was First Counselor, while Fred was only the Second. It is rumored that the Barlows demanded to know from Fred why he didn't take charge at that moment, the moment they all had been waiting for. But years of programming run deep when one has learned to be subservient to a "leader."

BARLOWS WORST FEARS REALIZED

Two years later, the Barlow's worst fears would come to pass when Warren began excommunicating many of them: Louis Barlow, Joseph I. Barlow, Dan Barlow, Sr, Nephi Barlow, David Jeffs, Hyrum Jeffs, Brian Jeffs, Blaine Jeffs, Roland Cooke, Val Jessop, Isaac Wyler, Leon Jessop, Roland Barlow, Evan Johnson, Carl Richter, Chuck Johnson, Tom Barlow, Orval Johnson, and Carl Holm.

Days after their excommunication, an anonymous letter by a Barlow was sent to everyone in town. It contained interesting information about what Warren had done at the time his father died. Excerpts follow:

"Remember Uncle Rulon died on Sunday, dissolving the First Presidency. Warren was still only an elder. The following day, at Monday morning meeting, Uncle Warren, besides giving us details on the passing of Uncle Rulon, made this statement. 'I won't say much, but I will say this, Hands off my father's wives.' Speaking to the newly bereaved widows, he said, 'You women will live as if father is still alive and in the next room.' I remember thinking to myself, 'Who in the world, at a time like this, would be lusting after Uncle Rulon's wives?' The thought sickened me.

"This was said on Monday. By that Friday, Warren moved in on those women so fast, and with such finesse, that only two of his 'mothers' had enough fortitude to stand up against him. Those stunned women, who had sincerely believed that their husband and prophet would live 350 years and give them children, went through the shock of losing their husband to death, seeing him buried, Warren proclaiming himself prophet quickly thereafter and then immediately receiving revelation to marry those women 'found worthy of him' in secret ceremonies.

"Before committing that kind of sin before the eyes of God, one of his mothers, seeing the futility of fighting him off, bravely fled the compound and left the community at a run. Another of Warren's young 'mothers' flatly refused to go along with the marriage. She was sent back to live with her father and told she would live the rest of her life out without ever being married." (End of excerpt)

GOVERNMENT PROGRAMS & THE POLYGAMISTS

In 1998, Tom Zoellner, reporter for *The Salt Lake Tribune,* investigated how government programs were used among the FLDS people. At the time, about half the FLDS were living in Salt Lake City and surrounding areas, which left the combined population of Colorado City and Hildale at a little over five thousand people, of whom thirty-three percent use food stamps. The rest of Arizona uses less than seven percent and Utah less than five percent. His report questioned whether parents could feed or clothe their children without government help.

Of federal housing grants to help refurbish homes for poor people, Hildale was given $405,006, but it was really UEP-owned land and the people lived in the homes as a Tenant at Will.

Dissidents from the FLDS claim that welfare has become a way of life. Zoellner found that the Cooperative Mercantile Exchange, the only grocery store in the twin cities, took in "$26,466.00 from the WIC food program in December 1997." And WIC has so many demands from the FLDS, the government pays Hildale $400 a month in rent for an office in town.

He reported that in 1998, Colorado City and Hildale had a combined budget of $13 million dollars to support a college, a small industrial park, a school district, a power plant, a radio station, and two city governments. Colorado City "received more than $1.8 million from the U.S. Department of Housing and Urban Development to pave its streets, upgrade its fire equipment and build a water-storage tank." Hildale received $94,000 to upgrade its fire station. An airport on the Arizona side received $2.8 million in government assistance.

John Dougherty of the *Phoenix New Times* conducted a six month investigation into FLDS financial practices and came up with an "array of unethical actions by the FLDS-controlled school board, district administrators and school principals."

"The investigation included an extensive review of thousands of pages of school district credit card records, travel vouchers, board minutes, district lease agreements and correspondence, all obtained under the Arizona Public Records Law."

The *Phoenix New Times* accused the Colorado City Unified School District, which has received state and federal aid in the amount of $4 million a year, of "operating primarily for the financial benefit of the FLDS church and for the personal enrichment of FLDS school district leaders."

On July 16, 2000, when Warren Jeffs had called all FLDS members to physically separate themselves from anyone not a faithful member of First Ward, the 800 FLDS students stopped attending public school. This left only the students and teachers of the Second Ward (Centennial Park). But FLDS school board administrators *still had control of millions of dollars of school district funds.*

The Colorado City school district has an annual budget of $5 million for a community of 5000 where there are "100 employees for 300 students, a 3 to 1 student to employee ratio." The average Mohave County employee ratio is one employee per 25 students. Because of a state law that protects school districts from sudden declining student attendance, "Colorado City has received more than $3 million since July 2000 in state funds for phantom students who were withdrawn from the school by religious decree." Although student attendance dramatically dropped, employee numbers stayed the same.

The Arizona State Auditor General's Office, the State Superintendent of Public Instruction, and the Mohave County Superintendent of Schools are investigating.

194

ANOTHER FIRST WARD SPLIT BEGINS

Determined to gain complete control over First Ward, Warren began to restrict privileges that the Barlows had enjoyed under Leroy Johnson and Rulon Jeffs. The community had always celebrated the birthday of the former prophet Leroy Johnson. On June 12, 2003, Warren would not allow this annual celebration to take place. On the 24th of July (Pioneer Day), the community had always sponsored a large parade down the main street of Colorado City. Warren did not allow this parade to take place. Fred Jessop had sponsored a Fall Festival Fair in October of every year. Warren would not allow this event to take place.

The controversy between the Barlows and Warren came to a head on the 26th of July 2003, the 50th anniversary of the Short Creek Raid. A dedication ceremony was held for the unveiling of a monument on the grounds of the old schoolhouse, and sponsored by Colorado City Mayor Dan Barlow. Inscription on this monument read: Early Morning July 26, 1953 The Prophet Leroy Johnson stood on this site with the people and met the raiding police officers. He later declared that the deliverance of the people in 1953 was the greatest miracle of all time.

WARREN JEFFS ORDAINED PROPHET

Ten days later on August 5, 2003, Warren Jeffs had himself formally ordained as President of the FLDS Church by his brother LeRoy Jeffs, whom he had just ordained to be the Patriarch of the church.

In the next church meeting on August 10, Warren Jeffs delivered a sermon that lasted more than an hour and a half. Severely chastising the people, he spoke to the Barlows but did not mention any of their names. He said they were going to be chastised by the Lord. Near the end of this sermon he read a revelation he said he received at his home in Hildale on Sunday, July 27, 2003. And he ordered the destruction of the monument that was unveiled two weeks earlier.

This is the revelation:

"Verily I say unto you, my servant Warren, my people have sinned a very grievous sin before me in that they have raised up monuments to man and have not glorified it to me. For it is by my almighty arm that my people have been preserved if they are worthy. I use men as instruments to perform my work.

"And my prophets of all ages who have endured faithful to the end have acknowledged me, as their lawgiver, their protector, and their God, and have taught and instructed my people the same. Those are some outward evidences.

"Reparations have to be made. What else is upon us? My people, let thee repent of their idolatry, which is covetousness loving anything more than God and His will; partaking of the world and its sins and all their wicked doings. For there are many elders who continue partaking of the spirit of the world and its wickedness.

"And behold I say unto you, my elders, beware, for what you do in secret I shall reward you openly. And you must seek my protection through the repentance of your sins, and the building up of my kingdom, my storehouse, my priesthood on the earth. And if you do not, I shall bring a scourge upon my people to purge the ungodly from among you. And those righteous will suffer with the wicked if I will preserve the pure in heart who are repentant. I the Lord have spoken it and my word shall be obeyed if you would receive my blessings. Honor me, through obedience to my celestial laws, and set your family in order, to abide the spirit of oneness, which is the spirit of the celestial kingdom.

"My holy love burning in your minds and hearts, bonding it together as one in a new and everlasting covenant, the laws of my holy priesthood. Hear the warning voice, oh ye my people, and repent and make restitution unto me that I may own and bless you in the day of trouble and also in Zion, if you will, for my arm of mercy is stretched out still unto those who will repent and come unto me with full purpose of heart, and I will preserve my servants among you to lead and guide you through my revelations and my power, otherwise you will remain unto those who will receive. Abide in my word. Let my people make restitution unto me, through the repentance of their sins and building up my storehouse and all other things, as I shall direct through my servants even so. Amen."

After reading this revelation, Warren then chastised the people again, accusing them of being unworthy of future blessings. He said there would be no more meetings held, neither priesthood meetings nor general meetings, no more marriages performed, no more baptisms, no more confirmations, but he would allow the people the blessing of paying their tithing to him and supporting his storehouse.

This meant that all men of the community would be forced to pay him $500 - $1,000 per month. He then said that the new monument commemorating the 1953 raid must be destroyed, broken into many pieces and scattered among the hills where no one could find it and restore it. He said this was because of the wickedness of those who had sponsored the monument, and that it was wicked to build monuments unto man and to do things in secret as the City Council had done this, without his permission.

Several weeks later on August 15, 2003, Warren said he had a revelation to call certain men as High Priests: James Allred, Fredrick Merrill Jessop, Edson Jessop, LaMar Johnson, Edmund Barlow, Steve Harker, Joseph Steed, Rulon Jessop, Gerald Williams, Boyd Roundy, Leroy Steed, and Paul Stanley Jessop, Sr. Wendell Nielsen would be his first counselor and Fredrick M. Jessop would continue to be the second counselor.

Jeffs then said that Kevin Barlow was the new superintendent of all priesthood schools and that LeRoy Jeffs and Richard Allred would act as his counselors. All these men clearly had made the kind of commitment to Warren that they knew he expected.

FRED JESSOP DISAPPEARS

In a church meeting on January 3, 2004, Warren Jeffs announced that he had released Fred M. Jessop as bishop and that Fred was in full agreement. But Fred wasn't in the meeting and no one had seen or heard from him.

At the time it was rumored that Warren sent Fred Jessop, with five of his wives, to a compound in Mexico, where he was being held against his will. By June 2004, a letter purportedly written by Fred to his family claimed he was in Eldorado, Texas.

Soon after Fred's disappearance Warren Jeffs appointed William Timpson, age thirty-two, to fill Fred's vacancy as bishop. Timpson moved into Fred Jessop's home, took over the rest of his family, and began teaching and directing them according to Warren's dictates.

Warren Jeffs knew he must remove Fred from the community in order to accomplish his next move. On January 10, 2004, in a Saturday morning prayer meeting at the LSJ meetinghouse, Warren Jeffs stood before a group of about 1500 people (men and women), berating them for their many sins and the lack of respect they rendered to the priesthood (himself). Then he read a list of names of about 20 people, asking them to stand up. He told them they were excommunicated from the church and must immediately remove themselves from UEP property and leave the community. Their wives and children would be reassigned to other men.

Most noteworthy in this group were Louis, Joe, Dan and Nephi Barlow. Also Louis's son Tom, and Dan's son Roland. Also included were four of Warren's brothers: David, Hyrum, Blaine, and Brian Jeffs. He asked those standing to show by uplifted hand that they accepted his action as the word of the Lord. All of the group raised their right hands. He then asked the audience if they accepted it as the word of the Lord. They all raised their right hands.

He then asked the audience to kneel while he led them in prayer. In the prayer he instructed those who had been excommunicated to repent, keep their nose to the grindstone, and continue giving him their money. If they were to faithfully do so, they may have a chance to someday return to the fold.

17

The Barlows Fight Back

On Tuesday, January 12, 2004, copies of the following letter were mailed to 453 random post office box numbers in Colorado City and Hildale. There is no question it was written by a Barlow.

> January 11, 2004
>
> I am a young man. I am simple and do not know the proper way to address you. But I have been commanded of God to stand upon the wall as Samuel and to tell you of a dream I had. For this reason I have chosen to send you letters describing this dream. I do this with humility and with trust in God.
>
> I beheld this valley before it became Short Creek – before it became Colorado City. I saw a stream that had cut its way into this sandy valley and I saw children playing on the banks of this sandy creek. And while they were children, I recognized them as the town fathers I have come to trust and love. I beheld the children of John Y. Barlow. And a voice that filled my soul and my heart spoke to me in this dream and it said, "Behold, these children are pure in blood and hold the birthright to this sacred valley. They were chosen by god to carve out of the very wilderness you see a community where the people can raise themselves up unto God's glorious work."
>
> And, I beheld this happen. I watched as our beloved prophet, Leroy S. Johnson, clung to John Y. Barlow's words. I watched as Leroy S. Johnson became the steward of these lands administering the just laws of God to this people. I watched him govern over the children of John Y. Barlow in a just and fair manner. And I saw how this place we live in was carved out of the wilderness by the will of God through these men. And I beheld that within their hearts they knew of their birthright and their duty to act as protectorates of this sacred place. And I saw that in all things they acted to this end, that by their sweat, their tears, and their very blood they stood true to their birthright.
>
> I witnessed the Fifty-three Raid. I watched in tearful reverence as Dan Barlow ran himself near to death to warn of the police cars he saw coming. I saw the tears upon the cheeks of the mothers of this community

who lamented for their husbands and feared for their children. I saw the life blood of this place in secret and strange places praying, pleading, and begging unto God that he might restore them to their sacred homes, to their sacred priesthood husbands. I beheld the sons of John Y. Barlow through these difficult times become true priesthood men, true defenders of god's work. I beheld, in particular, Dan Barlow apply himself to the building up of this kingdom unto God. And I saw that he was given great wisdom to understand the workings of government and man and that he did use his understanding to bring peace to this community, that he cultivated many important relationships of respect with the world.

I witnessed a great speaker raised up under Leroy S. Johnson and I witnessed this speaker fill the hearts of his children and this people with unbridled love and devotion to God. I stood in awe ready to stand the tide forever having been so moved by his words for he stood as Aaron stood to Moses. And I beheld that this man knew the prophet better than any man of his time. I beheld that he received special knowledge through the mouth of God and that many things he was told he held near and dear to his heart and that he has yet to reveal some of these things. And I beheld that this man carried the true birthright of John Y. Barlow; I beheld that it was Truman Barlow and that he was a just and true man worthy of his calling.

I watched as many men with their wives and children became disillusioned and left the care of our beloved prophet Leroy S. Johnson. And I saw that in this time of sorrow the sons of John Y. Barlow did hedge up the rift that formed in our prophet's heart having lost so many dear friends and that through the strength and love of the sons of John Y. Barlow he was able to continue on down the road together with the faithful, the pure, the meek and the mild.

I witnessed a great patriarch, Joseph I. Barlow, raised up unto God's work under the direction of Leroy S. Johnson. And I did witness this patriarch apply himself with a fervor to the defense of God's work and God's sacred land and to the institution of the UEP. And I saw that some were fearful and did resent him.

I watched as the sons of John Y. Barlow placed the mortal frame of their prophet into the ground and unto God. And I beheld that in this time the sons of John Y. Barlow did receive a new steward, Rulon Jeffs, to administer the laws of God unto them. And I saw that he was a just and fair prophet and administrator. And I beheld the mortal frame of this prophet also placed into the sacred earth.

And darkness crept into my dream and a great fog did form. I witnessed as many of the labors of our forefathers went unrecognized and unappreciated. And I did see the world's respect begin to whither for the people's work. I beheld a harsh time in which forgiveness was abandoned. And I beheld too many families destroyed for petty reasons. I beheld children torn from their fathers and mothers torn from their husbands. I beheld the people of God crying in the darkness for God to deliver them. Fear filled my heart and I too prayed for deliverance.

And in the darkness a light began to form and rays of light penetrated everywhere and bathed my heart in joy. I beheld the prophet John Y. Barlow before me and he did speak unto me and told me many things that did fill my heart with cheer, things that I cannot share. For this reason I shall not reveal my identity. The prophet then instructed me to look and I beheld a great meeting of men and I beheld the prophet Rulon Jeffs in glowing glory before me and I beheld the mantle of the prophet pass onto the pure blood of John Y. Barlow. And I beheld the eldest of the sons of John Y. Barlow, Louis Barlow, did receive the mantle and that his being was filled with wisdom and words of God. I beheld John Y. Barlow command unto his son to step up to his calling and to forsake his birthright no more, that his time remaining quiet has passed, that he was chosen before the world was created to do an important work and that the time for his calling has come. I then watched as he addressed each of his sons telling them in turn to defend their birthright and that God had marvelous plans for his people should they stay true, should they stay pure in heart, meek, and mild.

I beheld John Y. Barlow address our beloved bishop, Fred M Jessop who had been put away from the view of his people. And I saw that our bishop had become weak and feeble and that age had crept upon him. And I saw that through vices of man he was stripped of the right to share the love of God with his people and I beheld he wept. And my heart ached and I wept not alone for I saw the pure and the meek and the mild weeping with me. I witnessed the great prophet, John Y. Barlow, thank him for the lifetime of love's labor that he put into building this community. And I saw the bishop true and honorable in his methods, give this compliment to God. And I wept for I felt in my heart that he might pass from us too soon.

I woke and marveled at this dream and the sprit of God did burn in my bosom and I resolved to do as I had been instructed. I wish also to express my love and devotion to the prophet as shown to me by God and to commit myself to God through his wisdom. (End of letter)

A few days later another letter was mailed to people of the community. It is reproduced here as it was written. 1-15-2004.

A simple word to those in Colorado City/Hildale who are currently following Warren Jeffs. Never and nowhere, in the known history of God's work upon this earth, has He condoned the marriage of a mother to her son. It is an abomination in the eyes of God and should be shouted from the roof tops. In spite of Uncle Roy's teachings to all parties, the fact that Warren Jeffs, convincing his own mothers to wed and bed him, does not make a prophet of him. A true prophet of God has a testimony of Jesus Christ and <u>correctly</u> foretells the future. One of the many examples of Warren Jeffs (as proclaimed prophet at the death of his father) giving an incorrect prophecy quite some time ago was when he told us to flee California and come back to Colorado City/Hildale because California was to be immediately destroyed. We were so obedient that when the urgent call came, we rushed back home "to be spared of the destruction", dropping everything, jobs, contracts, obligations, materials, equipment, etc. By the end of that day not one of us was in the state of California and we still haven't returned to work in that state. Warren, in making a prophecy about Satan gathering his forces to come against us, then publicly thumbing his nose at the united states government, along with the continuing use of severe dictatorship-like powers as well as still giving and taking underage girls to wife after severe warnings, is a no-brainer. Of course "Satan will rage." Duh!!!

Uncle Roy felt concern for our future and so should we. He taught us something publicly in one of his last sermons, after returning from Salt Lake City, Utah, that he had never mentioned before. He said that he had run in to, or was almost overwhelmed by, a power in Salt Lake City that was almost stronger then he was. He told us that he would never go to Salt Lake again and he never did. While acknowledging how sinister this sounded, most of us didn't understand what he was talking about and just shelved this statement. Others, on our own, or perhaps at the subtle suggestions of others, bent Uncle Roy's words around until we thought the Mormon Church, who seemed to us to be leaving more and more of their original tenets and doctrines behind, was what he had been referring to. Had Uncle Roy been awakened to something subtle and insidious that we were not yet aware of?

Seeing things from hindsight is not so difficult. What is difficult is honestly admitting to <u>seeing things as they are,</u> not as what we are told they are, or as we wish them to be. One or two weeks after Uncle Roy made the statement, Uncle Rulon, the only other ordained apostle as well as the Salt Lake community bishop who we understood was to be the next in line if Uncle Roy died, in public sermon stated, " I hope and pray that I was not the cause of that statement by our prophet." We hoped so too. But did Uncle Rulon suspect that he, or something connected to him, was the cause of that statement?

Thru hindsight, we can recognize that there was indeed, an insidious new power gaining a foothold, that was slowly creeping into the fold. This wasn't an old established power that was easily recognized. This statement of Uncle Roy's occurred at the time in our history when Warren Jeffs had been given control of the Salt Lake City Alta Academy by his father, Uncle Rulon. This new school administrator began a somewhat foreign era of physically and mentally forcing young children to be righteous through fear. Fear of being physically whipped so bad by the principal of the academy that you could hardly walk and couldn't sit down comfortably for days. Fear of being publicly expelled from school and ostracized from your friends for small infractions of rules. This being done to scare the remaining children into being totally submissive and obedient. And, because of something you had said or done, (or not said or done) the fear of having our parents brought in and questioned by Warren about intimate things in their personal lives and beliefs they may have that may have conflicted with "correct teachings." The repercussions from this sort of treatment are traumatic and disastrous to a young person's mind.

As Warren's strength among the children grew, he fostered the need in these children to seek out what they were taught by him was evil and "humbly reporting" it in anticipation of a perceived position of superiority. This included, "humbly" informing Warren about any doctrinal or differences of opinion their own parents or family members might have had with those in authority. Warren planted small seeds in the minds of those young people that after "humbly and sweetly" informing on someone, they felt more elevated than those around them and "more worthy of building up the kingdom of God." These kinds of seeds grew and created a yearning for perceived power, position or authority, even at the expense of friends, neighbors, relatives, and even parents. Informants were everywhere. Children against parents, wives against husbands, and brethren against brethren. You didn't know who you could trust. Independent thinking, of any kind, was driven further underground. This force disguised as "love", began to slowly spread beyond the confines of the school and into our Salt Lake City community. During the administration of Uncle Rulon, it slowly, but surely, began to make its way into the Colorado City/Hildale community. This could go on and on, history repeating itself. The clues to our future are hidden deep in Warren's past, even preceding Alta Academy. Seek it and you will find it if you are earnest and are willing to put forth the mental and physical effort, in addition to prayer, that will be required.

Friends, this insidious wickedness has covertly crept among us, almost unawares, except for the many small hints that we were taught and trained to "just put on the shelf of belief" with the accompanying statement that "understanding would come later if we would just be obedient and go forward in faith, nothing wavering." This evil force, now among us, is a child no longer and needs to be exposed, Uncle Roy only warned us about this. He then withdrew from the saints in the Salt Lake community and permanently resided "down south." What knowledge did he suddenly acquire when he exclaimed, "oh, my God?!"

Uncle Fred, removed from power last month, and who has our bishop been for more years than most of us can remember, publicly said, "In case you elders haven't noticed, this work has done 180 degrees turn." Elementary students know that a complete circle is 360 degrees. If we do a one half turn 180 degrees, it is exactly the opposite of the way we were headed. Were we going to Hell under Uncle Roy's administration and to Heaven now? Were we going to Heaven under Uncle Roy's administration and to Hell now? You do the math. You can't have it both ways. Divide and conquer seems to be the motto of the day.

When Uncle Rulon was still alive and sitting on the stand, his son, Warren Jeffs, publicly speaking about John Woolley, (the father) and Lorin Woolley, (the son) both being prophets one after the other. Warren then made a revealing statement when he said, "then was the time for the reign of the Woolleys. Now is the time for the reign of the Jeffs." What exactly did Warren mean by the plurality of the statement? Slip of the tongue, perhaps?

Uncle Rulon had told us God revealed to him that his body would be renewed. His 67 mostly young wives, yearning for motherhood, would have children, and that he would live an additional 350 years into the millennium. He said he would be our last and only living prophet. That is why he didn't ordain any more apostles. With that kind of a life span there was no need to set up any chain of command. It simply wasn't needed. What was needed for the next 350 years was the trusted bishop and counselor Uncle Roy and Uncle Rulon had counted on for years to be with them. Before his stroke, Uncle Rulon said many times, "Uncle Fred and I are one." Uncle Rulon, at Priesthood meeting, in front of all the men, told Uncle Fred that God had also revealed to him, (Uncle Rulon) that Uncle Fred would also live to be an additional 350 years old and that his body would be renewed as well. He then asked Uncle Fred to move to the front of the stand and sit on a chair. He then requested that his new first councilor, Warren Jeffs, seal upon Uncle Fred, the same blessing of a renewal of his body and long life into the millennium that had been given to him.

From that time on, until the death of Uncle Rulon, believing in the actual bodily renewal of Uncle Rulon and Uncle Fred was an absolute requirement to staying in this religion. To even wonder if our beloved Uncle Rulon was getting old and feeble minded, after his terrible stroke, or that he may one day die, was cause to be turned into church authorities by those "humbly seeking out sin from among the people". If caught, the "heretic" would be called in and questioned by Warren and if found guilty of lacking faith that Uncle Rulon and Uncle Fred would be renewed, the offender would be cut off from the church and expelled from the community.

Warren constantly preached renewal of Uncle Rulon and kept it foremost in our minds. With the people truly believing that Uncle Rulon would be "our last prophet", as he said, and that he and Uncle Fred would lead us for the next 350 years, what was the need for the rule of the father and son Jeffs? Unless of course, one of Rulon's sons, beneath his "humble" pretense, was an aspiring man. Remember Uncle Rulon died on Sunday, dissolving the First Presidency. Warren was still only an elder. The following day, at Monday morning meeting, Uncle Warren, besides giving us details on the passing of Uncle Rulon, made this statement. "I won't say much, but I will say this, "Hands off my father's wives." Speaking to the newly bereaved widows, he said, "You women will live as if father is still alive and in the next room." I remember thinking to myself, "Who in the world, at a time like this, would be lusting after Uncle Rulon's wives?" The thought sickened me.

This was said by Warren on Monday. By that Friday, Warren moved in on those women so fast, and with such finesse, that only two of his "mothers" had enough fortitude to stand up against him. Those stunned women, who had sincerely believed that their husband and prophet would live 350 years and give them children, went through the shock of losing their husband to death, seeing him buried, Warren proclaiming himself prophet quickly thereafter and then immediately receiving revelation to marry those women "those found worthy of him" in secret ceremonies. Before committing that kind of sin before the eyes of God, one of his mothers, seeing the futility of fighting him off, bravely fled the compound and left the community at a run. Another of Warren's young "mothers" flatly refused to go along with the marriage. She was sent back to live with her father and told she would live the rest of her life out without ever being married.

As Jesus said, " Those who have ears to hear, let them hear. Those who have eyes to see let them see." This undercurrent of fear that we now have, but won't admit to having for fear that it proves us "wicked", has already been fully experienced by the first test cases at Alta Academy and is now being felt in full force by us as people.

Friends, there is only one power that governs or rules with the use of fear. The danger is no longer at the gate. The wolf is in the fold and the shepherds are down.

A Concerned Friend. (End of Letter)

These two letters were designed to win back the community for the Barlows. Their ability to speak persuasively, often manipulating the truth to serve their own goals, must be considered by the reader.

18

Violence Threatened

Anonymous Letter of Warning to Ben Bistline:

On the 22nd of January, I received the preceding "Concerned Friend" letter addressed to Ben Bistline. Apparently I was still on their mailing list. And on the same day I also received the following letter addressed to Benny Bistiline. It was one of a kind, sent to me only, and typed on lined looseleaf paper with holes on the edge. It is revealing as to the danger of potential violence that lies among the followers of Warren Jeffs.

The personal letter is now in the hands of the FBI. The letter is reproduced here exactly as it was written.

Cover Page to Letter

> Benny Bistiline
> I know that you're an evil man and that you're not a friend to the righteous in Colorado City or to the UEP but sometimes God uses the evil to do a righteous purpose. You stand for apostates and gentiles and you as well as your kind should take this letter as a warning. Hopefully after reading this the gentiles will understand our point of view and have a little more respect for us. When you take on God's chosen people you are playing with his fire.

The Letter:

> I'm from Colorado City and that means that you view me as a polygamist. We don't believe in polygamy. We believe in plural marriage which is the new and everlasting covenant of marriage as laid down by the prophet Joseph Smith. The difference is one is commanded of God and the other is not. I have a job to do. My job is to protect the prophet Warren Jeffs and the Lords chosen people from you cockroaches and scum. I'm sick and tired of the harassment we get here. It seems like every other day you gentiles and apostates are looking down our throats trying to make trouble. Why don't you just leave us alone! The truth is, you're jealous because you can't have what we got. We got priesthood and that makes our women and children obedient to us. We live a different more religious way of life and

you shouldn't hate us because of it. You're green with envy because your wifes argue and will leave you if you don't bow and scrape to their needs. Your children don't obey you. All they want to do is watch TV and play computer games. You gentiles don't know how to direct women and children because you don't know about priesthood. You don't understand what it takes to be the priesthood leader of a family. We have to raise our children like calves in a stall. Why do you think we don't allow gentile women as wifes or allow gentile people to move into our town. We work with our children everyday to make sure they don't know too much about you. You'd just destroy them in a matter of minutes. That's why were glad our prophet commanded us not to go to public school. We don't want our children being asked stupid questions that'll just destroy their lives. To much worldly influence destroys children. That's why we make our children dress with long dresses with jeans underneath them. The long clothes and all make them stand out so that you gentiles will leave them alone. Besides they'd never talk to you because they know that all you people are servants of Lucifer and that given half a chance you'd put your foot in the door and pry them wide open to sinning. That's another reason why you'd better leave us alone. You can't have these girls. They know better than to be associating with you all. You gentiles and apostates have no business here at all. Under the constitution we're guaranteed our religious freedom. We can do what we want here and you people should have nothing to do about it. We should be allowed to set up our own government and laws. The courts did not follow the headings of God and let us use our own laws. The courts accused us of trying to make a lawless society. The prophecies will come true to fix it. There won't be a yellow dog here to greet us or stand in our way when it comes time for the prophet to rule this world. Besides we already control everything here in the town anyways. You accuse us of marrying our cousins and relates. The Lord tells us who to marry not you. Rodney did the right thing. When it comes to choices you have to choose to do what the prophet wants even if you are sent to prison. The thing here is obedience. We're obedient to our prophet and in turn our wives and children are obedient to us. But that's none of your business because it's our religion!!! The world frowns on us for living our religion. But were not worried because God will protect us. We believe in following God's laws. Our prophet tells us that God's laws are more important than the laws of the land and so we choose to not follow the laws of the land. It doesn't matter what the people are doing here. It's a matter of principle. God brought these children into the world and he'll do with them what he wants. God raised these people up for this purpose. That's what the whole plan of Colorado City and the UEP is about. The UEP makes it so that if someone disobeys the prophet then he can make them leave so they don't destroy the lives of our children. These things are to keep our children protected. Our children must be protected from the evil ways of gentiles. We can't have people hanging around giving our children stupid ideas. Our children are scared of the world. They don't want to leave this town because they can see the ruined mess their lives would be if they do leave. God will curse them and destroy them. We've seen it time and time again that when people leave this town, satin possesses them and they go crazy. You gentiles don't have a right to get in the way with the way we raise our children or our women. The way we do things here is part of our religion and the constitution guaranteed freedom of our religion. You should know we don't force our children to do things like getting married anyway. Uncle Sam says in our priesthood meeting that we tell the world we don't force marriages. Is what we do is invite people to obey. The prophet then tells them which guy to marry. There's no force involved. People can choose to disobey. They have that right. Without perfect obedience we do not have priesthood. Obedience is the first law of heaven and when you disobey you break the first law of heaven. When they disobey they make a choice and the Lord tells the prophet to tell them to leave town. He has the right to forbid them to ever speak to even their families again. If a family chooses not to obey the prophet then they choose to disobey. If they choose to disobey then they make a choice to leave. They weren't forced because they made that choice. And their house wasn't theirs anyway it was the Lords. You see if they choose to disobey they turn themselfes over to Lucifer who will destroy them. The prophet says the only hope for a person who disobeys is blood atonement. He hasn't told anybody to kill anybody else. He's working very hard to get us to a point where God will clean up the world. That's why you see all the stuff happening here in our town. He's destroying the seeds of contention. If we're good enough then we'll get to help the prophet do his work. Then God will be able to order the destroying angels to go forth and they will kill off all the wicked. The only way you'll be saved is if you're wearing the priesthood garments and if you don't have the markings of the beast on you. We are ready to answer the call when our prophet asks it. He said it will be the young that will do this. We young priesthood boys have the most special privilege of getting to serve our prophet in the last days that are upon us. We meet in special priesthood meetings to learn special things that are special. This is the greatest time for a priesthood man to be alive. The prophet has promised us that the destructions are here and we will get to witness them.

I have a message for the person who wrote the letter in the newspaper. Uncle Louis supports our prophet with all his heart. You did a most evil thing in trying to stir up trouble with us. I hope you know the penalty for making false prophecies. If you really did have a dream then you are the most inspired man of satin I've ever known. God will reveal to the prophet who you are. I shudder to think what will happen to you. If I were you I would be shaking in my shoes with fear for your life because the Lords going to take your life. You have brought down a scourge and condemnation upon yourself. At this point there's no place you can hide that the prophet can't find.

The best plan for you gentiles and apostates is to leave us alone. It doesn't matter what you do cause the Lord will deal with you shortly. The more you gentiles bother us the harder you are going to get judged and the more terrible will be your destruction. We down to every single last man in Colorado City will gladly die to protect our prophet. As the mouthpiece of God on this earth we will do whatever the prophet commands us to do to protect the work of God. The best advice I can give you is to stay away from us and let us do Gods will as revealed to us by the prophet Warren Jeffs. (End of Letter)

In his new book *Polygamy Under Attack*, author and retired Sheriff's Lieutenant John Llewellyn devotes a chapter to the potential for violence that can and has occurred in some cults. And he was asked to make a similar presentation to several hundred law enforcement officers in a conference in St. George in January 2004, at the request of the Utah Attorney General.

He states: "The likelihood of aggressive violence initiated by 'leaders' of the prevailing organized groups is remote unless they are backed into a corner. Violence is more apt to come from deluded people . . . who without warning suddenly take it upon themselves to avenge the prophet or the principle of plural marriage.

"However, there is always the possibility of armed resistance on a grand scale much like occurred at Waco, Texas. The organized fundamentalists sects still believe in the doctrine of Blood Atonement that was preached by early leaders of the LDS Church." He then discusses other cult tragedies that have occurred in the past.

As they should, the FBI and law enforcement are taking seriously the possibility that someone, believing they act in the name of God or their prophet, will begin to avenge what they believe has been an assault on their leader. I called Ross Chatwin the day I received the threatening letter and cautioned him. And during his press conference, law enforcement was everywhere present.

ROSS CHATWIN

The next day, January 23, 2004, Ross Chatwin held a press conference at his home in Colorado City. Ross Chatwin is a young man in his early thirties who was recently told to leave his home and his wife and family, and leave the community. This message was sent to him from Warren Jeffs by James Zitting. The following is taken from a prepared speech that he read to about 50 reporters from all over the country who attended his press conference. It reads as follows:

Recently, I joined a growing list of men who have been told to leave their homes. I can't be sure as to why I've been told to leave behind everything that I've worked for.

I do know, however, that the owner of the UEP land trust, Warren Jeffs, has claimed to be receiving revelations of whom to evict. Typically he requires that the person in question quietly vacate their home and leave their family under the auspices that if they show complete humility he may restore to them what was lost. As part of the process, he requires the evictee to write a letter listing all of their sins. He says that if the list of sins does not match the list of sins that God gave him through revelation then their eviction becomes permanent. This is essentially the ultimatum that was given to me and it is the same ultimatum that was given former Mayor Dan Barlow and his brothers along with approximately 20 other men. My list of sins obviously did not match up with the list of sins Jeffs put together. I want James Zitting to know that what I have to do is stand up to Warren Jeffs and to the UEP. My family and I do not plan on leaving our home anytime soon. I am pleased to report that my wife has submitted to stay by my side regardless of Jeffs commandment to leave me. It was ultimately her choice to preserve our family. It is difficult for me to find the words that can express to her how much I appreciate her.

One of the messages I want to leave people of Colorado City is that they don't have to leave if they don't want to. I've come to realize that a few men stood up to the UEP, and paved the way for a better life for us all.

The young men of the FLDS church are taught that if they want advancement in the organization they must build a home upon UEP land. It's quite an exciting time for a young man. He knuckles down and puts everything he has into building his home all the while anticipating the possibility of marriage and of getting to start a family.

When I was a young, impressionable, a little ignorant, and maybe even a little over zealous, I wanted more than anything to build a home. As all marriages within the FLDS organization are assigned, I felt that as a 17 year-old boy at receiving a building lot from the UEP, it can only be matched by the dread of finally realizing the UEP might be used as an instrument to forcibly take my home from me.

If the UEP should try to evict you I would recommend that you resist leaving your home. The UEP has been known to send out notices asking that people move. I suggest that you ignore these notices. If you leave your home for more than 30 days, your home reverts back to the UEP.

While the possibility of losing your home is frustrating, the real travesty in Colorado City is the possibility of losing your family. The second message I would like to leave with the people of Colorado City is to not let some whimsical notion be the reason you break up your family. It's not fair to you and its especially not fair to your children. I've talked with individuals who, being stunned by the magnitude of the situation, allowed Jeffs to remove their families from them. They now deeply regret having allowed this to happen. Houses can ultimately be rebuilt. Once a family is destroyed, it leaves broken hearts that can never be healed. Please, give it some thought before you throw it all away. There are few systems of checks and balances to govern how Jeffs operates. One of the only ways we can affect what he is doing is by letting the world know about the things that go on inside this town. In this way, pressure from the outside world restricts to a degree what he can do. The Barlows have preached a concept of one man leadership that has come full round to ultimately remove them from the power. Jeffs has refined this doctrine even further. He claims to govern the FLDS church by way of a "benevolent dictatorship." Now Jeffs has been initially accepted, a renegade from Salt Lake City, to come into the position of the "one man" and have absolute power.

However, it is possible that Jeffs will abandon many of the members of the FLDS church. This does not mean that he plans on giving up the UEP anytime soon as it is his only source of income. My sources tell me that Jeffs is in the process of building a new community in a secret location and that he plans on taking a few of the elite to live there. Some evidence points to this compound being in Mexico. One of my resources tells me that the compound is being called Zion. In the last year, Jeffs has become extremely paranoid and is essentially gone into hiding. This is probably the actual reason as to why he's building a secret compound. Lately an entourage of bodyguards and wives attend him wherever he goes.

The compound as well as other responsibilities has obviously cost a great deal. The members of the FLDS church are being required to provide huge amounts of money to Jeffs. Last week on January 17 in the Saturday work meeting directed by the new bishop, the elders were instructed to come up with another thousand dollars each to give to Jeffs. Jeffs has obviously become increasingly frustrated with people being unable to pay. This latest demand also carries with it *a threat of being left behind* if you fail to come up with the money. And, this is just one of many required thousand dollar donations in the past little while. His need for cash has severely taxed the people of the FLDS church.

Overall, Jeffs' leadership has been reckless at best. It's shocking to realize that the owner of a 100 million dollar asset could act so carelessly. I am sickened by the number of families Jeffs has been instrumental in destroying. It's baffling to see the men who choose to stay around after they've had everything taken from them. At least 50 men have been essentially turned into eunuchs. They continue to consider themselves members of the FLDS church. They watch while other men take their children and wives. It is their lot in life to put their noses to the grindstone and hope that in the next life they may be given families again.

Jeffs' methods are cruel and final. He operates his benevolent dictatorship with a cold indifference. Most of the people he ostracizes are humiliated in public meetings before thousands of people. In my case, he told the congregation that I was a master deceiver. He said that he planned on publishing a list of names and that my name as well as two others would be listed in that publication. Jeffs defined what this meant by saying that "anybody who thinks they have priesthood when they don't are master deceivers." In the case of 20 men who were recently ostracized he told them to stand up in the audience of more than 1500 so that everyone could see who they were. He then publicly rebuked them. At the end of this meeting he required that the congregation get on their knees while he stood and prayed.

Some people are concerned that I might be endangering my life for sticking up for my rights. I do fear that some overly zealous person from within the FLDS Church might take it upon themselves to do something rash. But more than that, I fear what would happen if Jeffs was allowed to act unchecked. I feel it's my responsibility to let the world know about the situation here in Colorado City and that in doing so, I ultimately make things safer and better for everyone by limiting what Jeffs can do. Jeffs claims that "he fears no man or set of men." And yet he has walled his compound in Hildale with an 8 foot fence and has surrounded himself with bodyguards. I believe that Jeffs actions show that in fact he is afraid to face the troubles he has created. I believe that what I am doing here today does impact Jeffs in ways that are helpful to the people of the FLDS organization.

Some of the zealous young people within the FLDS organization need to be made aware of the implications of acting in a rash manner. Anything you do that might harm another individual will bring down a thorough investigation of this people. The very religion you are trying to protect will be exposed beyond your wildest imagination.

I know that most people within the FLDS Church will reject the advice I'm offering them. But at least the information will be out there. There may come a time they'll be able to use this information in order to react in an appropriate way. It is my hope that more people will stand up to Jeffs. If you are scared, just stand up and you will find that you have lots of support; just make sure that your family is standing with you. I'm your friend and will gladly help in any way that I can.

I am deeply concerned for the young people who are choosing to run away. I feel that these people need a tremendous amount of support. I am concerned that the world may not be aware of how sheltered these young people have been. They were raised in a culture that is quite different from what they are moving into and I fear that they are extremely vulnerable to some of the pitfalls of being a teenager. I would like to extend an offer of friendship to anyone who needs help. Please contact me and I will be happy to stand with you.

I want to say, "Lets stand up for what's right and help stop this evil dictator from destroying more families." Almost all the people here really are good people and I love them all. They just follow blindly and they are taught to not ask questions.

I just want to get the ball rolling and to help pave the road for others to add to. Almost all the families in this society are really good and hard working people. They are just taught (brainwashed) from infancy to just trust, believe, and follow like sheep and not to ask questions. If we don't understand something then we were told, "just put it on the shelf of belief."

When I'm tired of being kept ignorant, my shelf was so stacked up it broke.

We need your help to stop Warren S. Jeffs from destroying families, kicking us out of our homes, and marrying our children into some kind of political dollar browney point system.

This Hitler-like dictator has got to be stopped before he ruins us all and this beautiful town."

Ross then held up a book saying, "Warren has studied this book for many years. It is what he uses as a guideline to govern this community and control the people."

Someone then asked: "What is the book?"

Ross replied, "THE RISE AND FALL OF THE THIRD REICH."

ROSS CHATWIN WINS COURT DECISION

FLDS leaders tried to have Ross evicted from his home and this led to court action at Kingman, Mohave County, Arizona.

In May of 2004, Judge Chavez, Mohave County Superior Court Judge, ruled in favor of Ross Chatwin in the civil suit wherein the UEP was attempting to evict him from his home in Colorado City. Everyone was waiting to see how the judge would rule on a tenant at will issue, because the outcome would affect many other families on the throes of being evicted themselves. And, reportedly, there are more than thirty families at risk.

How ironic this is.

In the late 1980s and 1990s, when the dissidents battled in court to keep their houses, the judge finally ruled that to evict people from their homes without paying them for the home would be Unjust Enrichment. As these dissidents spent untold amounts of money for lawyers, and all the while being treated badly by other Colorado City residents, no one could have guessed that one day their exhausting battle would set a legal precedent that could free families yet to become dissidents. The first group paid a price for their own freedom, and for those to come.

And, on an interesting note, a federal authority recently told me that if an occupant is paying utilities for the home where he is living, he is not a tenant at will.

The ruling of Judge Chavez to allow Ross to stay in his home sets a precedence that will really hurt the cult leaders when they attempt to evict others. It has also given courage to others who have been told to move.   The more people who stand up and refuse to move, the more it will weaken the coercive power of the UEP leaders. If they have to initiate a lawsuit every time they attempt to evict someone, and they lose the lawsuit, it will become cost prohibitive to them.

It is my hope that rather than try to oust unbelievers, they will decide to take "their faithful followers" to one of the compounds being established elsewhere, thus making it more tolerable for those who remain.

19

Freedom & Industry Gaining Ground

The citizens of Centennial Park have worked to develop their community. In 2001, one of John Timpson's wives started a charter school called Masada for grade school age children. Jed Hammon still runs the Colorado City Academy, a private high school funded by tuition. One of John Timpson's daughters is a nurse practitioner and runs a clinic at Centennial Park. It is under her care and direction that the delivery of babies is overseen as she operates under a midwife license.

Several other businesses have been developed in Centennial Park: A cabinet shop; a separate cabinet distributing business; Joe Knudson's mortgage company, PRIME; and the sons of Jed Hammon established a concrete and sand business named Centennial Rock and Sand. These boys of Jed Hammon also own and operate a company that designs subdivisions, industrial parks, etc. And several private individuals do contract work outside the community.

Centennial Park is not incorporated, so it is not entitled to government funding for such things as sewers, roads, or sidewalks. However, some of the citizens have paved several roads, put in several sidewalks, curbs, gutters, and also a sewer system serving probably fifty percent of the town. This sewer system uses the Colorado City sewer ponds and sewage is pumped up to that pond from Centennial Park.

The city has their own water system supplied by wells, some as deep as 400 feet. Many of the people living in Centennial park have drilled their own wells, but they are still using septic tanks, because John Timpson has such a high fee to hook up to the sewer and water system, about $7,500 for each individual family.

Centennial Park citizens are notably more affluent than those in the neighboring cities of Hildale/Colorado City. This is due to owning their own property, so they are more free to make decisions and use their own initiative. There is no time in history that communism has ever worked. The United Order principles portrayed by the polygamists at Colorado City/Hildale is nothing but Communism. The leaders of First Ward are continually moving members from the homes they built into homes another family built. This is a protective measure so that if the UEP evicts a man and he contests it in court, the man cannot claim he built the house from which he was just evicted. This moving from house to house keeps people in a constant state of upheaval.

Centennial Park members are secure in their homes since they own their own property and their own home. Marion Hammon can be thanked for this. But it is a thorn for John Timpson to contend with. I think he would like to control the people more than he does.

If left to his own devices and through evolution of time, I believe he will attempt to have the people turn the homes back to him so he has more control over the people and their circumstances.

SUMMIT MEETING IN ST. GEORGE

During the summer of 2003, Mark Shurtliff and Terry Goddard, the attorneys general of Utah and Arizona, conducted a summit meeting in St. George, Utah. They were there not to attack polygamy, but to try to curb the underage marriages of young girls to older men. The wanted to discuss with local law enforcement what realistically could be done.

They conducted a public forum meeting and probably a hundred women from Centennial Park attended. The women were adamant in expressing that they were happy in their religion of living polygamy, and did not want interference from law enforcement, such as husbands being arrested on bigamy charges.

Mark Shurtliff tried to assure them that they were in no danger of such, saying that polygamy is an almost unenforceable law at this time. Constitutions in Utah and Arizona simply state that polygamy shall be prohibited. There has been no penalty set on the living of polygamy, therefore there is no legal means to prosecute.

The women of Centennial Park invited the attorneys general to meet with them at Centennial Park in a closed door session so they could air their grievances and try to persuade law enforcement that they were happy and just wanted to be left alone.

Prior to this meeting John Timpson, leader of the Centennial group, instructed the women that it was their fight. They must be the ones to enlighten the outside world of their intentions and wishes, and explain the situation at Centennial Park. In the closed door session Mark Shurtliff advised the women that it was not his place, in fact it was impossible for him, to change the law against polygamy. To bring about a change in the law, to make polygamy a legal choice, the people of Centennial Park would have to take the issue to the rest of America to consider.

CHANGING THE POLYGAMY LAWS

There are two ways to go about this. One is to take a test case before the U. S. Supreme Court to reconsider the decision rendered in the 1880s, and to have them rule that the anti-polygamy laws were unconstitutional. But there is a very small chance that the U. S. Supreme Court will hear a case concerning polygamy because no one is ever arrested on polygamy; therefore, it is never taken to court.

The other way of changing the law is that it must be ratified by a majority of the other states in the United States and this would be an uphill battle. The more reasonable approach in decriminalizing polygamy is to have the state legislators put a penalty on polygamy and class it as a low misdemeanor such as fourth class. Therefore the penalty would be very small and no arrests would ever be made. This does not set up a protection for polygamist wives in case of a divorce, however. But it would decriminalize polygamy, thus making it a non-issue in the minds of the Centennial Park women.

CENTENNIAL PARK WOMEN BEGIN TO SPEAK OUT

Some of the Centennial Park Women have begun to publicly come forth, making statements in defense of their religion, claiming that it was their choice that they married into polygamy and that they married at a young age, such as sixteen.

One of these women, Marlyne Hammon, had a guest editorial published in *The Spectrum* newspaper of St. George, Utah, on the 29th of April 2004. She was very emphatic that she made the choice to marry at sixteen and to marry the man she married, and she wants the world to know that it is her right to make such a decision.

However, there is issue to be taken with her statements. She would never have made the choice to marry at sixteen or to marry the man that she did if she had not been counseled by one of the priesthood brethren, most likely her husband's father, to make that choice.

It is true that she made the choice to marry at sixteen and to marry the man she married, but only after she was "assigned" by Marion Hammon to do so. This is really not freedom in its fullest. For example, if a girl were to go to John Timpson and express her desire to marry a certain young man, she would be given a severe reprimand for attempting to make such a decision on her own, without priesthood guidance and instruction. She would then be told who she is supposed to marry and she has little choice but to comply.

In First Ward, they claim that they grant freedom of choice. But that choice is simply to obey and stay in the community with family or not to obey and be forced to leave the community, their entire family, friends, and be ostracized forever. So the people of Centennial Park do live a much freer life than those in First Ward. And, of course, it is due to the fact that they own their own property and are free to choose what they want to do in business to support themselves. They are not forced to turn ownership of their businesses over to their priesthood leader, such as Warren Jeffs has commanded his followers to do.

To own and control their own businesses, to reap the rewards of their own labors is creating a freedom that builds a town. The women are more modern in their dress than neighboring communities; they are not forced to wear long dresses and never cut their hair, etc.

These are hard-working, honest-hearted people and, within the structure of their religious belief, they are a moral people. This was also true in First Ward until Warren Jeffs began taking wives from different men and changing them around. This, in my view, is very immoral. But it is the immorality of the leader Warren Jeffs rather than the immorality of the people, who are suffering at the hands of Warren Jeffs.

THIRD WARD

In addition to First Ward and Second Ward, there is another group referred to as Third Ward.

In the 1930s when John Barlow first came to Short Creek, two of his brothers accompanied him. Edmund was the older brother, and Ianthus, the younger brother. In 1938 these two brothers were the first ones to abandon Short Creek and move back to Salt Lake City. Ianthus Barlow came back to the group in the 1970s and pledged allegiance to Leroy. After Ianthus died in about 1980 and after the split that created Second Ward, a few of Ianthus's sons moved back to the area, and established themselves in Centennial Park. It was not long, however, before they were unable to agree with John Timpson's leadership.

About twenty families, sons and grandsons of Ianthus Barlow, built homes in Centennial Park where they were able to purchase property and could own their homes. These particular Barlows have become independent of any of the groups. Some of the Williams boys, some of the Hammon boys, and others have aligned themselves with these Barlows, and they hold meetings in one another's homes. They continue to live plural marriage, but they do not claim any priesthood authority, and make commitments only to one another and to living in polygamy. These Barlows are all located in approximately the same area on the south part of Centennial Park.

NEW ARIZONA LAW AGAINST MARRYING A CHILD

The Arizona Republic reported on May 21, 2004, that a state law banning child polygamy was passed by the Legislature and signed into law by Gov. Janet Napolitano. "The law makes religious marriages or cohabitation between a married adult and a minor a felony. It also gives the state the ability to charge church pastors who perform the ceremonies and the minors' parents with felony crimes. Modeled after a Utah law. . . It goes into effect 90 days after the Legislature adjourns."

Some suggest that the law will be hard to prosecute, however, because victims are unlikely to come forward to testify. There is hope that the law will act as a deterrent, causing men to be more cautious as they consider marrying underage girls.

20

An Interview with Ben Bistline

Q. It appears that Warren Jeffs is settling up other areas for his group.

A. Everyone now knows that Warren Jeffs has purchased property near Eldorado, Texas, in Schleicher County. Three apartment-type complexes have been erected on the 1300 acre site, and at least two more complexes are under construction. Allen Steed, ordained a patriarch by Warren Jeffs, is the man in charge of this compound, called Yearning For Zion (YFZ). His counselors are Roy Steed, Ernie Jessop, and David Allred. It is rumored that some of Warren's loyal followers did not want to go to Mexico, so the Texas compound was established to accommodate them.

It is believed that Fred Jessop is at this compound in Texas. The letter his family received sounds like Fred, his style, tone, and vernacular.

There is evidence that Warren Jeffs has at least two other developing compounds as well: one near Benjamin Hills, Mexico, south of Nogales in the state of Sonora; the other near Encinada, Baja, south of Tiajuana.

The FLDS has long been familiar with Mexico and there are other polygamy groups there. Back in the 1940s John Barlow tried to establish a colony in Mexico in cooperation with Dare LeBaron, father of Ervil LeBaron. But when Dare insisted on being the priesthood leader of the entire group, Barlow discontinued participation. Reportedly, newspaper reporters have been searching Mexico for FLDS compounds by air.

Q. Why Texas?

A. There are a number of likely possibilities. Presently Texas has no anti-polygamy law, and bigamy is defined as "state marriages." A sparsely populated county can avoid the public eye, and it is not that far from the border of Mexico. Also, the age of majority/emancipation in Texas is seventeen, unlike Utah, which is eighteen.

Q. They said it was a hunting lodge. Now they say there will be no more than 200 people living there, that they are building three buildings – each 21,600 square feet. How would anyone know how many people are actually living there?

A. Three buildings of 21,600 square feet have been completed, and at least two more are under construction. The people living in this compound will be living a type of united order, wherein they will share all commodities. I expect that probably each building will be

Dear - Very Dear

William - Martha Susan. Echo. et al. All my loved Cherished People
Men, Women Wives, Brothers, Sisters Babys. Children Father Mothers Whoever —
I have come to Know that "we" have been Selected to enter into the training for
Life eternal, Leaveing loved one friends Relatives. People, Set on a
Program Never to Return — As if dead to association except. You Come
to me. (if I can Qualify) for Eternal Life and you also. So don't despair
Just accept the plan. Gods Glorious plan which includes our
giving our energies to Heavenly Fathers Program of becoming Like Him.
Our Great Loving Father. We Accepted when we were Baptized.
"We" as here, "you" there. So we are alike engaged together (than the Lord)
Oh so thankful we should be. offering in Sacrifice all earthly things.
it is not a curse it is an eternal Blessing.
So Let us be of good cheer, get busy and Press on. Uncle Warren
Love us. and prays for us. Lots be happy I Love you truly truly Dear
                              NEXT MORNING

Fathers plan is perfect, so wonderful so eternal and Absolutly Necessary
O, if parents, adults, would Keep in mind how precious little ones are I am sure we
would treat them as God's very own, We would Save ourselves Later Concern and
Thus keep them in the path of eternal Life, which is their Right. and our sacred
Responsibility, May Heavenly Father help us change our ways before it is to Late.
Dear Family let us get on to Fathers plan, I Love you all. Let all the family
See My belated Warning. Starts with Keeping Sweet,
    Aspects of the Spirit of the Lord
First. it is True, it is firm, it is Kind, it is easy to understand, it is inclsive, it is adaptible to te
little children, it is good to feel, it uplifts, it is the Result of prayer. His gift

Please let all Read on hear this letter, Wives, Brother, Sisters Sons Daughters, friends.
                              Sure Do Love You

Letter believed to be written by Fred Jessop mentioned in first question of Ben Bistline interview.

220

under the direction of one man, one elder. Possibly there may be only one family in that building if he has many wives, or possibly there could be as many as five families in each building if it houses men with only one wife. Each building could conceivably house one hundred people counting men, women and children. Five buildings would hold 500 people.

The 200 number that they gave out is only a sidetrack so as to cause no panic in the area. I suspect eventually there will be more buildings constructed and more families moving in. If Warren Jeffs decides to wrest political control of the county, which is a conceivable concern, he would have to move in approximately 2,000 voting-age people. My estimation is that within a ten-year period, there could be over 2,000 people living at YFZ compound.

Q. Which members are living there?

A. The key men that are going to Eldorado at this time are only there to establish the community. Some will take one or two wives with them while the construction is going on. After the community is established, most of the key men will return to Colorado City or to another of Warren Jeffs' compounds.

A number of rank and file residents (not the key men in Warren Jeffs organization) will live there. Some of these have only one wife. Others with multiple wives will undoubtedly take their wives and children with them. This will be a permanent residence for a number of Jeffs' followers. There'll be one or possibly two high priests who will live in the new community with one or more of their wives and families. Their other families will remain in Colorado City/Hildale or move to Mexico, and the men will spend much time commuting back and forth. Warren Jeffs may possibly move some of his family to Texas also.

Q. *The Eldorado Success* newspaper quotes the FLDS as saying they won't go into competition with local people for contracting jobs. But if they decide to do so, what would stop them?

A. If the FLDS people at the YFZ compound would decide to go into competition with the local people at Eldorado, of course there would be nothing that could stop them. However, it would not be to their advantage to do so. First, there is not enough business in the small community to entice them. They will go to the larger cities such as San Angelo or San Antonio to do their bidding and contracting work. These workers would be young men ages sixteen to twenty who are on "work missions" and their income would be turned over to the FLDS.

Q. The FLDS in Texas say their intent is not to apply for government assistance.

A. The YFZ commune in Texas will try to be self-sustaining, raising their own food, and where necessary travel to cities such as San Angelo to purchase other groceries they need. But it is very likely that they will apply for food stamps and WIC, their common practice.

Q. Will a United Order work in Texas?

A. I suspect their attempt to live a united order, all eating at the same table and having no independent provisions of their own, is a system that will not work very long, as has been proven in Mormon history. They seem to be successful for a short time but soon people become very unhappy living under the strain. Everyone does not have the same tastes or the same desires for food, clothing, etc. There is also the issue of automobiles. What does one person do if he wants to take his wife, say, to dinner outside the community? That would almost be an impossibility. There will be squabbles with family members and with other families. I think the United Order type living could break apart from its own internal squabbling after a period of time. If Warren Jeffs still has any control over the Texas compound, at that time he will undoubtedly excommunicate those who are squabbling and attempt to move others in.

Q. FLDS leaders in Eldorado claim there won't be any child brides, but how will authorities know? It is a closed and gated community.

A. There is no way authorities will know whether there are child brides. In the rare case where there may be a problem with a young girl bearing a child and needing hospitalization, they would probably take her to a hospital in San Angelo. One thing to know about the FLDS leadership: They never tell the truth. They only say what is convenient to relieve the pressure at the time. Unless there is some system set up between the local authorities to be able to go into the community and conduct investigations or inquiries among the people, there'll never be any way to know of child marriages. But the FLDS will never allow this to happen.

   We know from sad experience that there will always be underage marriages. If a girl is allowed to remain unmarried until she becomes eighteen, it is much harder for the leaders of the cult to convince her to marry some man old enough to be her father or grandfather. It is much easier to convince a younger girl of fifteen or sixteen to do their bidding.

Q. Why does Washington County Sheriff Smith speak well of the people in Colorado City/Hildale when he talks to the authorities in Texas? And does he know any polygamist women?

A. The sheriff has jurisdiction only in Hildale, not in Colorado City, which is in Arizona. Kirk Smith, Washington County Sheriff, does not want to attempt to go into Hildale and try to prosecute polygamy unless he is absolutely forced to. He has made the statement that if he wants to know anything about Hildale, he calls Sam Barlow. I find this interesting, coming from a law enforcement officer. If you really want to know the truth about a particular group of people involved in illegal and criminal activity, why go to one of the leaders of that group? Sam Barlow is very adept at telling people what he wants them to hear. There is no way that Sheriff Smith can learn the true circumstances among the fundamentalists/polygamists unless he is willing to investigate sources other than those within the FLDS organization.

I doubt he personally knows any of the women. Any time that a young girl has been able to escape the community and make it to St. George, her parents will contact the sheriff and in all cases the girl has been returned to her parents at Colorado City/Hildale. Then before the girl becomes eighteen, she is generally married to one of the members of the community. The situation at Hildale/Colorado City is much bigger than any local sheriff or police can contend with. It must be done by either state or federal authority. Even then, it becomes a very complex situation.

Q. Knowing that they believe in blood atonement and knowing his people would do whatever is necessary to protect their prophet, do you think authorities will keep their distance?

A. No. The fact that they believe in blood atonement and are taught such by their leaders will not deter the authorities from eventually capturing Warren Jeffs. They are not interested in a standoff like Waco and will be very careful to avoid such. When they decide to capture Warren Jeffs, they will be able to do so without bloodshed, I believe. Law enforcement has learned a great deal about such situations and I have much confidence in the people who are handling the case. There is no way he can avoid them forever. Even if his bodyguards stand up to protect him, he will still be taken.

Q. Knowing Warren Jeffs and watching what he has done so far, what do you think may happen in the future as he plans for the end of the world?

A. I do not believe that Warren Jeffs himself is planning for the end of the world. He does, however, teach this to his followers and that is how he keeps them under his control, using fear of the end of the world coming. I believe that it will not be long before Warren Jeffs loses his position of leadership among the polygamists, either by attrition or by actions of the state and federal authorities to incarcerate him. When that happens, I believe that saner heads will be in control of the people and more freedoms will be extended to them and they can return to a more normal life.

As to the compound in Texas, I will be surprised to see it remain a polygamous stronghold for any more than about ten years. After that, there will be so many people in the compound that it will likely fall of its own weight. There will be some person or persons who will end up with ownership of the property and people will either leave the compound or make some arrangements to purchase the property, or to at least rent apartments.

This could become a normal situation if the children of those people were allowed to attend public schools, allowed to integrate into the community and be taught how the rest of the world lives; therefore, having a desire to better their lives and become rid of the superstitions taught to them since childhood.

Q. What is the future of the FLDS?

A. Warren Jeffs has created compounds in Texas and Mexico to escape prosecution that he fears he has to face if he remains in Utah or Arizona. At some point indictments and warrants may be issued for his arrest.

It is possible there will come a time when his own followers will become so disaffected with his leadership, because of his taking their wives and children away and giving them to other men, that there will be a rebellion. I would not be surprised to see Warren Jeffs suffer one day from the hands of those who are now his faithful followers. Looking back at the history of polygamy in the 20th Century and the many violent deaths that occurred in the name of religion, I also realize you cannot rule that out.

I do not believe that he would, of his own accord, abandon the project in Texas, since he has put so much effort and money into it. He will try to isolate it so that he will not come under scrutiny of local law enforcement. I do not believe the local people in Schleicher county will have the problem of YFZ people coming to them for public assistance such as food, clothing, or shelter. Those who leave the YFZ compound either of their own volition or because of excommunication will eventually gravitate back to the Colorado City area.

It is also my opinion that because of the things Warren Jeffs is doing and the course he is taking (alienating a good many of his followers), he will not be able to maintain control of the community and the people there. I believe that Warren Jeffs will soon lose his credibility not only among his followers but the outside business world as well and a new leadership will come into play.

Q. What will be Warren Jeffs future actions in the Colorado City/Hildale area?

A. Warren Jeffs main source of income at the present time is his extortion of the people. They are under an edict to pay him a monthly fee of from $500 - $1,000. Warren Jeffs has borrowed large sums of money from banks against the UEP property in Hildale/Colorado City and so long as he can meet mortgage payments and taxes on the property, he will remain an entity in Hildale/Colorado City. If payments cannot be met, he will abandon the community and the people. The United Effort Plan will be forced into bankruptcy and people living in the homes there will likely be given a choice of buying, renting, or moving out. And many of the men he has excommunicated are now in serious financial difficulty and are defaulting on loans to the bank.

As of July, 2004 more and more men are being excommunicated and from what I can determine, it is solely based on their inability to pay the monthly assessment.

Q. If Warren Jeffs leaves Colorado City, who would take over?

A. If something should happen to Warren Jeffs, convicted or incarcerated or death or something else, there will be someone who will rise up to take his place. The people will not be cast adrift, but it would be a blessing for them if they could gain their independence in such a manner. I have predicted that the Barlows would take over the leadership of the community if Warren Jeffs was out of the picture. Recent developments, however, leave a quandary in regards to this speculation.

The Barlow boys that have been excommunicated and told to leave the community now have had their wives taken from them and given to other people. This is a great surprise to me because I did not suppose the Barlows were serious in accepting Warren Jeffs as their priesthood leader. I still think that there is some planning on their part to overcome his oppression in their lives.

The Barlows are in a strained situation. The problems at Colorado City today can be attributed directly to the sons of John Y. Barlow and Martha Jessop. They are the ones that disrupted the natural sequence of events that brings the next leader of the fundamentalists into play. When they were able to alienate Marion Hammon from Leroy Johnson and have Hammon excommunicated and removed from the priesthood line of succession, that set the stage for Rulon Jeffs to step in; and through the appointment of his son as the leader, they are now suffering from their own actions.

Warren Jeffs has removed Fred Jessop from Colorado City/Hildale thus denying the Barlows access to him. He was their icon and he could have caused the majority of the people to fall away from Warren Jeffs and follow the Barlows. It is still not known for certain where Fred Jessop is today. Some speculate that maybe he is not even alive. Others speculate that he is being held in Mexico or Texas, against his will. Warren Jeffs has made the statement that Uncle Fred is no longer with us. Whether that means he is no longer alive or is just out of communication or access is not known.

Several people of the Colorado City area already have become dissatisfied with Warren Jeffs' leadership and have moved to northern Idaho and Canada, where they are giving allegiance to Winston Blackmore. It is possible that more people would turn to Winston Blackmore for leadership in the event that Warren Jeffs were no longer available.

Q. Why in the world did the Barlows just meekly lay down and allow their wives and children to be taken from them?

A. On May 24, 2004, Louis Barlow died at a home in St. George, Utah, where he was living. This will no doubt have a significant impact regarding whether or not the Barlows will assume the leadership of the group. Son of John Y. Barlow, Louis Barlow has been the patriarch of the Barlow clan and the leadership would have naturally fallen to him in the event of the Barlow takeover. There is a question as to which of his brothers would be as respected by other clan members as was Louis.

I have spent considerable time contemplating why Louis Barlow and his brothers so passively yielded to Warren Jeffs' actions, their excommunication, and their wives being taken from them. Such meekness just wasn't their style. Quite the contrary. I have finally concluded that Warren Jeffs must have some information about the Barlows that he is using to blackmail them. Information that would lead to their conviction of some alleged criminal activity that they may have been involved in. I can think of no other reason why they would submit so easily to his unreasonable demands.

I do not believe Louis Barlow accepted Warren Jeffs as a legitimate prophet. He only obeyed him until an opportunity presented itself for him (or his brothers) to move in and take over.

A surprising turn of events occurred. It has been the policy of Warren Jeffs to forbid the burial of those people who have died that he had excommunicated. He has made an exception in the case of Louis Barlow and allowed his funeral to take place in the LSJ meeting house and also allowed his remains to be buried in the Isaac Carling Memorial Cemetery. This is an unexpected honor.

However, Warren did not allow the grave to be dedicated, as is the Mormon custom.

Q. Some, including Ross Chatwin, have compared Warren Jeffs to Adoph Hitler. What do you think?

A. Well, I think Ross is referring first to the reputation Warren developed when he was in charge of the Academy in Salt Lake and the tactics he used to get children to come and tell him of anyone, friend or family member, mother or father, who said anything contrary to his strict interpretation of the doctrine. Then he would call the person in and "talk" to them. Then, of course, when he became First Counselor in Colorado City, he sent his thirteen-, fourteen-, and fifteen-year-old young men, he named them "Uncle Warren's Sons of Helaman" but they were more like the Hitler-youth program, and sent them into people's homes, forcing them to make a statement that they would acknowledge him as their leader and would accept whatever doctrine he preached to them.

And then when he had his brother ordain him as prophet, he began excommunicating his brethren and reassigning their wives and children to men more willing to completely commit to him and whatever he told them to do, or to believe.

And the newspaper reported that apparently Warren had been secretly taping sessions where people came in to confess their sins and then he used it later to blackmail them.

I suppose anyone can read about all that Warren is doing and draw their own conclusion.

Conclusion

Warren Jeffs has been clearing out people in First Ward he considers not perfectly obedient. When a dictator believes or purports to believe he is being led by God, and when he also believes that he too will become a God, no one can predict the lengths to which he will go or what he will do. It would be a serious error for the government or Texas to underestimate Warren Jeffs.

His top people have decades of experience in business, in hiding from and manipulating the government, and in developing strategies to keep people from knowing much about them. They know the law and how to use it to their advantage. These men are highly skilled, articulate communicators. They will publicly and persuasively state what local citizens and authorities want to hear, and then secretly carry out their own agenda, believing that any lie they tell is approved by God. They have done this for seventy-five years and there is no reason to think they will now change. The outward impression they make on strangers works. They are seen as decent and thoughtful men.

I've already talked about what I think may happen in Colorado City. And the answer may lie in what the federal government does with the case it is developing, while Arizona and Utah wait to see what happens there.

The way may be clear for the excommunicated Barlows to take over or start their own group. Unfortunately, almost all the wives and children of these excommunicated Barlows have already been re-assigned to other men. Still, the community was promised to them by their father John Yates Barlow as their heritage in the Barlow dynasty. The Barlows truly believe the Keys of Priesthood remain in their family. I think the Barlows have long waited for an opportunity to assume full leadership of the Group. I believe Rulon Jeffs and Warren Jeffs both knew this and it would account for why Warren has acted swiftly in excommunicating so many Barlows. An underlying power struggle has gone on for years. Because of the extremes to which Warren Jeffs has gone and because of all the public and government scrutiny, it would be politically smart for the Barlows to create a somewhat more open atmosphere within any group they create. Whether they will or not remains to be seen.

A number of women in First Ward have left over the years and they were able to do so because they had family members on the outside who were willing to help them restart their lives. They had a place to go, someone to help them understand the outside world, and how to create a life. Others have wanted to leave but had no one on the outside to help them.

The primary reason more women do not leave is because they have been taught from birth that their eternal salvation depends on being obedient to their prophet and his teachings. Deeply ingrained in them is the belief that to reach that place in heaven where families can be together, they must remain with a man who has at least three wives. For a faithful person, this is almost impossible to rise above. And to leave behind all of one's family and friends is simply more than some can bear. If a woman has school age children, trying to escape with them is almost impossible. She must slip away by herself and then go to the government for help in getting custody of her children. If, in fact, the government will help her do so.

Because of the almost impossible challenges in leaving, very few polygamist wives will leave the community to seek a different life. It would be as difficult for them as any person coming to America from a third world country. So they need a compelling reason to make such a drastic change. If help services are funded and put in place, perhaps the next generation will begin to consider a different future.

Arizona is planning a justice center in Colorado City, which is expected to be open in the summer of 2004. This will provide a presence of the outside world so those needing help have a place to turn. And they have plans to advertise an 800 number manned twenty-fours a day by experts in child abuse. Many services have been put in place in the past few years to help victims of domestic violence leave their abusers and restart in society, and similar services are needed for our people. Safe houses, education, child care, learning a skill or trade – all are needed to help these polygamist girls, women, and boys enter mainstream society. Those helping must remember that these people have been compelled to live as someone else has dictated, their whole lives. Such people may still be easily misled, easily manipulated. Mentors are needed. Coaching is needed. Patience and kindness are needed. Creating a new life structure in which they can live day to day is essential.

And even in Second Ward where they have more freedom, the girls and boys are still under the control of their priesthood leaders. They must marry who they are told to marry, or leave the community. Better than First Ward, but not the freedom our forefathers fought and died for.

The bottom line solution that may produce the greatest gain is to decriminalize polygamy. We can see what making polygamy illegal has done, not unlike prohibition in the last century. Let these people come out into the world. And as they do so, they will see clearly that they have choices. Stay in polygamy. Or leave. But the choice is theirs. And I suspect fewer people will enter plural marriage.

If it is decriminalized, over zealous leaders will have less control. It would remove the power of self-proclaimed religious leaders in controlling people and their marriages, particularly of young girls. A girl must be allowed to mature so she can make a legitimate decision about her future. And I wish First Ward children could return to public school. I wish the government-funded schools were not allowed to teach religious doctrine.

If the UEP doesn't go bankrupt, the next step would be to dissolve it, placing ownership of the homes and property in the hands of those who paid for and built the houses.

A comparison between First Ward at Colorado City and Second Ward at Centennial

Park does show a significant difference. The people living in Centennial Park are much freer and live a more normal lifestyle. Their dress is more modern and less conspicuous than their First Ward neighbors. Two reasons for their freedom and open-mindedness: Young girls are not forced to marry older men, and the people own the property on which their houses are built. Thus they can't be threatened with losing their homes for disagreeing with or for perceived lack of devotion to their leaders; but, of course, this could change.

In associating with the people in both communities (my wife and I are related to 90 percent of them), the attitude and feelings we encounter are many times more friendly and truly warmer among those of Centennial Park Second Ward than those of Colorado City First Ward.

We have a daughter living in a polygamist relationship in First Ward and another living in a polygamist relationship in Second Ward. We have a good relationship with both. They each chose their lifestyle and are happy and satisfied with their choice. They feel they have the right to make this choice and desire to be left to pursue their own mode of happiness. This is not the case with all polygamist wives living in the society, however. There are many human rights abuses of men, women, and children, and these abuses must be addressed. Evicting people from their homes must stop.

It is my hope in writing this history that those of my many relatives, friends, and others in the community who are living in unhappy circumstances might read it, and that it might have some influence in giving them the courage to take the necessary steps to change their lives for the better.

And now that Warren Jeffs is expanding into Texas, their citizens, law enforcement, and government officials need an in depth understanding of the FLDS, how they have developed over the years, the strategies they employ, and how they deal with outsiders.

Not unlike Iraq, our country faces a serious violation of freedom and human rights. This is America, after all, – and in America, we defend freedom.

Bibliography

The references given here are among the main ones utilized in the preparation of this book. However, they are by no means a complete list of all the works and sources consulted; rather, the list merely indicates the substance and scope of reading upon which some of the material is based. The bibliography is intended to serve as a convenience for those who wish to pursue further the study of fundamentalist polygamist history, and related issues.

Allred, Byron Harvey. *A Leaf in Review*. Salt Lake City: Caxton Publishers, 1933.

Anderson, Max. *The Polygamy Story: Fiction or Fact*. Salt Lake City: Publishers Press, 1979.

Baird, Mark J. and Rhea A. Kunz. *Reminiscences of John W. Woolley and Loren C. Woolley*. 4 vols. Draper, Utah: N.p,n.d.

Bradlee, Ben, Jr. and Dale Van Atta. *Prophet of Blood–The Untold Story of Ervil LeBaron and the Lambs of God*. New York: G.P. Putnam's Sons, 1981.

B. H. Roberts. *Comprehensive History of the Church of Jesus Christ of the Latter Day Saints*.Provo: Brigham Young University Press, 1965.

Jeffs, Rulon. *Purity in the New and Everlasting Covenant of Marriage*. Privately published 1990s.

Jessop, Edson, with Maurine Whipple. "Why I Have Five Wives: A Mormon Fundamentalist Tells His Story." Colliers, 13 November 1953, 27-30.

Johnson, Leroy S. *Sermons*. 6 vols. Hildale, Utah: Twin City Courier Press, 1984.

Journal of Discourses. 26 vols. Liverpool and London: Latter-day Saint Book Depot, 1854-86.

Musser, Joseph W. *Celestial or Plural Marriage*. Salt Lake City: Truth Publishing Co., 1944.

------, Joseph W. Musser Journal. N.p., n.d. These published excerpts are available from Pioneer Press, Salt Lake City.

____, *The New and Everlasting Covenant of Marriage an Interpretation of Celestial Marriage, Plural Marriage*. Salt Lake City: Truth Publishing Co., 1934.

Musser, Joseph W. and J. Leslie Broadbent. *Supplement to the New and Everlasting Covenant of Marriage.* Salt Lake City: Truth Publishing Co., 1934.

Newell, Linda King and Valeen Tippetts Avery. *Mormon Enigma: Emma Hale Smith.* New York: Doubleday and Co., 1984.

Short Creek Historical Calendar. Hildale, Utah: Twin City Courier Inc., 1992.

Smith, Joseph. *Teachings of the Prophet Joseph Smith.* Salt Lake City: Deseret Book, 1976. Joseph Smith

Solomon, Dorothy Allred. *In My Father's House.* New York: Franklin Watts, 1984.

Van Wagoner, Richard S. *Mormon Polygamy: A History.* Salt Lake City: Signature Books, 1986.

About the Author

Benjamin G. Bistline was born in Logan, Utah, on April 21, 1935, the son of John Anthony Bistline and Jennie Johnson Bistline. He was the sixth of ten children. His parents were active members of the Mormon Church but became involved with a few polygamist families in Millville, Utah, and were excommunicated by LDS Church authorities in 1937.

The family moved to Short Creek, Arizona, in 1945 to join a united order movement, also known as The United Effort Plan. His father soon became discouraged by Barlow's ineptness in governing his Order, and by 1948 he had repented of his decision to join with Barlows' group at Short Creek. He then decided to rejoin the Mormon Church, but his wife refused to leave, taking a firm stand. Ben's father died in April of 1949, before rejoining the LDS Church because of their policy of a one year repentance probation period after being excommunicated.

Ben's mother had always wanted to live polygamy and this gave her the opportunity to do so. She married Richard Jessop as his fifth wife and they moved into his large household of four wives and about thirty children.

Ben lived in this polygamous household for the next three years until the raid on Short Creek in 1953. While living with his stepfather, he became romantically involved with one of the daughters, but the Raid interrupted the courtship. Ben was eighteen and Annie was fifteen. All minor children in the community were declared wards of the state of Arizona, and were transported with their mothers to Phoenix, Arizona, in 1953. They were released and allowed to return to Short Creek in 1955

Annie and Ben were married June 24, 1955, and remained in the society where they parented and raised sixteen children. He was never allowed to marry any other wives, after being deemed unworthy of the privilege by polygamist leaders because of his "rebelliousness." He refused to take what he was told at face value, he refused to join one of the cliques, and he refused to live in blind obedience. Thus he was never a polygamist. He and his wife would have accepted plural marriage.

In the early 1980s Ben became discouraged with the polygamists due to their changes in religious doctrine. He was a plaintiff in a lawsuit filed in 1987 in an attempt to win title to the property on which he had built his home. The court granted him equity ownership in his home but not ownership of the property (land). In March of 2003, Fred Jessop, bishop for the polygamists, negotiated an equity agreement with Ben whereby he was able to move away from the community. He now lives on his own property in an area called Cane Beds, about two miles south of Colorado City. He and his wife are still very much involved with the polygamists due to extended family relationships.

Ben and his wife Annie joined the LDS Church in 1992. They believe the same doctrine as the LDS Church in regards to polygamy. They are members of the Kaibab Moccasin Ward where they have served in several church callings. Ben has served on the high council of the Kanab, Utah Kaibab stake.

Since the FLDS began a compound in Texas, authorities and media there have counted on Ben to provide insight and experience, so they know what they are dealing with.

Books on Polygamy

The Polygamists: A History of Colorado City, Arizona
  by Benjamin G. Bistline – ISBN: 1888106743

An 8 x 10 soft cover of 446 pages, the book provides deep documentation of the history of the religion and the town.

Polygamy Under Attack: From Tom Green to Brian David Mitchell
  by John R. Llewellyn – ISBN: 188810676X
Polygamy expert, former polygamist, and retired Salt Lake County Sheriff's Lieutenant John Llewellyn provides a dramatic inside look at each of the polygamist groups, how they began, how they rule their people, and their beliefs. He explores serious human rights abuses that occur such as forcing young girls to marry men old enough to be their father. A former friend of Tom Green, the author provides deep background on Tom's life and polygamist activities. John explores the fascinating underground fraud by the various groups, and evaluates Brian David Mitchell's efforts to turn Elizabeth Smart into a compliant plural wife.

And finally, he takes a hard look at the possible value of decriminalizing polygamy so that the many hidden abuses, including tens of millions of dollars of welfare fraud when polygamist wives pose as single mothers with children, can be brought out into the open and finally be dealt with realistically.

Table of Contents: Brief History of the Mormon Fundamentalist World, A Profile of Each Group and the Independents, Anti-Polygamy & Pro-Polygamy Movements, An Inside Look at AUB Fraud, An Inside Look at TLC Fraud, Tom Green and His Wives, Bleeding the Beast for Your Tax Dollars, Authority versus Love in Mormon Fundamentalism, Legal Issues and Four Attitudes Towards Polygamy, Are There Realistic Solutions for Polygamy Abuses, Rights of Children vs. Rights of Parents, Decriminalizing Plural Marriage, From Tom Green to Brian David Mitchell, The Potential for Violence

John R. Llewellyn appeared on *The Today Show with Matt Lauer & Katie Couric, NBC Nightly News with Tom Brokaw*, Fox News Channel's *The Edge* with Paula Zahn, MSNBC, *Inside Edition*, and *Good Morning America*.

Murder of a Prophet: Dark Side of Utah Polygamy
  by John R. Llewellyn – ISBN: 188810693X
A riveting story of intrigue, murder, and sex. Lusting for worldwide power, the fanatical leader of a Utah polygamist group launches a plan to become the "prophet" over the entire

Mormon Church. Detectives fear a doomsday Waco-type standoff with women and children. Investigator John Llewellyn, polygamy expert, creates a fascinating tale taken from real-life events, based on the Rulon Allred murder by Ervil LeBaron.

A Teenager's Tears: When Parents Convert to Polygamy
    by John R. Llewellyn – ISBN: 188810659X
The publisher and the author wanted people to be able to walk in their shoes and feel what they feel, to be on the inside looking out. An emotionally charged and tender fact-based story.
    Review by Laura Chapman. "Llewellyn accomplishes the incredible task of exposing the many diverse dynamics of Utah polygamist groups and their members in *A Teenager's Tears*. The characters of the women, children, men and self-proclaimed apostles are both astounding and precise. The display of male privilege, abuse of power in leadership, and struggles within families is triumphantly accurate. The feminists within the groups are still captured in a basic belief that without a man there is no heavenly glory in the hereafter."

Printed in the United States
109907LV00005B/33-34/A